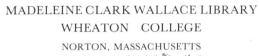

Reasonably
Vicious

CANDACE VOGLER

HARVARD UNIVERSITY PRESS

Cambridge, Massachusetts
London, England
2002

For Lisa

Library of Congress Cataloging-in-Publication Data

Vogler, Candace A.
    Reasonably vicious / Candace Vogler.
        p. cm.
    Includes bibliographical references and index.
    ISBN 0-674-00741-7
    1. Ethics.   2. Practical reason.   I. Title.

    BJ1031 .V64 2002
    170′.42—dc21   2002027250

Contents

Acknowledgments

I have been at work on this book for some time and have been tremendously fortunate in my interlocutors all the while. Early drafts of bits of some chapters were presented at the University of Wisconsin at Milwaukee and at Madison, Northwestern University, Vanderbilt University, the University of Illinois at Chicago and at Urbana-Champaign, Illinois Wesleyan University, the University of Chicago, and Princeton University. I am grateful to my audiences for their helpful comments on work very much in progress. I developed the first full draft while participating in a philosophical writing group with Lauren Tillinghast and Jessica Spector, both of whom helped me hammer chapters into their first form, as did Carol Voeller, Michael Thompson, Leonard Linsky, Adrian Cussins, David Lloyd, and Hilary Bok. Before sending it off, I had the benefit of several days' intensive discussion of the whole with Elijah Millgram, and the penultimate draft could not have taken such shape as it had without him. Once it was set, I was guided in my final revision by comments from two anonymous reviewers for Harvard Press, Beth Povinelli, Martha Nussbaum, Josef Stern, Dan Brudney, and Ian Mueller. Two additional writing groups, one with Scott Anderson and Mark Jenkins, the other with Jeremy Bendik-Keymer, gave me places to air revisions in progress. I have been helped by discussions about Anscombe's work and mine with David Gauthier, with Doug Levin, Colin Patrick, Christopher Ferro, George Streeter, and Joe Schear. Lauren Tillinghast and Dan Brudney stepped in again at the end to have a look at some of the most revised chapters, and helped me to make some final corrections and additions.

Throughout this rather long haul, I have been cheered on and supported by many friends, colleagues, and associates. I have already thanked some for their critical comments on the text. Lindsay Waters at Harvard University Press took an interest in the project very early on, and continued his interest even after it became clear that I was reversing entirely the position I had developed in a doctoral dissertation. Working with him has been a great joy. I want especially to thank the Garbanzis, Lauren Berlant, Roger Rouse, Beth Povinelli, Hank Vogler, Michelle Jensen, Khalif Malone, Peter Enger, and Lisa Roraback. Lisa, my sister, saw me through multiple drafts in more ways than I can count. The book is dedicated to her, in love and gratitude.

Introduction

Here are two remarks drawn from recent work on ethics:

> In contemporary philosophy of action, there is a fervid debate about whether any intentional action must be prompted in part by a desire, or whether it is possible to be moved to action by a belief—such as the belief that doing so-and-so is morally required—alone. The debate all takes place against the background of the assumption that beliefs and desires are as different as gold and oxygen.[1]
>
> —Rosalind Hursthouse

> [My opponents] will insist that the fact of an agent's having reason to do something (say to keep promises) is itself dependent on his feelings, passions, or desires.[2]
>
> —Philippa Foot

Here is a third taken from work about practical reasoning:

> I conjecture that the cause of this failure of percipience is the standard approach by which we first distinguish between "action" and what merely happens, and then specify that we are talking about "actions." So what we are considering is already given as—in a special sense—an action, and not just any old thing which we do, such as making an involuntary gesture.[3]
>
> —Elizabeth Anscombe

It is the aim of this book to argue that if we take Anscombe's suggestion to heart, and if we attend to some of her sources carefully, then the contemporary philosophical wrangle over desire will look much less interesting, the discussion of reasons to do something will become more

1

focused, and the trouble about explaining the connection between ethics and reason—addressed by both Hursthouse and Foot in different ways—will stay with us in its old familiar form.

Hursthouse's observation concerns moral psychology (that region of philosophical psychology concerned with the aspects of subjectivity that inform rational agency). Foot ties the relevant form of moral psychology to an associated picture of practical reason (reason directed at action or policy). The target they share has many names: "Humeanism" or "neo-Humeanism," for instance, or "noncognitivism." Following one standard American practice, I call it *instrumental views* of practical reason—instrumentalism, for short. Instrumentalism takes several forms (discussed at length in the first chapter). What they all share is the thought that effective reasons for acting must engage both belief and desire, that belief's role in rational action lies in finding means to ends, in scheduling pursuits, and in making trade-offs when one cannot get everything one wants. Desire's role, on the other hand, lies in setting the ends of human action. Desire is further distinguished from belief this way: whereas belief is by its nature open to rational criticism and assessment (it is a cognitive state, a state that aims to track the truth of its matter), desire is to some extent immune from rational criticism (its aim is rather to make its matter come true). Instrumentalism about practical reason involves a family of what I call (following Anscombe) *calculative views* of reason in action: views that locate the exercise of practical reason in taking means to ends, doing parts of an activity in order to do the whole. Ethicists care about instrumentalism because many think that, if instrumentalism is true, then there can be no rational grounding for ethics. Suppose, for instance, that bad people have no desire to change their ways. If desire is needed for rational motivation, then it follows that they will have no reason to change their ways.

The most curious feature of instrumentalism in practical philosophy is this: instrumentalist views are usually described as standard theories of practical reason—theories philosophers can take for granted in their work—but hardly anyone believes that instrumentalism is true, and there has been an enormous amount of philosophical work in the past quarter century suggesting that such views are not only false, but wildly implausible.

When most people in a field of philosophical inquiry take it that the standard theory of their topic is a view no one could seriously maintain if he thought about it carefully (John McDowell derides it as the "hydraulic" picture of rational motivation),[4] when refuting that view has become so much a part of academic life that scores of doctoral dissertations continue to appear devoted to defeating the position in new ways, and when experts in the field continue to give every indication of believing that the view remains worth arguing against, it is time to practice philosophical diagnostics.

The need to do so here becomes more acute the more closely one attends to the controversy, for the many refutations of instrumentalist views often turn on arguing that some exercise of noninstrumental practical reason (practical reason that aims to *set* or to *evaluate* ends rather than figure out how to attain ends we are already determined to pursue) is vital for people because employing it is a means to attaining some very important end or a part of realizing some deep practical commitment we can be assumed to share. Sound exercise of noninstrumental practical reason, we are told, enables us to develop (solidly coherent or duly flexible) selves leading authentic lives,[5] or enables us to live ethically in the company of our fellows by regulating our passions and interests for the sake of realizing the ends of individual stability, interpersonal concern, and justice.[6] Anti-instrumentalist practical philosophers continue to experience a kind of magnetic pull toward traditional suggestions that practical reason, properly exercised, directs us to the end of producing and maintaining well-ordered individual and social life. And, really, what *other* sort of account of the place of practical reason might one give that could show why practical rationality is an excellence worth striving for? The thought that such goods are the nonaccidental outcome of practically rational lives *ought* to attract our interest. But in the current philosophical climate, the old-fashioned thought that the due exercise of practical reason (as an important power of human maturity) improves life only produces a puzzle: right at the center of stories about why calculative pictures of practical reason are false, we often find the thought that the noninstrumental exercise of practical reason is required as a means to or part of attaining important ends. And this in turn suggests that, far from being outgrowths of an impossibly crude moral psychology, calculative views owe their force to something on the order of an *ur*-form of practical justification.

When this sort of situation arises in practical philosophy, it is often a good idea to look backward—as Jack Spicer once put it, surveying surviving versions of Arthurian legend, "Plainly we are dealing with materials distorted from their original form."[7] This brings me to my third quote, Anscombe's suggestion that we ignore action at our peril in work on practical reason. The old source I will turn to in sorting things through and bringing action into focus is one of her sources, Thomas Aquinas. Much of this book is devoted to taking Anscombe's warning seriously, using it to locate the strength of calculative views of practical reason, and, drawing on Aquinas, defending one such view, a view that I call the *standard picture of practical reason*.

The Project

I see my first task as unearthing the foundation of instrumentalist views, the buried but sensible source of current doctrine. Current instrumentalist views are, I think, erected from fragments of a much older position. Accordingly, I urge that instrumentalism gets such force as it has from an old insight into the nature of rational action, one that (in spite of Anscombe's steady efforts) has never quite fully reared its head in modern secular theories of practical reason. The insight is just this: (representation of) intentional action, as such and paradigmatically, has a means–end or part–whole calculative form.

Aquinas sees the insight about action in Aristotle. And, following Aquinas's lead, I suspect, Elizabeth Anscombe displayed much of it in her work on intention. I leave to scholars the question whether the saint was right about the Philosopher, and to Anscombe's intellectual intimates the question how far her position is Thomistic. What matters for my purposes is Aquinas's brilliance as a theorist of reason in action, not how true he was to his sources. And while removing some bits about practical reason and ethics from the larger theological context of Thomism mangles the account, these bits all on their own represent a decided advance over more narrowly Aristotelian work.

The advance comes, I think, in part from the fact that Aquinas gave serious and systematic attention to culpable wrongdoing (a focus that owed much to the need to theorize sin). That is why I draw more from Aquinas's discussion of vice than from his work on virtue. It is the work on vice that presents an ongoing and serious challenge to any attempt to get ethics to drop straight out of secular work on practical reason. Aquinas gives us something on the order of a theory of immorality: an account of acting ill that takes the question "Why be immoral?" as seriously as it takes the question "Why be moral?" If you attend to this theory, and are, for whatever reason, committed to doing secular work in practical philosophy, you are left with an explicit, systematic account of the rationality of many varieties of individual immorality, conveniently taxonomized according to the point of doing evil in this way and that, with extensive discussion of the ways in which the ends of some modes of viciousness are best served by developing subsidiary vices. Worse yet, it is easy to recognize the sort of characters Aquinas describes when he discusses the vicious. This is a dreadful thing to stumble across if you seek a secular answer to the question "Why be moral?" that will show how every adult who acts ill thereby acts irrationally. I do not see any essential flaw in Aquinas's treatment of evil. If anything, he provides approaches that could be profitably extended in the direction of thinking through the myriad varieties of human badness that have developed over the ensuing seven centuries.

Standard secular ethical treatments of wrongdoing these days chalk up wrongs to rashness, weakness of will, or ignorance of the greater good. All three sources of wrongdoing display some failure of practical reason, although the third sort of failure may be excusable if an agent has no way of knowing better. I take from Aquinas an account of vicious conduct in which, shorn of a substantive account of the human good, viciousness betrays no failure of practical reason at all. My assumption is that relatively determinate, substantive accounts of the human good are inherently controversial. I motivate this hunch by giving numerous examples of views of how it befits a person to conduct herself, each of which makes some sense but many of which give contradictory advice about how to live. What I mean to show thereby is that the rabbit we have most wanted to pull out of the hat of practical reason—an account of unethical conduct showing that everyone who acts ill thereby sins against reason—cannot be conjured from a calculative account of practical reason. Since I defend a calculative account of practical reason, this is tantamount to arguing that if I am right about practical reason, then you won't get an uncontroversial grounding for ethics in thought about practical rationality.

This is not to say that we cannot do ethics. It is not to say that ethical conduct is irrational. The standard picture leaves room for moral or ethical volitional elements, and the space made for these is, I think, the right sort of space: they are some among the many sources of human ends. For all that, faced with a deeply vicious man who is doing an excellent job of realizing his vice in practice, the version of the standard picture that I defend finds no error of practical reason. The man's conduct is ethically deplorable, and this is no small thing. But he can be held accountable for the badness of his conduct precisely because he has made no error in calculative practical judgment. On my view, as one says in law, he has a guilty mind because he is in possession of his faculties, is intent on attaining his ends, rightly takes it that he thereby stands to gain something, rightly takes it that unethical conduct will get him what he is after, and so displays malice aforethought. This sort of malice need not imply any bad feeling. It is in the calculative structure of what he does, in the means that he is prepared to take in order to attain his ends.

In short, the advocate of the standard picture is driven to insist that reflection on practical reason unhindered by controversial claims about the human good will not establish that individual unethical conduct is irrational. I base this insistence in Aquinas's account of the worldly, human goods at issue in the deliberate cultivation of vice. Aquinas is a metaphysical realist about value. I stress that, shorn of theology and rendered in plain realist naturalism about the good things in human life, realism about value is compatible with seeing practical reason at work in individual habituation to viciousness. Naturalist metaphysics about human good of the kind found, for example, in contemporary neo-Aristotelian virtue theory or contractarian moral theory may ground claims about how collective flourishing requires that some of us be, say, just, prudent, brave and temperate. But, from the much-touted first-person perspective, naturalist reflection on human good could likewise ground cultivation of the vices.

As will doubtless come clear, I am drawn to realism about value. My point is that this tendency, married to a calculative picture of practical reason, is not enough to support an argument that individual bad character or bad action betrays a failure of individual practical reason. Since we Anglo–North American ethicists are all of us inclined to see practical reason as an individual human capacity (rather than a power to be sought first in congeries, corporations, or collectivities of individuals), we are also inclined to suppose that the answer to the question "Why be moral?" must be pitched to the individual and must address his sense of himself and of what matters in life. In these terms, in light of Aquinas's work on vice, the question may well have no satisfactory answer (I consider, of course, many candidate answers as I go along).

My insistence that the standard picture of practical reason provides the philosophical foundation of instrumentalist doctrines is, then, not merely archeological. It has several of the features that have led many (myself included) to inveigh against instrumentalism. For example, it crucially involves internalism about reasons for acting. What one has reason to do or pursue, on this view, depends on one's ends, and on such features of one's character or temperament as tend to give rise to ends or to set the terms in which doing things is, say, sometimes delightful. Relatedly, perhaps the most important way in which a secular version of the standard picture is like contemporary instrumentalist views is that it offers no principled way of insisting that individual unethical or immoral conduct is invariably irrational.[8]

It is because I think that a whole view of practical reason can be spun from a simple insight into the structure of intentional action, and that this view (unlike instrumentalism) really *could* do duty as a standard or default account of the topic, that I am willing to defend a position with this exceedingly unpalatable consequence. Accordingly, a large part of this book is given over to arguing that the point about (representations of) intentional action is a truth, and that, while there are such things as noncalculative sources of action and motivation, taken in isolation from calculative reasons for acting, noncalculative practical considerations are not full-fledged reasons, offer no insight into practical reason at all, and could not, all on their own, form the core of any sound theory of practical reason. The other part of my task is to argue that a calculative account might be sufficient for understanding practical reason.

The Plan of the Book

In Chapter 1 I discuss the varieties of instrumentalism, point out that they share a tendency to bifurcationist moral psychology (the sort Foot and Hursthouse have in view), and begin formulating the standard picture by stripping away the bothersome psychology from the calculative core of instrumentalist views. This core then becomes the basis for the standard picture.

Because an advocate of the standard picture can find no necessary fault with simply taking life as it comes along, doing this and then that, without trying to make the whole add up to much of anything, with cultivating vice, with having a life plan of the sort rarely considered in contemporary work on practical reason (for example, being willing to sacrifice security for the sake of adventure), and so on, the question will arise: In what sense and how is the standard picture normative?

I answer this question in a roundabout way, beginning even before defending the standard picture. The answer first involves giving an account of reasons for acting. Because a question about normativity is often a question about how an "ought" arises in connection with good, I take it that one way to answer the question is to supply and motivate the relevant account of good. The story about good that I tell is based in a system for sorting reasons for action into three very general categories. These categories will direct our attention to three ways in which intentional action can have a point, that is, three kinds of desirability characterizations that can be accurately adduced in support of what one does. The division is formal and pleasingly principled. I take it from Aquinas. It turns out that the three sorts of desirability characterizations do different work in explaining intentional action, and attach to and justify what they explain in different ways. Chapters 2–6 are devoted to the task of laying out, motivating, and explaining the threefold division of practical good. By doing this I mean to argue that the threefold division provides nonarbitrary criteria for thinking about good in action, and, hence, normativity.

In the course of discussing the last of the three regions in Chapter 6, I give the first half of my main argument: that noncalculative practical considerations all on their own cannot give us a grip on practical reason. Chapter 7 is devoted to presenting and defending the standard picture in light of the threefold division. I argue that the standard picture all on its own might be an adequate account of practical reason. The whole of these chapters is rather haunted by ethics. In my final chapter, I return to ethical practical considerations and talk about what is left of them in light of the preceding work. Finally, in a series of appendices, I address several points or issues that arise along the way.

I confess that I have neither the hope nor the expectation that this book will convince anyone that the standard picture is defensible. What I do hope to show, however, is that no sound action theory can do without an account of calculative volition, that a calculative theorist might be able to operate without leaving room for deeply noncalculative reasons for acting, and that the way to find out what calculative reasons are like is by attending to the calculative order in intentional action. This is also where one ought to go to understand calculative accounts of practical reason, I think, not to some doctrine about wanting in general, or the faculty of desire, or a story about passions, or work on the metaphysics of value.

Instrumentalism about Practical Reason

A casual survey of the Anglo–North American philosophical literature on practical reason produced over the past twenty years will introduce the reader to the term "instrumentalism." The reader will learn a few things straight off. First, instrumentalism is the view that all of one's reasons for acting express, engage, or otherwise involve one's desires. Second, desires are not necessarily amenable to rational criticism or correction. Third, instrumentalism is, as Robert Nozick puts it, the "default theory" of practical rationality, "the theory that discussants of rationality can take for granted, whatever else they think" because it "does not seem to stand in need of justification, whereas every other theory does."[1]

The astute reader ought already to smell blood in the water. Here is a view that *reasons* for acting owe their effectiveness to an arational source. And not just any arational source—not, say, biological processes or evolution, not the weather or the physical environment or the causal structure of the world—but a contentful psychological state of which one has some awareness, *desire* (or, as I often put it, *wanting*). You do not need an elaborate psychological theory of desire to notice that human wanting is sometimes unending, wild, and unruly. I mean, here is a hard truth about human life: you can want almost anything. You can want people you've never met to do things you cannot get them to do. You can want to be the sort of person who has worked with his hands since he was a child, or who craves raw vegetables and exercise when he is depressed instead of cake or bourbon. Like Groucho Marx, you can want never to join any club that will have you as a member, or long to belong to any group that won't have you. Indeed, lively, imaginative people have sometimes been known to envy (a species of wanting) the contentment of the dullard. Nothing about human wanting seems to require that human wants restrict themselves in any convenient way—for example, to objects that are in principle or in practice get-able.[2] One might suggest that this is part of what elevates us above the lowly shrew who seems to want mostly to eat n-times its body weight daily, to avoid death, and, when circumstances dictate, to mate.

It is easy to understand how the expansiveness of human wanting could explain something of human misery. It is harder to see how endless, unsatisfiable wanting could give anyone a reason to do anything, except, perhaps, to extinguish wanting. In this vein, notice how odd it would be to find a major, highly influential teaching about the human condition whose first noble truth was, "All suffering comes of having reasons to do something" and continued by outlining some steps you might take in order to rid yourself of the basis of this condition. We don't suppose that the explanation for Buddhism's enduring and widespread popularity is that it panders to sloth, after all.[3]

But this is just the beginning of the trouble, for not only do human wants range throughout the describable, they change, sometimes from hour to hour, sometimes for no other reason than that one has grown tired of oneself or one's mood has shifted. Reasons for acting come and go, but it is highly unlikely that every such shift can be explained by a mood-swing hypothesis, just as it is highly unlikely that fickleness changes one's reasons for acting willy-nilly.

Reflection on such phenomena would lead you to think that this view, instrumentalism, must be some kind of red herring. But no. It is, you are assured, the *standard* philosophical view about reasons for acting. Moreover, it is a view whose viability philosophers can take for granted, because *it does not stand in need of justification*. This is an exciting claim. What could the philosophers be thinking in making it?

Instrumentalism

In order to answer this question, the astute reader will keep on reading. But the more closely one reads, the harder it is to find any single topic or tenet that philosophers have in view in discussing instrumentalism. At the heart of the debate seems to be some thought that reason's role in human life is limited. That is why instrumentalists hold that some range of psychological states treated under the rubric "desire" (crucial ingredients to motivation) are at least partly immune to rational criticism or correction. Now, many roads lead to the conviction that something in human life betrays the impotence of reason. Here is a list of subjects and positions most often associated with instrumentalism:

1. *The metaphysics and epistemology of value.* Instrumentalism involves the claim that there is a metaphysically grounded distinction between our apprehension of facts and our evaluative judgments. Value has its source in human nature, culture, or inclination, whereas the facts are what they are quite apart from these. Because of this, no amount of information about how things are (information acquired through the operation of plain reason) can settle questions about how things ought to be (an evaluative judgment reflecting our needs, wants, or culturally relative patterns of appraisal).

2. *Moral psychology.* Cognition is the function of plain reason. However, two similarly situated agents with equal powers of plain reason may act very differently when faced with the same kinds of circumstances. The instrumentalist explanation for such divergence is that motivation is not a function of reason alone. Rational motivation divvies up into two components—a volitional component and a cognitive component. The volitional component may involve an intention, a plan, a pro-attitude, a preference, a desire, or some affective state or sentiment. The cognitive component may involve knowledge, skill, belief, an estimation of the likely outcomes of various courses of action one might take, or the conclusion of a practical inference. Here, instrumentalism insists that volition without cognition is blind, while cognition without volition is idle.

3. *Practical reasoning.* Practical reasoning, as the term suggests, is an exercise of reason directed at figuring out what to do. Deciding what to do issues in having some objective or end in view, and having some thought about how to attain that end. Reason's impotence here shows itself in its failure to set the ends of human action. Hence, instrumentalism about practical reasoning teaches that there is no rational deliberation of ends, but only of means.

4. *The structure of rational justification in practical contexts.* Let *A* and *B* be actions of different types. Instrumentalism claims that one is justified in *A*-ing only if one takes it that *A*-ing is a means to (or

part of) attaining (or making it possible to attain) a further end, *B*-ing, and one wants to *B*.[4] In short, the structure of rational justification in practical contexts is calculative.

Notice, first, that *none* of the four seems equivalent to the initial thought about wanting and reasons for acting. (2) comes closest, but the list of volitional elements includes some items that would not usually be taken to be psychological states of any particular kind. "Preference," for example, is an economist's term of art introduced precisely in order to remove from economics the claim that welfare or utility involves specific psychological satisfactions. Similarly, the philosophical term of art "pro-attitude" points to no single kind of psychological state. Likewise, a corporation can demonstrate its intention to make good on an agreement, suggesting that intentions need not be psychological states (corporations as such do not have psyches).[5] What the philosophers are thinking, then, is a bit obscure.

Next notice that, while one can hold variants of all four of these positions without falling into an obvious inconsistency, one need not accept all four in order to accept one or more of them. For example, a metaphysical realist about value will deny (1). Suppose, however, that he thinks that some regions of the psyche track truths about how things ought to be, whereas other psychological departments keep track of how things are.[6] He will accept some version of (2). He could then insist that there is no deliberation of ends because having an end is setting out to make things as they ought to be. There are truths about how things ought to be, on his view. It is not up to us to deliberate about these any more than it is up to us to deliberate about whether we should be subject to gravitational forces on Mondays. He accepts (3). Nevertheless, he could deny (4) if he thought that we were sometimes moved to make things as they ought to be unwittingly. I might do the right (that is, justifiable) thing on instinct, or through the operations of evolutionary mechanisms that I do not understand, or under the unanalyzed pressures of an unconscious motive, or while possessed by spirits. (4) ties the rational justification of action to what agents think and to what they knowingly seek. Our realist could allow that I may have no clue what end my act *really* serves, and nevertheless hit on exactly the right thing to do. My act is justified, but I could not tell you how or why. This man accepts (2) and (3). He denies (1) and (4).

Of course, one could take up a different subset of the views. Say that our man is an antirealist about value and a bifurcationist about motivation, but insists that there *is* deliberation of ends. Sometimes we are not merely in the dark about how to attain our ends, he might point out, but unclear about which ends we should pursue. There are no facts about what we *ought to* pursue, on his view. It is up to us what to seek. Indeed, he insists, that is *why* we need to figure out what to pursue. For all that, our antirealist may deny that we have any reason actually *to do* anything without some determinate end in view. This man accepts (1), (2), and (4), but denies (3).

Neither of these two positions is widely held. The next one is. Here we meet the philosopher who is an antirealist about value and a belief–desire bifurcationist about motivation. He denies that there is strictly rational deliberation of ends. Ends are, he thinks, expressions of desire and you cannot simply decide what to desire. He does not think that the mere fact that A-ing is *a* means to (or part of) B-ing is enough to justify A-ing. Instead, he takes it that an agent will have to believe that A-ing is the best, or most efficient means to B-ing (or else a necessary part of B-ing) if she is to be justified in A-ing. The third man accepts (1), (2), and (3), but denies (4). This last assemblage of positions is extremely common among avowed instrumentalists,[7] and appears to involve the (suitably interpreted) subset of our four theses that anti-instrumentalists have argued against most frequently, often by targeting *one* of the component views.[8]

In short, part of the reason that it is hard to get a read on instrumentalism is that the four sorts of views associated with instrumentalism in practical philosophy, while mutually consistent, are *not* mutually entailing. Given some time for reflection, the astute reader could fill in a matrix of sorts in which one accepts only one, only two, only three, or else all four of these "instrumentalist" views, mixing, matching, and interpreting as suits, perhaps while refusing to take any stand at all on one or more of the topics. The "standard view about practical reason" seems to have dissolved into loosely related clusters of positions on disparate subjects, none of which need be identical with the view that reasons for acting depend on desires.

The reader tries another tack. Perhaps a careful search will reveal that *one* of our four theses is especially important to instrumentalism in practical philosophy. Instrumentalism *can* involve many things. On the face of it, however, there seems to be no agreement about which topic (or, for that matter, which position on the relevant topic) is paradigmatically in-strumentalist.[9] Happily, *this* appearance deceives. Friends and foes of instrumentalism alike think that instrumentalism assumes the need for a separate volitional component to motivation in its treatment of reasons for acting. Often philosophers go so far as to insist that a reason for act-ing consists of an amalgam of psychological states. For example, philos-ophers will treat a reason for acting as a belief-and-desire, or a belief-and-pro-attitude. That is, otherwise unrelated versions of (2)—the view that rational motivation requires separable cognitive and volitional com-ponents—enjoy special prominence in the literature.[10] (1) and (3) are often taken as, respectively, the ground and the consequence of (2). The most common variant, then, emphasizes moral psychology partly be-cause of a position on value, denies that there is deliberation of ends be-cause of the moral psychology, and may ignore, deny, or accept the claim about justification.

And here we drift back to where we started. Having a rational motive for action, having *effective* reasons for acting, requires both cognition and volition. That these are separable ingredients of motivation suggests that volition is not a matter of cognition alone. *If* cognition is the sole province of reason's operation, it will follow that volition always in-volves some arational element. Add to this a claim that genuine reasons for acting are effective, and that, to be effective, a practical consideration (a potential reason) must bear some nonaccidental relation to an agent's motivational set (perhaps because reasons for acting explain action, and no one does anything on purpose that she cannot be motivated to do). Insist that practical considerations have a nonaccidental relation to one's motivational set just in case they do or could engage the *volitional* ele-ments in the set. (Notice, here, that the cognitive elements in a motiva-tional set can be shared among agents who have very different motives.) Finally, note that *desire* is the preferred candidate separable volitional el-ement in instrumentalist moral psychology. We get that reasons for act-ing depend on desires, and that desires are, to some extent, arational.

The Story So Far

Instrumentalism may be any of several bundles of theses tied together by strands of moral psychological speculation. The moral psychological views in question give bifurcated accounts of rational motivation. Instrumentalists think that one aspect of motivation is strictly cognitive; the other is not, strictly, cognitive. The latter element is immune to rational criticism and correction, insofar as noncognitive. Philosophers often call the cognitive element *belief* and the volitional element *desire*. It is hard to tell how closely philosophical use of such terms corresponds to commonsensical psychology about thinking and wanting. But, on the side of desire, anyway, the fit seems close—sometimes, after all, just wanting to do something *is* reason enough to do it. Anti-instrumentalists, however, deny that this is enough basis for a theory of practical reason. Indeed, some anti-instrumentalists deploy insights about wanting in arguing against instrumentalism,[11] and such criticism has inspired the instrumentalist backpedaling you may have anticipated initially, having noticed what wanting is like. Instrumentalists nowadays most often hold that, while all reasons for acting are based in desire, not all desires generate reasons for acting.

Minimally, then, instrumentalism centers on the claim that if you have a reason to do something, you must want to attain some end. For all that, some wants fail to provide a basis for rational motivation. There have been, along these lines, very interesting instrumentalist accounts of the kind of wanting that is relevant to action, and arguments that such desire can be more susceptible to rational correction than some anti-instrumentalists allow. There have been many arguments that the species of wanting that generates reasons for acting gains this status by surviving one or another mode of rational reflection. And, of course, anti-instrumentalists have met such amendments with new counterexamples and newer, deeper, better arguments that instrumentalism is made vulnerable at its core by the role it accords to (at least partially) arational wanting. Most recently, there has been a lot of work asking how it is that instrumentalism involves any genuine principle of reason, produced with the suspicion that any appearance that the theory makes sense is entering in by way of all kinds of assumptions about belief, knowledge, inference, and thought (aspects of cognition) and that, if instrumentalists really are committed to the arationality of their source material (wanting as a necessary volitional element), they do not get to help themselves to "norms of theoretical reason" in order to rein in desire.[12]

The astute reader's first impression was right. There is blood in the water, and many species of the flailing theory have been attacked and picked over from as many directions as one might care to mention. I suspect that the proliferation of points of attack owes much to the fact that the four "instrumentalist" theses are not mutually entailing. Defeating one may have no implications for the other three, and there are many possible interpretations of each of the four. The sheer variety of practical philosophical views gathered together under the rubric "instrumentalism" virtually guarantees an endless field of anti-instrumentalist engagement.

A Question

Interestingly enough, however, philosophers who continue to take calculative theories of practical reason seriously are likely to suspect that the recent attacks miss their marks, that the source of instrumentalism is much deeper than the refutations allow, and has not only not been injured, but has scarcely been touched by the minor industries that have sprung up in the service of destroying first this, then that instrumentalist view. And those who continue, privately or openly, to subscribe to some version of instrumentalism have this much going for them: surely in light of all the work suggesting that this view has almost nothing to recommend it, the question to ask is *not* whether a view that tends to see all reasons for acting as arising from pools of desire can be refuted. We should rather ask *what* might have accounted for instrumentalism's having the status suggested by calling it the *standard* or *default* theory in the first place.

Some Candidate Answers

Various sociological answers suggest themselves (for example, we have somehow got into the habit of thinking that a doctrine about wanting that no one would believe if he stopped to think out what it meant is the theory to beat, perhaps because of some peculiar features of academic culture). These answers are not to the point, and, anyway, not the sort that philosophers are especially equipped to give. It might be thought that the status of instrumentalism instead is one more instance of the notorious tendency of philosophers to remain steadfast in views that look pretty implausible on the surface, owing to the fact that there is impressive argumentative support for those views. But the odd thing about instrumentalism is that there is *not* strong argumentative support given in its favor.

This is not to say that people don't point to its virtues. These, we are told, are several. It is sometimes suggested, for example, that a properly modern, thoroughly scientific worldview leaves no source for reasons for acting *but* wanting, where what people want is not invariably utterly idiosyncratic, but can also be shaped by such more orderly forces as culture and education and nature. The point about value under conditions of modernity has been debated at considerable length. And anyway, as I mentioned in my survey of the four topics, one could be a metaphysical realist about value and still adhere to all other aspects of instrumentalism in practical philosophy.

Some think that the success of the belief–desire model of motivation is all by itself a reason to embrace instrumentalism. This cannot be right. For if the volitional element, desire, is in some respect arational, it becomes increasingly hard to understand why we would expect the requisite transfer of volitional force from end to means needed in order to generate action on the belief–desire model.[13] Instrumentalists hold that desire gives us ends and belief tells us how to attain them. Desire is an unwieldy force in human life. But it must moment-by-moment be brought under the sway of calculative reason if instrumentalism is to have *any* point of application to human action.

Here is what I mean. Whenever anybody does anything on purpose for a reason, according to this model, she desires to attain an end and believes that her act is a means to or part of satisfying this desire. But "end" and "means" are relative terms. I walk to the market in order to buy apples. Attaining my end (securing apples) is made possible by taking these means (heading off to shop). I buy apples (means) in order to make apple pie (end). I make an apple pie (means) in order to give a pie to Sarah (end). I give the pie to Sarah (means) in order to cheer her up (end). What is an *end* relative to some means is often a *means* to a further end. Indeed, it is possible to subdivide the active components in any such example, generating still more points of prerequisite volitional transfer—I put one foot in front of the other (means) in order to walk to the market (end). And so on. Hence, if "desire" is the name of whatever moves one to act, then the force of desire will have to be transmitted along calculative chains of means and ends, parts of an activity and the whole of it, in order to generate not only whole courses of action, but any intended *bit* of a whole course of action. The agent will have to desire to attain not just the last end, but the linked *series* of means and ends, parts and wholes. Otherwise her cognitive grasp of the calculative relation in action will be idle.

Why would we expect desire to be transmitted along the lines sketched out for it by calculative cognition? We know, for example, that this does not always happen. Sometimes discovering what it will take to get what you want dampens your enthusiasm considerably. Here, desire wanes in the face of reason. Other times, you are tremendously excited over a thing you might get but take no steps to get it. Here, desire embraces its object, but does not motivate. The instrumentalist will object that these cases may involve irrationality of some sort. But this response begs the question. The question is, recall, given that desire needn't inspire action, why does desire *ever* move us along smoothly from means to end, part to whole?

The instrumentalists claim that the "success" of the belief–desire model of motivation provides independent support for instrumentalism about practical reason. In order to assess this claim, we must look at how an instrumentalist could explain the transfer of desire from end to means. Two accounts are hinted at in the literature.[14] Neither is much help.

The first is that evolutionary mechanisms grease the wheels of motivational transfer, for if no one ever took steps to get what she wanted, then no one would survive long enough to see another generation into being. This is scarcely enough to explain the end–means desire transmission, however. There are three reasons why.

First, notoriously, it is precisely in matters of looking after one's own health (or other long-term interests) and of doing one's bit in collective enterprises that will benefit all concerned—matters where evolutionary explanations *gain purchase* on the practical lives of other animals—that the transfer of motivation from end to means is hardest for us to effect. Instrumentalism's appeal comes partly from our widespread unwillingness to put such matters as our own health or the general welfare ahead of other interests. This unwillingness tends to persist even when we acknowledge the sense of doing things to these ends, and would very much like it if the ends could be attained effortlessly. What evolution explains in the life of the Arctic tern is not widespread enough to provide similar explanation in the life of the human.

Second, presumably one reason to suppose that there are arational forces at play in human motivation generally is our capacity to display sublime indifference to good sense about how to improve our lot. In short, the unruliness and destructiveness of human wanting is a *datum* for instrumentalism. Given the wildness of human wanting, it could instead be argued that *failure* to effect end–means volitional transfer might give us more adaptive advantage than a smooth end–means desire transmission mechanism would. The quick invocation of evolutionary mechanisms to ensure the transfer of motivation from end to means, that is, looks like a kind of dodge. Very little about human wanting would lead one to detect the hand of biological evolution in its range of objects. How, then, will reproductive advantage explain transfer of incentive from object to act? As a holdover from an earlier, simpler era in the life of the species—somehow akin to hairy backs and longish little toes?

The whole direction of explanation seems the wrong way around. For, third, what is an evolutionary explanation if not an account of how some trait was a *means to* or *part of* securing adaptive advantage? Evolutionary explanation, notice, is calculative in form. Our question is why should volition *also* have this structure, if the belief–desire model explains volition? We know that volition does not always ensue when calculative reason meets desire. We know that human desire floats free of considerations of health, long-term interest, and collective welfare. If the belief–desire model is right, then whenever action follows on the heels of desire, this will be because desire thus liberated travels smoothly in accordance with calculative reason. Why?

The second sort of answer goes like this. "Belief" and "desire" are technical terms. By definition, any psychological state or process governed by cognition goes into the belief box. By definition, the desire box holds whatever aspects of human psychology explain why we sometimes set out straightaway do what we take ourselves to have good reason to do, sometimes procrastinate, and sometimes set out to do anything *but* what reason recommends. The resulting model of motivation will doubtless apply no matter what we do. In this sense, it will be "successful." But it cannot supply independent support for instrumentalism. Here's why. Allow that the unruliness of desire tells in favor of motivational bifurcationism (it is hard to get people to do things that they don't want to do, after all, and people's wants can be extremely inconvenient). Allow that desire is there whenever motivation is. Allow that desire sets the ends of action. Allow that belief's job is to suggest means to these ends. Allow that both elements must be present in rational motivation. That is, accept a common instrumentalist picture. It now turns out that desire must be at once *sensitive* to the deliverances of cognition (hence transferable from end to means) and *insensitive* to the deliverances of cognition (that is, otherwise arational). We want to know why desire should have *both* of these properties, and why the influence of reason on desire should be so singularly limited. Resorting to stipulation at this point again begs our question.

Claims about the explanatory success of belief–desire motivational bifurcationism do not support instrumentalism. The model only works when desire transfers from end to means. Either this transfer is merely some glad *accident* in the otherwise arational business of wanting (hence inexplicable), or else the transfer is simply *assumed* by the model (hence unexplained). I conclude that the so-called success of the belief–desire model of motivation is not in fact a distinctive virtue of instrumentalism, largely because the model is not a success apart from the assumption that instrumentalism is true, and conceals many mysteries even if instrumentalism is true.

Instrumentalism is supposed to have other advantages. For example, many favor instrumentalism because, arguably—I mean, this is one of the points that has been hotly disputed of late—it lends itself to formal treatment of the sort one finds in Bayesian decision theory and economic models of rational choice.[15] The elegance of the math and the imprimatur of mathematical social science are supposed to be a point in favor of the doctrine about practical reason. It is hard to understand this thought. Surely it would be the *soundness* of the theory that would be its best attraction. An unsound theory, no matter how elegantly packaged, would be no great find, and anti-instrumentalists have been keen to point out (a) that there are big questions about the descriptive adequacy of Bayesian decision theory and neoclassical economics, and (b) that anyway it is doubtful that either is, strictly, instrumentalist. Neither, for instance, turns on any particular descriptive account of human psychology, moral or otherwise.

Finally, instrumentalism is sometimes thought to be attractive on grounds of ethical neutrality. Instrumentalism promises to account for reason in action without importing any tendentious or moralistic claims about what people are supposed to want. It takes people as they are, leaves it up to them what they want, and analyzes practical reason as reason in the service of getting those things. The suggestion is that instrumentalism proceeds from a stance of tolerance, and so embodies an important liberal ideal. But genuine instrumentalism would have to leave room for all kinds of intolerant, outright hateful desires as well as the gentler, live-and-let-live variety. The fact that the *theory* is ethically neutral does not mean that the *practices* thereby theorized would be. In this case, there is reason to suppose that the reverse will be true. For while it is hard to imagine a nonhuman species coming to ruin over its members' own vicious acts, it is easy enough to sense the possibility for us.

And the question becomes more acute: What is it about instrumentalism that is in any way compelling?

A Proposal

In what follows, I attempt to answer this question and, in trying to answer it, produce a limited defense of a view about practical reason. I do not call the view *instrumentalism,* partly in deference to John Dewey, who invented the name but never dreamed of baptizing this sort of position with it, and partly in order to distinguish my view from some contemporary work.[16] Rather, I call it *the standard picture of practical reason*—the *standard picture,* for short. (By "picture" I mean something more crude and less grand than is suggested by "theory.") The standard picture has it that practical reason is centrally the power to match means to ends, or parts of an activity to the whole of it, in action. That is, practical reason is primarily calculative. The sort of primacy in question is this: I argue that any sound view of practical reason must account for the goal-directedness of reason in action, that, for example, without a calculative framework in place there could be no such thing as rational assessment of human acts.

The standard picture turns on no particular moral psychological thesis. Many different moral psychological doctrines are consistent with the view, because the view says nothing about the distinctive psychological sources of human ends or reasons. My own moral psychological commitments are relatively insubstantial. I take it that the standard picture invokes a special variety of human wanting—*calculative wanting*—that restricts its objects to things that are in one's power to do, to make happen, or to make possible and has this feature: its structure mimics the means–end, part–whole order, earlier described in the fourth instrumentalist thesis, which concerned practical justification. It went like this:

> Let A and B be actions of different types. One is justified in A-ing only if one takes it that A-ing is a means to (or part of) attaining (or making it possible to attain) a further end, B-ing, and one wants to B. In short, the structure of rational justification in practical contexts is calculative.

Calculative wanting, that is, seeks to A in order to B, where A and B are actions of different kinds that it is in one's power to do, and the wanting tracks the calculative relation between A-ing and B-ing.[17] As such, calculative wanting is only in place once the transfer of motivation along calculative lines is in place, and its object is an action or course of action in prospect. Very few wants take calculative form. Moreover, while I emphasize calculative wanting, the emphasis does *not* imply that reason is impotent in practice. Quite the contrary. I argue that the standard picture outlines the conditions that *must* be met if we are to have a topic worth writing about in writing about *practical* reason. In this vein I argue that any episode in the life of a human mind that could count as practical reasoning will have a means–end or part–whole *form*, no matter what its content. In short, not only is calculative wanting *permeated* by reason (which is why there's no mystery about its sensitivity to calculative cognition), the calculative form that such wanting takes is the *primary* form that rational justification takes in practical contexts. On the standard picture, that is, it isn't that volition without cognition is blind. Rather, volition without cognition is impossible.

Put bluntly, the red herring in contemporary debates isn't a calculative view of practical reason; it is instrumentalist moral psychology. Indeed, it is the centrality of bifurcationist moral psychology to instrumentalist doctrines that makes instrumentalism seem shockingly weak for a position described as needing no justification. But instrumentalist views circle around topics pertinent to practical reason generally, and can also be read as various accounts of how or why reason in action principally tracks means and ends, parts of an activity and the whole of it.[18]

Let's reserve the term "instrumentalism" for calculative views of practical reason that turn on moral psychological doctrines that explicitly or implicitly involve the division of the mind into distinctive departments—reason and passion, thought and feeling, cognition and affect.

Now look what happens: the fortunes of calculative views of practical reason will *not* hang on the fortunes of instrumentalism, since instrumentalism may compass unusually weak calculative accounts of practical reason. This would explain why it is so easy to criticize instrumentalism.

And why doesn't instrumentalism simply go away, given the many refutations of it? Perhaps because, for all its weaknesses, instrumentalism turns on *calculative* views of practical reason—indeed, instrumentalism provides the going calculative accounts of practical reason. The plot thickens. For suppose that practical reason is primarily calculative, and that this claim, suitably interpreted, can be given argumentative support. Suppose that the claim that practical reason is primarily calculative is not a claim about the psychological antecedents of rational action, but is rather an abstract, philosophical claim about the role of thought about ends in setting the terms and structure of practical justification. The MacGuffin in our story then turns out to be the most abstract and least discussed point—namely, the fourth thesis, the thesis about the structure of rational justification in practical contexts.[19]

In giving a limited defense of the standard picture, I defend a picture of reasons for acting rooted in the fourth thesis. More precisely, I argue that calculative practical reason is so important that even if there are deeply noncalculative practical considerations, their standing as reasons for acting will depend on their role as sources of ends, means, or constraints on ends and means in human action. No practical considerations detached from thought about ends and means could count as a reason for action. In terms familiar from contemporary debates, I argue on behalf of a *non*-desire-based version of internalism about reasons for acting.

That most discussion of instrumentalism turns on the first, second, or third topic (or some combination of these) is why the many refutations of instrumentalism seem to miss the mark. Although moral psychology is very important to work on ethics, calculative views of practical reason need not turn on *any* specific moral psychological commitments. Neither need they turn on views about the metaphysics and epistemology of fact and value. Nor need they involve quasi-empirical claims about whether we sometimes think about what to pursue rather than how to attain such ends as we are already determined to pursue. Hence, the claim that practical reason is primarily calculative cannot be defeated by recourse to claims about practical reasoning, claims about the character of fact and value, or claims about moral psychology. And since the character of rational justification in practical contexts is crucially important to practical philosophy, the contributions to understanding motivation, affect, and so on made in the course of twenty years of disputation about instrumentalism have not got rid of the inchoate sense that a calculative view of practical reason must somehow be something we can take for granted. The many refutations of instrumentalism out there *could not* get rid of this half-thought because they have not addressed it adequately.

I begin my defense of the standard picture by giving an account of practical good. The strongest arguments against its poorer cousin, instrumentalism, turn on the thought that calculative accounts of practical reason fail to explain the normativity of practical reason. Since accounts of normativity concern ways that an *ought* arises in connection with practical or theoretical good, I work to forestall this objection by providing a suitable account of practical good.

2

In Some Sense Good

Primum principium in ratione practica est quod fundatur supra
rationem boni quae est, Bonum est quod omnia appeteunt.
—Thomas Aquinas

"The first principle in practical reason is founded on the meaning of
good," Thomas Aquinas wrote. *"Good is what all things pursue."*[1] Beginning from Aristotle's remark that "[e]very art and every inquiry, and similarly every action and pursuit, is thought to aim at some good; and for
this reason the good has rightly been declared to be that at which all
things aim,"[2] Aquinas argues that the good has the character of an end.
He thereby ties wanting both to good and to the calculative form of justification. From such a starting place an account of the *normativity* of
calculative reason might be spun.

It was a late medieval commonplace that everything pursued is pursued as good—omne appetitum appetitur sub specie boni—and Aristotle's text suggests that it was an ancient commonplace as well. But
Aquinas's argument in support of the point is unlikely to strike contemporary philosophers as especially compelling. Ends are still ordinarily
understood as the objects of pursuits. What will give us pause is treating
ends in general as even *apparently* good, unless this move is flatly stipu-
lative and, hence, empty. In this vein Bernard Williams complains:

> In any ordinary understanding of *good*, surely, an extra step is taken if
> you go from saying that you want something or have decided to pursue
> it to saying that it is good, or (more to the point) that it is good that
> you should have it. The idea of something's being good imports an
> idea, however minimal or hazy, of a perspective which can be acknowl-
> edged by more than one agent as good. An agent who merely has a cer-

tain purpose may of course think that his purpose is good, but he does not have to.[3]

I take up contemporary opposition to the idea that thought about the good and thought about intentional action are bound up together at the conclusion of this chapter. Before addressing the complaint, however, it is important to consider how thought about good and thought about action could seem inextricably bound together. The obvious possibility is that we are working with a practical account of good.

Throughout the following four chapters, I work to motivate a practical understanding of good, taking my inspiration from Aquinas. Much of the work in this chapter involves laying out a sketch of a formal division in kinds of reasons for acting drawn from some of Aquinas's remarks on good, and using this to respond to Williams's complaint.

A Practical Account of Good

I mean "practical" to carry more weight in the phrase "practical account of good" than it has for a long time. I mean the term to direct our attention straight off to doing things, to intentional action. Intentional action is action that can be explained and justified by giving one's reasons for so acting. A practical account of good, then, has to do with reasons for acting. The one I give proceeds from consideration of intentional action.

The more usual starting place these days in thinking about reasons for acting is moral psychology. Intentional action and mental life are not unrelated: one's intentions both shape action and give what one has in view in so acting. Elizabeth Anscombe directed our attention to this feature of intentional action initially by noting that "if you want to say at least some true things about a man's intentions, you will have a strong chance of success if you mention what he actually did or is doing," because, "whatever else he may intend, or whatever may be his intentions in doing what he does, the greater number of the things which you would say straight off a man did or was doing, will be things he intends."[4] Her interest in intentional action is unusual. We are more inclined to suppose that the operation of practical reason is most readily detected by examining what goes on when people think about what to do or pursue. In short, we often treat the term "practical" as marking out a region of topics *about which* one can think, and practical reason as what is at work when one thinks about such topics. The region of practical topics consists in topics pertaining to action in general, with considerations pertinent to one's own doings as a kind of subdivision. The latter are of special interest since they are most likely to be brought to bear on what one does.

Contemporary focus on practical topics as objects for critical reflection has the unfortunate consequence of rendering reason *in* intentional action rather opaque. The *mise-en-scène* of reason becomes the mental theater and the operations of practical reason become head work that is separated from, and often taken to be temporally prior to, the work of enacting one's will. We have, one might say, a white-collar vision of reason in action. Mental labor and manual labor were not in this way distinct for Aquinas. Accordingly, to begin to get a sense for what distinguishes an old-fashioned practical account of good from some other variety, we need to imagine that practical reasoning is not just thought *about* action, but rather reasoning *toward* (paradigmatically extramental) action. The force of *toward* is at least this: not only does practical deliberation issue in doing something and concern topics pertinent to what one does, the fit between the two must be such that the reasoning is undertaken *in order to decide what to do* and what is done is done *on account of* and *in accordance with* the grounds provided by deliberation.

Old-fashioned work on practical deliberation sees the objective of practical thinking as action. On many contemporary views, it looks as though it will count as a coincidence if reason ever reaches this destination.[5] It is as if we have become so interested in what a rational agent takes it into his head to do (and why) that we are unconcerned about how it all turns out, as though he could be a perfectly realized practically rational being without all the fuss and bother of engaging in extramental activities, without lifting a finger, really. We are driven to this kind of view by imagining that excellence in the exercise of practical reason—practical rationality—is attained by developing, say, a beautiful character, or a deep commitment to morality, or a sound understanding of what matters, or very fine principles (where "principles" is understood not, in the first place, as sources of what people do that give shape to their lives in practice, but as considered opinions about what ought to be the case, opinions that one is occasionally called on to actualize), and that the way one *gets* principles, knowledge, commitment, or character is by critical reflection on oneself and on practical topics. Whereas I think that any theory of practical reason that locates practical reason first and fore-most in moral psychology (and so renders doing things a simple adjunct to the rich inner life—a little bit off to the side that is no part of the real topic of interest) is not a theory of the excellent exercise of *practical* rea-son at all.

To begin with, then, in order to see what the medievals were getting at, I concentrate on intentional action, with the thought that reasons for acting both shape it and are what one has in view in doing what one does. This gives the right sort of sense to practical reason. Additionally, by thinking about reasons in and for acting, we attend to what one might say on behalf of doing what one does. And *this* is the way to think about "good" in "practical account of good." A practical account of good be-comes an account of reasons for acting. To say that good is what people pursue is to say that intentional action *as such* is subject to reasons-for-acting-seeking questions, criticism, and the like. Getting a grip on this requires thinking about reasons for acting generally, rather than only moral ones or only prudential ones—the two sorts Williams seems to have in mind. By focusing on only moral or only prudential practical considerations, we fail to notice a great deal of what people do and why.

I begin motivating a practical account of good with a remark about practical deliberation.

The Threefold Division

When you reason about what to do, you do so on the assumption that sound practical reasoning will point you in the direction of one of the better alternatives available to you. "Better" means: in some respect "more good." There are many ways in which some alternatives can be better than others. Some of the things you could do might be easier than others or riskier, more scandalous or less conspicuous. Whether any of these would count in favor of an action in prospect for you will tend to depend on other things about you, about what you are after, about what you can do, and about your situation. Contrary to what Williams sug-gests, this sense of "better" need not have anything to do with morality or long-term interest. The good implied by such use of "better" likewise has no obvious necessary link to overall well-being or morality.

I focus on three very general ways in which some of your alternatives might be better than others, taking a cue from Aquinas. First, some of your alternatives might promise enjoyment in prospect. Second, some might help you to attain or (make it possible to attain) the whole or some part of your immediate or further ends. Third, some of your alternatives might square better with how you think people in general, or people in your position, should conduct themselves. In general, some things you can do are better than others in the sense of being more fitting, some as more useful, and some as more pleasant. These are the three senses in which one alternative can be more good than another. All three concern the sense in which your ends are, from your point of view, choice worthy. And, of course, in giving an account of how your pursuit is useful, fitting, or delightful, you will be supposing that others (namely, those others who ask about your reasons for acting) can understand what you offer on behalf of doing what you do.

Any of these three ways in which an end can be good might be at work in determining you to risk, ease, scandal, or inconspicuousness in action. For example, if the plain fact that something is risky counts in favor of your doing it, this could be because you are an occasional thrill seeker who takes pleasure in tempting the fates or because you think that taking chances leads one to live life to the fullest by requiring that one focus all of one's powers and attention on what one is doing (that is, you take it that it befits one to live on the edge). In rare cases, that a thing is dangerous to do can even make the pursuit useful. For example, if you are one of the few people who make very difficult climbs without safety equipment, and only exceedingly perilous climbs allow you to develop your skills, then the fact that the Golden Gate Bridge is very dangerous to climb in this way will count in favor of climbing it.[6] In a slightly less exotic vein, if you seek to prove that you are not a coward, then you will favor a testing ground where you stand to lose something important. Again, some of your alternatives might be more good than others in the sense of being more useful, more fitting, or more pleasant. Call this way of seeing the good at work in practical reason the *threefold division* of good.

Aquinas took up the threefold division from Ambrose, and saw it at work in Aristotle's remarks on the three objects of love and the three kinds of friendship.[7] Thomas may have drawn the correspondence between Aristotle and Ambrose this way: what one seeks or moves toward is good, the object of love in friendship, according to Aristotle, likewise is what's lovable and, hence, good; the three bases of practical love are found in the three kinds of friendship, and the three forms of friendship—friendship for the sake of attaining common goals, friendship for the sake of pleasure, and friendship pursued for its own sake—corresponds to a threefold division among practical considerations.[8] In general, the threefold division provides a framework for explaining intentional action, one that takes seriously the fact that the questions "*Why* are you doing that?" and "What's the *point* of doing that?" and "What's the *good* of doing that?" are basically the same question. This question, in turn, seeks out your reasons for so acting. Asking about your reasons for so acting is asking about why you are pursuing the ends you are pursuing.

The threefold division, then, is about how the point of doing something can enter into explaining what one does. Explaining by showing the point of what one does is crucial to justifying what one does. Aquinas wrote:

> [I]n the movement of appetite, the thing desired that terminates the movement of appetite relatively, as a means of tending toward something else, is called the *useful* [*utile*]; that sought after as the last thing absolutely terminating the appetite, as a thing toward which for its own sake the appetite tends, is called the *befitting* [*honestum*]; for the *befitting* is that which is desired for its own sake; but that which terminates the movement of appetite in the form of rest in the thing desired, is called the *pleasant* [*delectatio*].[9]

He meant this as a general remark about movement. For creatures with rational appetite (humans, for instance) Aquinas's thought involves both a division among desirability characterizations that can be given for an action and a division among sources of action.[10] That is, it is about considerations that simultaneously explain and justify intentional action as such.

Appetite is, roughly, what characterizes an agent as a pursuer or seeker. There is no contemporary equivalent for "appetite" in widespread use. The closest one might get is by taking up a term coined by Michael Thompson: "end-orientation."[11] Rational appetite (our sort) becomes a species of what Thompson calls *concept-involving end-orientation*.[12] The movement of rational appetite becomes an individual's concept-involving, end-directed action. That is, the movement of rational appetite becomes individual intentional action.[13]

On this reading, Aquinas's remarks about the terminal points for the movement of rational appetite are remarks about where intentional action reaches its intended destination, its happy conclusion, its end. For Aquinas, the point of an intentional action is the desirability of the intended end or term. The end or term is an object of pursuit *qua* desirable. (This is the sense in which practical good is the *aim* of practical reason.) And the point of an intentional action as such is given by adverting to the threefold division of good. When what is sought in action is sought because it is useful, the agent has set her sights on some further, future end, and what she does is done in order to attain or make it possible to attain that further end. When what is sought terminates in lingering enjoyment of what she is up to, of the present action, then the agent seeks rest in the thing desired; the good at issue is good in the sense pleasant. Ultimately, pursuits stop when the agent has got all that she seeks—at her last end, her final destination. What can be said in support of attaining her ultimate end will involve the overarching practical direction of her life—a direction that determines whether her life was a good human life in Aquinas's system. In that sense, what stops the movement of appetite in what is wanted for its own sake is what fits the agent more generally, given the sort of practical being she is and works to be. Such pursuits are good in the sense fitting.

Notice that all three regions of practical good concern the ends of intentional action *as such*. Aquinas insists that there is a difference between merely going for one thing rather than another (as very young children do), and pursuing an end as such (as only animals with linguistically informed rational appetite do). Philippa Foot discusses this point at some length.[14] She treats the two topics (pursuit of an end as such and pursuit of good) separately, but because Aquinas is treating pursuit of an end as such *as* pursuit of practical good, the two stories have the same moral:

> [W]hat Aquinas says about animals and small children being able to have ends but not see them as ends seems comprehensible and acceptable. And the same point could be made in terms of what is seen as good.[15] For it can be said that while animals go for the good (thing) *that they see,* human beings go for *what they see as good.* . . . It is for this reason that while no animal can be said to "know the better and choose the worse," it makes sense to describe a human being as doing this. We can, to be sure, mark hesitation in an animal that is, for instance, torn

between hunger and fear; but nothing in [a nonrational] animal's be-
haviour could lead us to say that it saw that one alternative was better
than another but that its action did not match its thought! The problem of *akrasia* (incontinence, or so-called weakness of will) concerns a
description belonging only to rational beings. . . .[16]

Human beings not only have the power to reason about all sorts of
things in a speculative way, but also the power to *see grounds* for acting
in one way rather than another; and if told that they should do one
thing rather than another, they can ask *why* they should. Quite early
on, a child learns that a "should" needs a ground, unlike an order,
which may simply be reiterated or backed up by a threat.[17]

What we have here is an *end-based* account of reasons for acting, inextricably bound up in an account of the as-such ends of beings with rational
appetite as (at least apparently) good.

Because good is being treated as the object of pursuit, the justification
of the act in the Thomistic account is also end-based: you describe
where you are going, what you are headed for in doing what you are doing, what will count as the successful conclusion of this turn in your
practical engagements, and the description of your destination is meant
to show the good of your practical direction. Sometimes the good at issue will be obvious (as when one seeks a fair resolution to conflict, plans
a splendid meal, or purchases a good tool for a task). Other times, the
good at issue will not be obvious. But practical reason primarily tracks
practical good, and understanding intentional action as such is understanding the good at issue in it.[18]

On this view, reason is both in the action and in the agent. Practical
reason aims at ends that are desirable. The desirability or goodness of
what I am doing here and now is drawn from the desirability or goodness of the end (which is good insofar as useful, pleasant, or fitting).
And these matters enter into the explanation and justification of action
in three different ways, drawn from the rational structure of the completed act and its place in the agent's pursuits. Aquinas holds, further,
that is not just that some ends are good. Rather, practical good is the
constitutive end of practical reason, and practical good—good as the object of pursuit—is the primary sense of "good": "primum principium in
ratione practica est quod fundatur supra rationem boni quae est, Bonum
est quod omnia appeteunt."[19]

Throughout the remainder of this chapter, I work both to underscore how different this view is from most contemporary secular accounts, and to show how it finds reason first off in intentional action. I begin by glancing at Aquinas's work on evil, in order to consider the place of evil in this kind of treatment of good. This provides a gateway to rethinking befitting-style desirability characterizations, the sort that Williams seemed to have in mind.

A Touch of Evil

In what sense can we treat good as the object of human pursuits when it is abundantly clear that people sometimes knowingly and deliberately do bad things? Happily, this is a question to which Aquinas devoted a lot of attention. And his answer to the question resembles one kind of answer that some contemporary secular ethicists give: immorality involves an error in judgment, and the character of the error is clear if we think about how it befits one to live.[20]

What is *truly* befitting on Aquinas's account is ethically sound intentional action. This accords with contemporary sensibilities. But secular theorists interested in this account of practical good—this way of thinking about reasons for acting—cannot help themselves to Aquinas's account of the befitting and should not assume that what is, formally, befitting will be ethically sound. Here's why. In Aquinas, there is a single last end for people, which is, in a very strong sense, given by our place in God's plan. Consideration of the last end provides a deep unity to Thomistic thought about the threefold division of reasons for acting. Where we are meant to wind up is in Paradise, occupied in everlasting contemplation of God. The prospect of resurrected life draws together all three regions of good for Aquinas: it is the ultimate end-in-the-sense-stopping-place in human life, that is, it is the destination toward which each of us is headed if all is going well and to which this life is (in a way) a means; it is how it befits a man to end up, and living as he must live in order to get there (by God's grace) is living as it befits him to live; finally, it is ecstatically pleasant. Aspects of divine providence unify all three regions of the good. Because of this, Aquinas can see the useful, befitting, and pleasing orders in human life as bound together by a divinely ordained calculative order that allows us to give a relatively clear, relatively direct assessment of actions of particular kinds under their circumstances: the account of practical reason is set in a substantive, calculative ethical frame.[21] The pleasures of the wicked may explain and show the point of what the wicked seek, but pale in comparison with the pleasures of holiness. The prospects of short-term gain might attract our interest and show the point in doing some of what we do, but because our long-run is very long indeed, there could not be a sound way of discounting the future in favor of the temporally proximate (where temporal proximity might involve the whole of worldliness). The life of the virtuous on earth might be rough going, but, by God's grace, beatitude is virtue's ultimate reward, so virtue remains useful and fitting, even when it looks as though acting from it will bring disaster to one's mortal life.[22] Roughly, the formal account of practical reason is calculative, and the irrationality of anyone in possession of revealed truth determining himself to an unethical life is clear.[23]

What I hope will strike the non-Catholic student of Aquinas's practical system *is not* the image of so many cogs and wheels set fortuitously spinning in a single direction by the hand of a foreign, premodern God, but rather how difficult it will be to motivate *any* such satisfying unity without the theology.[24] What *unifies* an end-based account of reasons for acting, hence the good in action, hence practical good, is *the ultimate end.* When we conceive the whole of a human life as going in a determinate direction, we can discuss each bit or stage of that life in terms of whether and how it contributes to reaching the destination in question. The three divisions are distinguished in terms of the temporal relation a practical consideration bears to the act it explains. Useful-style considerations look to the future. Pleasant-style considerations look to the present. In Aquinas's system, befitting-style considerations bridge past, present, and future by directing our attention to how what we do serves the last end. But there is no reason to suppose that what serves determinate *future* ends, what tends to lingering enjoyment in the *present,* and what lends order to ends that shape everydayness in the *whole of a life* will invariably come together in secular work.

Traditionally, the difficulty in giving a unified account of good in action lies in understanding the relation between acting well (acting from and for the sake of ethically sound befitting-style practical considerations) and faring well (pursuing private advantage or pleasure). It is relatively straightforward to get things going if moral reasons turn out to be inextricably linked with calculative reasons for acting. Then the distinction between acting well (acting for and from morality or virtue) and faring well (successfully acting in order to attain one's ends) are tied closely enough together to show acting well to be in one's (long-term) interest. (In effect, Aquinas takes this route.) Similarly, if you deposit in some agents a practical orientation that favors acting well (for example, virtue), and treat both the ends that arise from this orientation (for example, virtuous ends) and the constraint these agents show in their other pursuits as the normal outcome of the good practical orientation, then your agents will tend to act well even in pursuit of private gain. A less subtle strategy involves crediting agents with an inclination toward acting well, such that they will be unhappy with ill-gotten gains, and hence will not be able to fare well unless they act well. Variants of all three are around these days.[25]

But if you take seriously the thought that acting well can lead to significant personal loss (and is anyway no guarantee that good things will come one's way), then getting calculative considerations, considerations pertaining to broad patterns in one's life, and considerations of pleasure to come together will not be easy. Consider: Kant, who is the source of some of the best arguments about the frequent failure of fit between calculative reasons and considerations of pleasure on the one side, and considerations pertinent to morality and virtue on the other, holds that faith is necessary for practical reason. Without it, given that we are necessarily interested in our own happiness and know full well that Nature does not reward us for virtue or morality, we have no reason even to *hope* that a virtuous or dutiful life will be a happy one. You can't set your sights on faring well in proportion to acting well in your life (that is, you can't *will* it) if you have no reason even to *hope* that a virtuous and dutiful life will have some measure of happiness in it. Neither virtue nor morally fitting conduct is any insurance against getting struck by lightning, or falling rocks, or stray bullets, or the bomb. Any natural or manmade disaster that befalls you can wipe out your happiness for a long time, should you survive.[26] Practical faith is faith that acting well and faring well will not come apart entirely.[27] Getting these two to work in concert is a task even Kant thinks requires faith in a divine order of justice. This aspect of Kant has received very little contemporary attention outside the circles of Kant scholars.

But things look even worse than the contemporary debates suggest that they are if we press the topic in a different direction than Kant did. The trouble with getting calculative practical reason to hook up with

ethics becomes most acute if we think carefully about individual immoral acts (sins, in Thomas's system) and vice (with special emphasis on
capital vices—vices that ordinarily operate as the ends of various other
vices).[28]

Armed with the threefold division, an account of the good things in
life, and revealed doctrine about the last end, Aquinas theorizes not only
ethically sound intentional action, but also ethically deplorable intentional action. Both revolve around pursuit of *as-such desirable* things.
Both involve desirability characterizations falling into at least one of the
three regions. Both display practical reason, that is, reason in action.
And Aquinas's account of culpable wickedness provides unflinching
treatment of the reasons for and sources of first-rate and lesser varieties
of human badness. We have neither a modern nor an ancient equivalent
for this work among the standard sources for contemporary secular
moral philosophy. One half suspects that faith gave Thomas the courage
to do it. I mean, once you appreciate the power of the work on viciousness, and if you are committed to secular ethics, it really does seem that
all the king's horses and all the king's men couldn't put reason and ethics
together again in a way that shows individual wickedness to be necessarily irrational, or even unfit.

It is depressing to have to pay attention to viciousness. Contemporary
secular ethicists do not, as a rule, but some of what people deliberately
do is very unethical, and blinding ourselves to what can be said on behalf of what people in fact deliberately do is blinding ourselves to what
they are up to in action, to the *nature* of their purposes. This is no minor
limitation for a theory of practical reason. It is something more on the
order of willful refusal to look at our chosen topic from the aspects it
presents to us. The aspects in question are those in light of which a pursuit presents itself as desirable in the eyes of the pursuer and in terms
that make sense (even a veritable witches' brew of vice is heated by the
flames of incentives to pursue genuine goods). The threefold division of
good sorts these aspects in terms of how they contribute to understanding and explaining action. Seeing reason in pursuits, seeing their points,
is seeing what is desirable in them. And seeing this is seeing the *good* of
doing them, from the individual's point of view, even when the pursuits
are vicious.

I pause here to discuss some of Aquinas's work on vice. This is intended partly to introduce the reader to this work, and partly in order to

dispel a powerful contemporary philosophical prejudice. The prejudice is that:

(1) All objective theories of good will show that individual unethical action is irrational (Aquinas is an objective theorist of good who theorizes reason in viciousness).

(2) True befitting-style desirability characterizations will give moral or ethical reasons for any individual's actions under the relevant circumstances (they only do so in Aquinas in light of revealed doctrine, and secular theorists cannot bask in that light).

(3) What is good in action is what is morally, prudentially, or ethically sound (Aquinas theorizes the place of pursuit of genuine good in acts of utter depravity, and the account makes sense).

Dispelling the prejudice leaves secular theorists without an obvious account of what is individually irrational in vicious conduct. It also makes it harder for secular theorists to restrict their accounts of befitting-style desirability characterizations to practical considerations that earn high marks ethically.

In the aggregate, the trouble with vice is clear. But part of the work of, say, capital vice consists in removing unreflective inclinations to avoiding wrongdoing, thereby derailing such individual tendencies to ethical conduct as may have been picked up along the way. Moreover, capital vices take genuine goods as their objects.[29] Finally, capital vice is cultivated—one habituates oneself to it rather than being afflicted by it. It shows *strength,* not weakness, of will. That is why it is possible to treat the reason in viciousness systematically, both substantively and formally. Aquinas points out:

> Now that one sin be directed to another can occur in two ways: in one way on the part of the sinner himself, whose will is more inclined to the objective of one sin than of another; but this is accidental to the sins themselves [that is, however statistically widespread among people, the link between kinds of wrongdoing is idiosyncratic rather than calculatively sound], hence no vices are called capital according to this; in another way, from the very relationship of ends, one of which has a certain affinity with another, in such a way that for the most part it is ordered to that other, for example, deception which is the end or aim of fraud is ordered to amassing money which is the end of avarice; and in this way the capital vices are to be taken. Therefore those vices

are called capital which have ends principally desirable in themselves in such a way that other vices are ordered to them.[30]

The ordering of one vice to another in capital viciousness, that is, is impersonally and calculatively tied to the character of the vices in question. There are seven capital vices. Pride seeks the excellence of honor and renown. Avarice has as its object acquisition and control of wealth. Gluttony fixates on eating, which is crucial to the preservation of the individual. Lust has sexual pleasure as its object, which (at least) pertains to the good of preserving the species. The relation of the remaining three—anger, acedia,[31] and envy—to good things is less in the pursuit of an as-such desirable good as in the avoidance of a bad thing. The man who is in one of these ways vicious sees a spiritual good or the good of some other person as an impediment to his own good, which in turn makes the perceived genuine good painful to behold. The operation of envy, acedia, and anger involves a self-protective aversion to the pain that comes of seeing a good not one's own as a threat or as an obstacle to one's own well-being.

Whether we agree with the catalog of capital vices (for example, lust is not everywhere taken to be a vice nowadays) or the specific analyses of their operations (for example, a secular theorist might make humanity the source of the good that becomes aversive in acedia), what we find in Aquinas is something on the order of a *theory* about immorality. Without the theology, what the theory shows is the sense in which it befits a vicious man to act viciously.

This is not to say that there are no genuine human goods that become inaccessible to the deeply vicious. It is merely to notice that the very habits that place these good things out of the vicious person's reach tend also to suppress her inclinations to pursue them. The envious person, for instance, who is inclined to see in others' well-being a painful reminder of all that she lacks and an outright impediment to her enjoyment of what she has, will not be much moved by an argument that our collective well-being demands that we jointly seek justice (and, hence, that she ought to support justice), even though collective well-being almost certainly demands some measure of justice. Rather, relations of justice established for the sake of widespread well-being hold out the prospect of indefinitely multiplied sites of pain for an envious person. Others' misery *soothes* the envious like few things can. This is part of why the envious are not merely unhappy, but toxic. It will not do to insist that happy anticipation of her own increased well-being ought to carry an envious person over the hump. As Aquinas points out, capital vice is corrosive. The vice that erodes the envious person's ability to enjoy what she already has produces so acute an awareness of the inadequacy of what life brings that even a decided improvement in her fortunes is lost on her. And it is not that her failure to be moved by our arguments is rooted in imperfect reason. If we seek to show her that justice is in her interest, we must take into account her own understanding of what is in her interest. As she understands it, collective well-being is not in her interest. If justice will produce collective well-being, then justice is not in her interest either.

As ethicists hope will be the case, the wicked *do* turn out to be making an error in practical judgment on Thomas's account, but this is a conclusion drawn in light of the larger theological system, centered on a discussion of our last end. In short, the wicked miscalculate—not about what they are doing here and now, exactly (although wickedness tends to disorder even in this life, on Aquinas's view), but rather about what they can expect to gain by their deeds. There is in wickedness "a turning towards a transitory good and a turning away from an unchangeable good."[32] That is, the lives of the deeply vicious are disordered at root with respect to their last end. And no matter how wanton the individual has become, no matter how deeply corrupted his character, it remains true of him, *qua* member of the species lowest in the order of intelligent beings and highest in the order of organisms, that his last end is otherworldly and that he needs the virtues in order to live well in light of this larger order in life. In this sense, part of what is wrong with cultivated ethical badness—vice—is that it betrays a failure of calculative practical reason with respect to the last end. Thus, it befits even a confirmed scoundrel to change his ways.

Notice that there will be no such straightforward link between ethical conduct and a claim about how it befits every one of us to live if it is implausible to credit the vicious individual with *having* an end that might be served by virtue. If we are strict about "ascribing" ends to people—if, rather than supposing that the envious person *has* proper ends about which he is in a muddle, we notice that some of his ends are unethical—then we are not going to get this sort of account of the irrationality of acting from envy. The Thomistic account of why it does not befit a man to act from capital vice depends on the character of the last end. Lose the last end and you lose the moral science. Lose the moral science and, in light of the theory of vice (which has, I take it, independent plausibility), you lose the claim that practical good is singularly unified. Faced with one man leading a harmless, drifting life and another leading a splendidly disciplined vicious life, one might rather prefer the former, even though the latter displays more self-culture. Given the theory of vice, minus the theological frame, individual immorality need not be rash, weak-willed, or ignorant. That is, none of the traditional philosophical accounts of bad action still floating in contemporary literature need apply.

Fit and Ethics

In its theological context, there are various direct links between the threefold division and an account of ethical good. There is, moreover, a set of principled relations between the three regions, a deep unity to them, and a way of getting ethics to come straight out of the insight about practical reason (it comes via consideration of what Denis Bradley calls "the natural endlessness of human nature,"[33] revealed in doctrine about our last end). What remains of the threefold division taken out of this context is a clean formal classification of practical considerations and good reason to suppose (a) that its employment will be piecemeal in principle and in practice, and (b) that the insight it gives us into practical reason will not yield any straightforward argument that unethical conduct is inevitably irrational. What does this leave in the befitting region of good for secular work?

There is no longer philosophical agreement that individuals *have* last ends in the sense of final destinations, toward which their doings tend in general and, hence, to which their daily lives are means. Neither is there complete agreement that individuals must conceive their whole lives as going in the kind of determinate direction that is required to get talk about last ends off the ground. The current popularity of the thought that people must have some sort of definite plan covering the main points of their maturity supplies a version of ultimate end talk: the ultimate end consists in realizing the plan. But there are indefinitely many sorts of plans one might have for one's maturity, backed up by views about what's good in life that make a kind of sense. Consider: live fast; die young; leave a pretty corpse behind.

What secular theorists can salvage from this bit of the Thomistic framework is the thought that *some* of what one does is expressive of the general shape of (the whole or some part of) one's adult life. One's larger practical orientation sets some of the terms (that is, ends) of what one does as parts of realizing a pattern, even if one aspires not to outlive one's own youthful vigor and beauty. While secular work on practical reason cannot keep a grip on Thomas's understanding of the ultimate end, it at least can retain calculative thought about how it befits one to live: some ends find their source and desirability in aspects of one's character, role, identity, plan, or what have you. This interpretation of fit replaces talk of the last end with discussion of such patterns in adult human life as the agent works to establish, develop, and maintain in practice. This gives us the formal character of the last of the three regions of good.

Why There Are Three Regions

The reader may well be asking "Very well, but why *three* regions of good? Why wouldn't there be more ways of approaching good in action than these three?"

The quick answer to the question is that it's hard to see where we would look for *more* concluding points for intentional action. We have: the conclusion is in the future and doing this is a way of getting there (the useful). We have: the conclusion is attaining this very end, which expresses or is otherwise rooted in more enduring, patterning features of my life (the befitting). We have: the point in doing this is to savor the doing of the present action (the pleasant). The threefold division concerns that with a view toward which you act. It identifies the attainable end of your act with the desirable direction of your doings. You can have a further goal in view, or you can have in view attaining this end on account of how it fits with an established pattern of some sort, or you can have in view what you are here and now doing, not primarily with an eye toward the future and not necessarily from patterns you have been concerned to establish in the past and seek to maintain, but just because what you are here and now doing is delightful or satisfying. Formally, the different kinds of practical considerations have different *temporal* relations to what you do. It is hard to see what has been left out.

One possibility is a case where the good or bad you respond to is in the *past*. Anscombe, for instance, adds cases where I mean to kill Donald because he murdered my brother, or I want to bring Lauren flowers because she did me a good turn. Here, the good or bad at issue in the action was in a past event. Accordingly, Anscombe calls revenge and gratitude *backward-looking motives*.[34] What we would get by having a *fourfold* division instead of a threefold division is this: reasons that draw their force from the past (backward-looking motives), reasons that cling to the present action (pleasures), reasons that look to the future (considerations about what's useful), and reasons that are meant to show the place of what one does in some larger scheme of things (befitting-style considerations). This covers *all* possible temporal relations, as near as I can tell, and in that sense, backward-looking motive is a pleasing addition. But I fold backward-looking motive into the useful. One does what one does from backward-looking motives *in order to* address a past good or bad. One is *finished* with action from backward-looking motive when one has adequately addressed the past good or bad in question. The "in order to" form of reason is what is at issue in useful-style practical considerations. As such, backward-looking motive adds nothing especially relevant to my larger project.[35]

The Threefold Division Again: Locality and Terminability

Put somewhat differently, befitting-style reasons for acting are *nonlocal* (explain a lot of different things that one does) and *interminable* (unending; without a built-in natural stopping place). Useful-style reasons for acting are *local* (attach to a specific action or course) and *terminable* (specify a further end and vanish when one has accomplished what one set out to do). Pleasant-style reasons for acting are *local* (attach to the present action) and *interminable* (while pleasure eventually flees, nothing about the kind of reason in question determines when this ought to occur).

Now, if we were filling in a matrix, we might wonder whether any kinds of practical considerations are nonlocal and terminable (it is, after all, the remaining possibility).[36] Steps one takes to ensure attainment of recurrent ends (like the ongoing need for food, clothing, and shelter) or that concern the stages in realizing a pattern or whole life plan may be cobbled together to get useful-style practical considerations that in fact explain a lot of different things that one does. Such considerations are, by natural extension, nonlocal (explain/justify many different kinds of action or course) and terminable (do so by showing that each is a means to or part of attaining a specific end). For example, throughout the duration of my life I will need to eat now and again. Perhaps I explain a lot of what I do in my job as directed at securing a stable income, hence, a routine source of food money. One end of teaching, then, is providing myself with food. Some backward-looking motives are likewise nonlocal *in practice* and terminable: for example, avenging my brother might explain many things I do for years (nonlocal) but will come to an end when I have finally accomplished the act of vengeance (terminable). We can get a complete "matrix" of sorts by noting that sometimes an act is useful because it plays a part in a much larger scheme of things, secures conditions necessary for attainment of recurrent ends, or belongs to the playing out of epic-scale backward-looking motive.

The reason that there are three regions, then, is that it's hard to see what is left out of account in the threefold division *except* cases where you didn't have anything much in view in doing what you did. The exceptions, notice, just *are* the cases where there is no desirability characterization to offer in support of something that you are up to, so it is unsurprising that a formal system for sorting desirability characterizations has no cubby for them.

In short, if you accept A-ing as a description of what you are doing, and you are A-ing on purpose, then answers to a reasons-for-acting-seeking question "Why are you A-ing?" will give a reason falling into (at least one) one of the three regions, or else be something on the order of "No particular reason/just thought I would/just felt like it."

The real beauty of the threefold division is that it provides a non-arbitrary and exhaustive system for sorting reasons for acting in terms of how each type contributes to explaining/justifying intentional action. The kinds of explanation given in the three terms are distinctive: useful-term explanation shows that what you are here and now doing is a means to or part of attaining one or more determinate further ends; pleasant-term explanation points to the pleasure in doing what you are here and now doing, whether or not doing it leads anywhere else; and befitting-term explanation situates what you are doing in a larger pattern of pursuits; moreover, sometimes, befitting-style explanation involves recurrent or long-term usefulness. The three sorts of favorable light in which one might view intentional action strobe different aspects of the act. And, best of all, in *each* aspect, there is a link between justification and explanation (we are explaining intentional action, note, by means of desirability characterizations).

Finding the Threefold Division in Action

Secular ethicists and philosophers of practical reason are unaccustomed to thinking about reason in intentional action. If we were to draw a crude diagram of the theoretical tendency in contemporary work on practical reason, we might depict a very large human head with many things going on inside it (the scene of reason) plus a kind of external flash-mark (the action). A tight connection is assumed between the two: what goes on in the big head is *expressed* in the flash of action; the flash of action *proceeds from* the reasoning in the big head; we look to the flash in order partially to determine what commitments and norms shape processes in the big head; the big head's identity, operations, and powers are partly displayed in the flash; and so on. For all that, as would be indicated by the spareness of the flash-mark, "intentional action" functions as a kind of unanalyzed primitive in contemporary work. Paradigmatically, an intentional action is an event of some kind. In the big-head approach, it is the event caused and explained or justified by some sort of mental process. In premodern work as I read it, on the other hand, understanding what matters in the psychological aspect of intentional action is partly a matter of understanding the structure and place of the intentional action as an end-directed process in a life. The character of the purpose is read *first* from the character and articulation of the act, not from the mental states that likewise exhibit the kind of character in question.

The contemporary theorist most likely to have been read by secular ethicists who has attended to the stuff of the flash-mark is, as I mentioned, Anscombe. She is nearly unique in her insistence that we focus on intentional action in trying to understand intention and reasons for acting. And, in investigating intentional action, she isolates something on the order of a criterion for determining whether some proceedings involve it.[37] In this section, I explore Anscombe's criterion and link it to the threefold division of good. I thereby show how the threefold division is bound up with thought about intentional action. It is appropriate to turn to Anscombe's work both because it is related to Aquinas's and because many non-Catholic Anglo–North American philosophers have read her.[38] Admittedly, although Anscombe is read and cited often enough, she is hard to understand. Why this should be so is, I suspect, partly because she draws on the kind of premodern work that I am urging us to take up again.

Anscombe argues that an intentional action is a datable event in a man or woman's life history to which

> the reasons-for-acting-seeking question "Why are you A-ing?" (where A-ing is a kind of thing you are doing), has application.

This is the criterion for determining whether an event involves an intentional action of some type.[39] The reasons-for-acting-seeking question "Why are you A-ing?" "has application" to what one is doing when one accepts A-ing as a description of something one is doing and

> the answer to "Why are you A-ing?" either terminates in a desirability characterization of one of our three sorts, or else is something on the order of "No particular reason / just thought I would / just felt like it."

Anscombe doesn't argue for the threefold division. It is, however, clearly at work in her discussion of desirability characterizations. While the desirability characterizations she discusses sometimes involve wanting a good object of some kind (she considers doing something by way of getting a good kettle because one wants a kettle, for example),[40] she is relying on the connection between having a standard purpose in seeking out an *a* and wanting a good *a*.[41] That this is a good *a*, in light of the presumed standard purpose, points to the usefulness of getting one's hands on it.

The threefold division is generally much closer to the surface. Anscombe devotes most of her attention to cases in which the answer to the characteristic question "Why?" mentions a further intention with which one acts (that is, shows that what one does is a means to or part of attaining some further end, in other words, shows that what one is doing is *useful*).[42] But she also discusses befitting-style practical considerations,[43] and notes that one way of showing how what one is doing is desirable is by pointing to the respects in which what one is doing is pleasant.[44] The threefold division informs her essay, even though she does not make of it the studied centerpiece I favor.

What it is for the question "Why are you A-ing?" to have its characteristic sense—what it is for that question to be a *reasons-for-acting-seeking* question—is for it to be answerable and made intelligible in terms of how A-ing serves a further end, in terms of the pleasure of A-ing, or in terms of what's fitting or suitable about A-ing under these circumstances given some larger scheme of things in one's life. The fourth sort of answer, some variant on "No reason," also gives the question application— "['Why are you A-ing?'] is not refused application because the answer to it says that there is no reason, any more than the question how much money I have in my pocket is refused application by the answer 'None'"—it is just that there's no desirability characterization to give on behalf of the proceedings under the description A-ing.[45] Giving answers in one of these four sorts of terms *is* giving the characteristic question "Why are you A-ing?" application to the proceedings under the relevant description (A-ing). So there is a very tight connection between intentional action as such, on this view, and the threefold division. Tight enough, I think, to mark "intentional action" as a kind-term and to employ the threefold division in determining whether some proceedings count as involving intentional action.

The Larger Thesis Revisited

With the threefold division in place, it becomes possible to amend the fourth thesis from the preceding chapter, the thesis about the structure of rational justification in practical contexts, the basis of the view I want ultimately to defend. That thesis was:

> Let A and B be actions of different types. One is justified in A-ing only if one takes it that A-ing is a means to (or part of) attaining (or making it possible to attain) a further end, B-ing, and one wants to B. In short, the structure of rational justification in practical contexts is calculative.

But if we leave the larger claim about justification to one side for the moment, and allow that practical reason aims at practical good in the way that the threefold division suggests that it does, we can convert this thesis into a thesis about reasons for acting:

Let A and B be actions of different types. One has reason to A only if one takes it that A-ing is a means to (or part of) attaining (or making it possible to attain) a further end, B-ing, and one wants to B (for no particular reason or because B-ing is pleasant, useful, or fitting).

Call B-ing the *primary* end, A-ing the *secondary* end. But, now, doesn't it appear as though we have introduced reasons for primary ends? The difference between calculative and noncalculative accounts of reasons for acting would, after all, appear to be just this: in noncalculative accounts, there are reasons for primary ends; in calculative accounts, there are only reasons for secondary ends.

The simplicity of this way of dividing the territory is inviting. But I think that we ought to resist it. The temptation to say it probably has its roots in bifurcationist moral psychology (the kind that informs instrumentalism). If you hold that desire is (at least partly) immune to rational criticism, and that desire is the source of primary ends, then you will hold that primary ends are (at least partly) immune to rational criticism. It is a short step to saying that there are not proper reasons to pursue primary ends, that reason is a matter of belief, not desire, that belief is what is involved in apprehending the calculative relation that rationalizes A-ing in light of one's attachment to B-ing, and so forth. Bifurcationist moral psychology is what makes instrumentalism—in light of the excellent work that has been done in the service of refuting it for many years now—untenable. Neither the fourth thesis, nor the thesis about reasons for acting, nor the picture of practical reason that I defend requires subscribing to bifurcationist moral psychology.

Philosophical diagnostics to one side, there is good reason to reject the simple characterization of the difference between calculative and noncalculative views of reasons for acting. Consider: whether the "reasons for B-ing" at issue in the threefold division of good threaten a calculative account of practical reason will depend on how we construe those reasons. We have our four kinds of remarks that might be offered in response to Anscombe's question directed now at B-ing: no reason, because B-ing is useful/pleasant/fitting. That B-ing is useful merely means that it is a means to or part of attaining some further end, so we can leave those "reasons for B-ing" to one side, along with the "no reason" case. Taking a cue from Aquinas, I argue that considerations of pleasure themselves provide a distinctive end (that rationalizes, for example, unplugging the phone in order to avoid potential interruptions). And while I will give extended treatment to *one* kind of befitting-style desirability characterization that does take us well beyond anything that a calculative theorist can cope with adequately, much of this region can also be read as providing desirability characterizations that are merely interminable in practice (that is, considerations of long-term use, given that one seeks to realize a pattern or plan in practice).

In short, on this view of reasons for acting, the justificatory structure remains *calculative* because it remains end-based: without some determinate end in view, there is *no* reason to do anything. Moreover, it is *because* of the calculative relation obtaining between A-ing and (desirable or merely occupying) B-ing that one has reason to A. Finally, by admitting the full range of intelligible, reason-giving responses that can be given when asked "And why do you want to B?" we produce a picture of practical good that shares the ethical neutrality of instrumentalism without tying this to a doctrine about arational human desire. One can discuss the aspects in which B-ing is pleasant, useful, or fitting. There is nothing arational in the claim that a calculative relation obtains between A-ing and B-ing, nor need one's attachment to B-ing be arational (instrumentalists take attachment to the primary end as the bit of motivation pertaining to desire, the noncognitive part, so there is a significant shift here—a shift from brute desire to desirability, if you like). Nevertheless, the mere fact that many things might be said on behalf of Sally's B-ing does not mean, on this view, that there are many reasons for Sally to B somehow floating around out there, entirely independent of her other ends and larger practical engagements. Rather (as I argue in later chapters on the three regions of practical good), whether considerations pertaining to the desirability of B-ing count as reasons for some agent to B will depend on such matters as her skills and circumstance (pleasure), her other, determinate future ends (use), or whether B-ing is a part of realizing some larger pattern that she means to have shape some part of her mature life (fit). Of course, all three sorts of desirability characterization she might offer on behalf of B-ing may themselves be criticized as claims about B-ing in just the way that one might criticize an agent who insists that she is A-ing in order to B, when A-ing is neither a means to nor a proper part of B-ing. But this kind of criticism stays with what is in her will and shaping her action. The difference between noncalculative views of reasons for acting and calculative views becomes:

Noncalculative theorists insist that there can be reasons for an agent to B quite apart from her plans, projects, particular attachments, character, skills, habits, or further ends; the calculative theorist denies this.

Returning to the Complaint

Aquinas's thought about the three regions of good in action is best grasped as a thought about three senses in which what we do can have a point. One reason to embrace it is that it provides clear links between the explanation and justification of intentional action as such. I began this chapter, however, by noting that the thought that the most basic principle in understanding human action draws in considerations about good and bad has become controversial. To this end, I quoted Bernard Williams's complaint about the medieval commonplace. Williams took it that having a purpose was one thing while thinking it good was quite another, and that the latter, but not the former, implicitly involved a style of thought that evoked a perspective from which what one intended to do could be seen as good by more than one person. He went on to claim that the shared perspective "goes somewhere beyond an agent's immediate wants, to his longer-term interests or well-being."[46] We are now in a position to sort through the complaint and answer it.

It is true that thought about good in action involves a perspective from which the point of what one is doing can be recognized by more than one person. More than one person ought to be able to grasp the sense in which, say, getting one's hands on a kettle is useful if one means to make tea, or savoring a splendid meal is pleasant, or it suits an envious person to be a spoilsport.

It is also true that one sometimes does things for no reason.

It is false, however, that long-term interests and well-being, or ethics, or some such, are *always* involved in seeing the point of doing something. Consider getting the kettle, enjoying a meal, and ruining a rival's fun—you can grasp the point of doing these things without taking any particular view about the way the actions at issue concern the agent's long-term interests. While you can tell many different stories about how such actions *might* find their place in an ethically or otherwise sound larger scheme of life, the sheer recent proliferation of very different stories in this genre ought to be enough to show that you need take no one definite view of such matters, and this is no surprise. From an agent's own point of view, there is often little beyond the end of ordinary intentional action to point to in explaining and justifying what gets done.

Finally, it is false that the medieval commonplace must be read as implying that all pursuits are good in the sense conducive to promotion of one's long-term interests, ethical or otherwise. As I am using it, the medieval commonplace means that rational pursuits are the kinds of events to which the reasons-for-acting-seeking question "Why are you *A*-ing?" (where *A*-ing is a kind of thing you are doing) has application.

The good at issue in the threefold division is *good* in the sense of being to the point, *good* in the sense of being skilled, *good* in the sense of being relevant to answering the question "What's the good of doing that?" Again, what the medieval commonplace says on my reading is that intentional action as such is the appropriate subject of reasons-for-acting-seeking questions. And *that* sense of "good" is at work in *every* department of the threefold division and in the presumption that when one does something on purpose, one can be asked to give reasons for what one has done. The practical considerations sorted by the threefold division are *all* things that can be offered on behalf of what one did in order to show the sense in which what one did was desirable, hence, good. The region of good they fall into says how the point enters in to explaining/justifying the act. Giving an intelligible desirability characterization *is* giving the point of what one does in terms that can be shared by more than one person. Saying "No particular reason" in response to the reasons-for-acting-seeking question is *not*. But in saying "No particular reason," you *still* give the question application, so it remains true that what you are doing, under the description in question, was the appropriate subject of a reasons-for-acting-seeking question.

The medieval insight covers four sorts of responses to a reasons-for-acting-seeking question: a desirability characterization falling into at least one of the three regions, or "No reason." Giving any of these is giving the question about reasons for acting application. Giving that question application *is* implicitly acknowledging that intentional action as such can be discussed in terms of its good/its desirability/its point. Moreover, because the division into regions is formal, almost any concrete practical consideration can be functioning as a useful-style one, as a pleasant-style one, or as a befitting-style one in some setting. (I foreshadowed this point by considering how considerations of risk, scandal, ease, and inconspicuousness might prove decisive in practical deliberation.)

Reclaiming the whole of the threefold division (rather than letting ourselves become fixated on a subdivision of the befitting) isn't just a way to preserve old-fashioned thought about good in intentional action. Besides providing a clear method for categorizing and understanding desirability characterizations, the threefold division allows us to distinguish cases where the agent is just doing something for no particular reason from cases where her pursuit serves a further purpose, is undertaken from or for pleasure, or is fitting for someone of her sort to do. And *this* is the way to mark the fact that not everything you do is, by your lights, in some sense desirable.

Suppose you are doodling on a pad of paper while chatting on the phone, and though you wouldn't say doodling is useful, pleasant, or in any other sense good, you nevertheless know perfectly well what you are doing and do it on purpose: "Why are you making those marks?"—"I'm doodling." "Why are you doodling?"—"No reason." This is perfectly intelligible. One thing that the threefold division of good makes clear is the distinction between this kind of case and others where the agent has more to say on behalf of what she does than that she means to do it.

And so we see that Williams has conflated two different thoughts: (1) not everything one does is by one's lights desirable; (2) not all of what one does is desirable in the sense fitting. Both are true. But they are not the same idea. Williams fails to notice that our topic is reasons for acting *generally,* and that having nothing much in view in A-ing is *not* the same as refusing application to a reasons-for-acting-seeking-question "Why are you A-ing?"

3

Medieval and Modern

The threefold division is a very old, very powerful piece of philosophical machinery whose operation will be unfamiliar to many Anglo–North American practical philosophers. In the spirit of clearing a bit of ground on which to wheel it out and set it to working, I devote this chapter to contrasting it with more familiar work on good and action.

Goods and Good

Usually, when philosophers think about what's good, they have in mind things or states of affairs—*goods*—or else morality. In this vein, recall Williams's complaint: "surely, an extra step is taken if you go from saying that you want *something* or have decided to pursue *it* to saying that *it* is good, or (more to the point) that *it* is good *that you should have it*."[1] Williams just renders the medieval commonplace as a thought about goods.[2] Many contemporary readers expect that a view about good in action (whether or not it is a view about morality) will boil down to a view about making or bringing about a good thing, or about how one responds appropriately to such goods as there are in the world. Both of these interpretations have to do with goods. The threefold division, however, concerns processes. For the most part, how goods are involved in these processes will depend on the character of the processes.

Specific Good and Reasons for Acting

The most obvious links between practical good, the good in intentional action as such, and goods involve discussion of specific good. Specific

53

good is what is at issue when we notice, for example, that a good horse has nothing much in common with a good essay. Aquinas distinguishes the threefold division from what makes a thing *a good one of its kind,* that is, from specific good.[3] However, because he also holds that our last end is given by our kind, he treats virtuous action as specifically good for humans, and so finds a direct link between action theory, motivation theory, and thought about our kind.[4]

In the medieval work on which I'm relying, the threefold division connects to thought about specific good in three ways (corresponding to the three regions). First, there are various views about pleasure holding that a being takes pleasure in what perfects beings of its kind. The link is sometimes direct (the pleasure of a good night's sleep owes something to the fact that humans need sleep), sometimes more remote (the pleasures of grammatical studies are not for everyone, but the exercise of intellectual powers generally, and this way of exercising them in particular, is a thing that it belongs to us to do). Second, if you want to get or use things of some kind (fishing nets, say) for a standard purpose (catching fish) then you will want to get or use good things of that kind (nets strong enough to hold the fish, loose enough to permit water and some debris to flow through the mesh, free enough of tears and of a tight enough weave to trap fish—that is, good nets). Third, thought about how it befits one to live turns on what sort of being one is, and is in that sense relevant to one's "kind."

Pleasure and Perfection

First things first. Whether we agree that pleasant activities are perfective of kinds of being, this link between specific good and reasons for acting concerns a single region of the threefold division, not the whole of it. That suggests that it will only help us explain and justify what gets done when the kind of reason for acting at issue is local and interminable (that is, underwrites doing this very sort of thing under these very circumstances and looks ahead to no further, future end). Not everything we do will be desirable in these terms.

More to the point, it is hard to see *why* we would think that what a being enjoys is normally perfective of it in virtue of its kind, however indirect the link might be. People, for instance, sometimes delight in activities that don't seem to be expressive of human good, either directly or indirectly. For example, I once read a sort of treatise on the pleasures of consensual erotic play involving cutting or being cut with very sharp knives.[5] The essay was at once an encomium to the activity and a manual on how to do and sustain it for a long time in a way that produced calculated patterns of scars without risking more serious damage. It is very hard to see erotic knife play as even remotely linked to the appropriate exercise of characteristic human powers, except in the sense that one does not imagine that members of many other species would go in for this sort of thing. But that is not usually enough to give us the kind of characteristic human engagement that goes with talk about what is good for humans as such. We are also the only species that damages the ozone layer.

Erotic knife play that produces scar patterns is *not* chosen as one means among many to get a pattern transferred to one's skin, and so has no obvious share in human love of ornament. While one gathers that it demands tremendous powers of concentration from all participants, it is not exactly meditative. Because it requires that everyone maintain a tense pattern of attention and steadiness, it would be a mistake to assimilate it to free-flowing expressions of sensuality. In short, although this activity involves exercise of many human capacities in a highly controlled setting, and may incidentally involve all kinds of goods we associate with people, it is not thereby expressive of specific good.

Specific good *does* enter into the erotic cutting equation, but at an entirely different point. It isn't that erotic knife play is perfective of the human as such, or of the individual person in light of her skill in a *standard* area of human endeavor (for example, grammatical studies, cookery). Rather, the elaborate system of *precautions* set forth in the treatise is made in light of an understanding of the heightened vulnerabilities adult humans will face when engaged in erotic blade play, and the psychological complexities that may afterward ensue. The *engagement itself* is supposed to hold the pleasure. The cautions—the considerations that really do belong to thought about our kind—instead establish a set of guardrails around this mode of intercourse.

Could we get the considerations of specific good back into the picture by denying that risky cutting is pleasant? Again, this distorts the case. We can leave to one side examples in which one or more of the participants is so anxious about health as to be incapable of enjoying unguarded erotic cutting. It would be odd to find the hyper-health-conscious going in for knife play in the first place, and there is additionally a lot of evidence that less anxious people often accept health risks for the sake of sexual pleasure. Leaving the faint of heart out of it, it seems safe to suppose that the pleasure of blade play with merely washed instruments need be no less than the pleasure of blade play with perfectly sterile knives. It is just that the risk of subsequent infection increases in the former circumstances.

I hope we would not respond to the example by deciding to treat lovers-who-go-in-for-cutting as the name of a distinct species of being and apply the whole apparatus of medieval metaphysics to it, understanding the pleasures of erotic knife play as what is perfective of erotic cutters. This would be more a joke than conceptual progress.

We might instead try to deny that erotic cutting could be pleasant to do or undergo. Denying that the essay has pleasures as its topic at the very least calls for argument. Participants describe it as a uniquely delicate and absorbing activity best conducted in light of a sound, rudimentary understanding of anatomy and contagion. In the idiom of higher and lower pleasures, *this* one is complex enough to attain a certain height. But unless we take the route of multiplying species or else denying that some pleasures are pleasures, the treatise provides a counterexample to any straightforward revival of the old-fashioned link between considerations of pleasure and considerations of specific good. I take it, then, that we have no good reason to buy the traditional link between pleasure and specific good wholesale. Moreover, reflection on dark pleasures suggests that part of what is covered by the threefold division (that is, those very pleasures) has *no* direct link to thought about what's good for humans as such.

What of considerations about what's useful or fitting? Do these have any direct link to thought about specific good? Here, we can draw not only on old-fashioned thought about reasons for acting, but also on some contemporary work that bears its influence.

Specific Goods, Choice, and Use

Considerations about specific good animate Foot's discussion of goods and their use.[6] Foot argues that there is no necessary link between choice and good examples of various kinds of thing. Instead, whether I want a good *a* depends on what I want *a* for. A good dinner table is solidly constructed (however graceful), strong enough to bear the weight of food, dishes, and diners who lean on their elbows while chatting, long enough to accommodate those who will dine there, narrow enough to permit conversation across it, low enough to put food within reach (which may be very low or rather high, depending on seating arrangements), and so on. If I mean to hold dinner parties, a good dinner table is choice-worthy. But if I am looking around for a dinner table to use on stage in the production of a play involving squalid, cramped life circumstances, then I will hunt for a very bad dinner table (too small, too light, unstable, and so on). Specifically good things are not always choice-worthy.

Good Action and Being a Good Person

Nevertheless, there is some overlap in topics when we turn to thought about what it befits a person to do. For one thing, befitting-style practical considerations apply in virtue of the sort of being one is, specifically or individually. We can ask what makes someone a good human being (an adult who is good *qua* human being, and in that sense, specifically good). Such thought is sometimes involved in work on virtue. More generally, practical concern about *being* a good F, where "F" names some sort of thing one is, shows itself in one's practical concern to avoid conduct unbecoming to an F, and to engage in conduct befitting an F.

To make the link to traditional thought about specific good via thought about what makes one a good F, we need rather to restrict the domain of kinds of things one might be. Not just any skill- or role- or occupation-related considerations will get us to reasonable conclusions about the human good. What makes someone a good parent or teacher, for example, will count. Unlike salmon, people have to be taught to do many things in order to make their way in the world, and it falls to the older to teach the younger. In this sense, it is fitting for adults to have qualities that conduce to the ends of teaching or care-taking. Having developed skills that fit one to teach and look after others marks one, in this sense, as specifically good. There are, however, not merely types of human action (for example, erotic cutting), but types of human occupation (for example, some kinds of soldiering) that require one to develop skills and qualities that are at odds with traditional understandings of human good. And notice, again, that this sort of thought about action and substantive good concerns only *one* of our three regions: it is the *good* stage dresser, the man who is good *qua* stage dresser, who chooses a *bad* dinner table for the set.

In short, reflection on specific good cannot replace the threefold division. Rather, the threefold division was traditionally thought to have various links to considerations of specific good, some more plausible than others.

A Good Intentional Action

But now suppose that one attempts to assimilate the threefold division to thought about specific good in a different way. One might suggest that what is at issue in the threefold division is what makes something a good *intentional action*. An intentional action is a kind of event, and saying what kind of event it is will involve understanding what makes an action a *good* one, just as understanding what makes a thing a dining table involves understanding what makes a dining table a good one. The thought is that talk of kinds enables apprehension of specific good, that "intentional action" is a kind-term, and that the threefold division might tell us what makes one of these a good one.[7] I have already suggested that "intentional action" can be treated as a kind-term. In Chapter 2, I gave Anscombe's criterion for determining whether an event involves intentional action, and the threefold division picks out three ways in which the point of concept-involving, end-directed events of this sort enters into explaining and justifying what happens. However, while "intentional action" may be a kind-term, and while the threefold division is relevant to determining whether an action was in some respect good, simply understanding that a process involves intentional action is not enough to tell us how to evaluate it. "Intentional action" is not *that* kind of kind-term.

In short, construing "intentional action" as a term for a kind of event is not going to give us the variety of kind-talk that enables discussion of specific good. *That* sort of kind-talk belongs to discussion of natural kinds, artifact kinds, hybrid kinds, role-related kinds, and so forth (for example, the good horse, the good essay, the good *F*). These kind-terms are sortals. "Intentional action" is not a sortal.

For starters, notice that intentional actions themselves come in kinds, and what makes one sort a good instance of *its* kind will defeat another sort entirely. The things that mark an able and successful life-saving effort, for example, spell ruin to an assassination scheme.

Here it could be objected that dogs and wolves are, alike, canines. Moreover, some dogs come in distinctive breeds, and what makes a miniature poodle a good one of its kind would be so out of place in a Newfoundland hound as to cast doubt on the lineage of a dog born as a result of a Newfoundland hound breeding program and bearing some distinctive marks of a miniature poodle. For all that, just as we have criteria for determining whether an event involves intentional action, we have criteria for determining whether an animal is a dog. Why not treat "intentional action" by analogy to "dog," and act types as the lesser "breeds" by analogy to "Siberian husky"? Why not treat "intentional action" as a sortal?

As a softening-up point, notice that identifying instances of kinds picked out by sortals makes it possible to count or otherwise measure instances of the kind. "Intentional action" doesn't function this way. As Anscombe argued, like "thing" and "event," "intentional action" is not a term that operates as a count- or measure-noun, although discussion of specific sorts of intentional actions, events, or things enables counting or measuring.[8] Consider: it is not clear that there could be a sound answer to the question "How many events were there in Chicago this week?" (Do we mean rain storms? hittings of rain drops on the pavement? intervals of hard rain or claps of thunder occurring during storms? city council meetings? motions passed in chambers? raps of the gavel or side conversations during meetings? utterances? tuckings-in of children at night? the operations involved therein? and so on) However, at least in principle, we *can* answer such questions about *kinds* of events—for example, how many human deaths were there in Chicago this week? how many car crashes? Notice that, even if we restrict our attention to kinds of events, possible overlap between kinds of occurrences precludes getting an answer to "How many events?" by summing instances of the various kinds. One suicide, for instance, may also be counted in the tallies of homicides and car crashes if a despairing driver, overcome by rage, veered suddenly into oncoming traffic in order to commit suicide, in order to murder his passenger and thereby prevent her from inheriting his estate, and in order to injure the driver of an oncoming car who failed to dim high-beam lights at rush hour. What we can say is that the account of what happened at t on that stretch of highway presupposes that the same intentional action was suicide, murder, and the cause of several traffic fatalities. At least some of the traffic fatalities were intended. We could also say that his act ruined his tires, spread shards of glass over the daylilies in the meridian, caused a sudden breeze, made a noise that spooked the cat in a nearby apartment window, and so on. These were not part of his intention. (*Ex hypothesi*, had it been possible to ask "Why are you damaging your tires?" as he was crashing into the oncoming car, and had he been willing and able to respond, he would have explained that destroying the tires is not the point of crashing his car; he is crashing his car in order to commit suicide, kill his passenger, and so forth; he merely foresees, but does not intend, the collateral tire damage—that is, he would refuse to give the characteristic question "Why are you *A*-ing?" application where *A*-ing is damaging your tires.) Paradigmatically, actions are intentional under several descriptions, unintentional under indefinitely many more. It belongs to praising, criticizing, and, more generally, assessing intentional action that we can discuss the same action in various ways. But that does not mean that we can count up intentional actions. Was turning into oncoming traffic *one* action—turning—or *many* actions: aiming for a break in the meridian, easing off the accelerator, cranking the wheel hard to the left, speeding up again, straightening out, and so on?

Not all sortals are count-nouns, of course. But it goes along with sortal-style classification of things and events that we have identified something that is in principle measurable. There may not be an answer to a question about how *many* waters there are, but there are ways of calculating how *much* water there is in some region. Notice: it makes no more sense to ask how *much* intentional action was involved in the traffic suicide than it does to ask how *many* actions were involved in it. This lends some initial plausibility to the suggestion that "intentional action" is not a sortal.

Instances of kinds picked out by sortals are in some way measurable. They are also things the good of which can be assessed in terms of their kind, that is, specifically. We can ask how pure a sample of gold or water is. We can ask whether a human being has the right number of fingers and toes, or (to borrow an example from Aquinas) the natural faculty of laughing.[9] We can ask whether this instance of cake-baking displayed a sound exercise of the baker's art, or showed someone new to baking to be good at following directions. Sortal-style apprehension of kinds sets the terms for an investigation of what marks off instances of the kind substantively, of what provides something on the order of *differentia* or essential features of the kind rather than mere accidents. And this is why having a grip on a natural or artificial kind both enables measurement and enables assessment of the relevant sort of soundness of instances of the kind. "Intentional action" may be a kind-term, but it is not a sortal. Act-type terms, however, are rather like sortals.

All that we get by knowing that some proceedings involve intentional action is that they were intentional under some descriptions and not others, and were the sorts of things that might have been done for reasons. In order to assess the soundness of proceedings involving intentional action, we need more than this. We need to know at least one of the descriptions under which the action was intentional—that is, not just *that* it was intentional, but what *kind* of intentional action it was. It is in light of such a description that it becomes possible both to count or measure, and to see how well or badly the agent did a thing of that kind.

It is not as though we have, one the one side, three ways in which a kind of action might be desirable, and on the other side the class of events called *intentional actions* to which we apply the division. They come to us bound up together, as it were: to understand intentional action as such is to understand that the proceedings might have a point; the threefold division is about the three senses in which intentional action can have a point. But you have to know what *kind* of action is at issue in order to be able to determine whether it was sound. The traffic suicide attempt, for example, might have been sound in some respects, unsound in others. Suppose the collision killed everyone involved *but* the suicidal driver, and this can be explained by noting that his aim was off. That is, knowing that an event involves intentional action opens it up to reason-for-acting-seeking review (as it were), but the *content* of the ensuing judgments will rely upon the *kinds* of action involved, the circumstances of the act, and what the agent had in view in doing it.

The threefold division is about what people deliberately do and deliberately omit to do. It is about the sorts of considerations that jointly shape and justify action and intention. The account is to this extent irreducibly practical. And the distinctions among divisions are, largely, formal. The formality in question both lends the account its general applicability and prevents us from substantively assessing action simply on the basis of our understanding that it was intentional.

Various Goods and Reasons for Acting

Work connecting goods and reasons for acting need not confine itself to thought about specific good. Contemporary work on incommensurability, for instance, involves discussion of many goods. Suppose we were to assimilate the threefold division to discussion of the many-more-than-three incommensurable goods. We know about lots of goods. Why not treat use, pleasure, and fit as three among the many incommensurable goods?

Incommensurable goods are good and they are related to action and choice. The central thrust of work on incommensurable goods is that, on the face of it, they cannot be weighed on a single scale, hence, that one cannot make weighing-style trade-offs between them when deliberating about what to do.

There are three ways in which the threefold division is different from contemporary thought about incommensurability.

1. There are incommensurable goods *within* each of the three regions of the good. This is obvious in the case of the useful. I might love high, long tables and dislike the fuss and bother of chairs, but if I intend to hold an ordinary sort of sit-down dinner party, I need both, and, moreover, need enough chairs and enough table to allow my guests to dine in relative comfort. I can't trade-off chairs in favor of ever-greater expanses of table—at least not if I have a fixed guest list and wouldn't dream of stacking several guests on each seat. Lap-pyramiding is not the sort of intimacy to which one aspires at standard dinner parties, nor the way in which one hopes that one's dinner party will be memorable. In the furniture shop, chairs and tables are commodities whose exchange values at the time of purchase are conveniently commensurated and displayed on price tags. In my dining room, table and chairs are use-values. That one beautiful chair costs as much as two elegant tables should not obscure the point that useful things *as such* are not commensurate.

The point is equally obvious in the case of what is pleasant. In Thomistic/Aristotelian parlance, the pleasure of sexual congress is "alien" to the pleasure of speculative grammatical studies, as can be seen by noticing that, should you become distracted by the one at the point you are engaged in the other, you will find it difficult to continue in your former occupation. For at least some pairs of pleasures, you can't have both at once because you can't do the things involved at the same time (scuba-diving and smoking come to mind).

Finally, there are incommensurable practical considerations about how it befits one to live. The most familiar contemporary example is the Frenchman's quandary about whether to stay home and look after his mother or go off and join the Resistance. His problem might involve a conflict in life projects, in fundamental values, in core understandings of self, and so forth—any of which suggests that some overarching pattern of practical engagements is at stake rather than a question about how to complete different projects (a problem about what is useful) or a question about how to keep a good thing going (a problem about sustaining pleasure).

Incommensurability *within* each region is one reason to suppose that the threefold division does not give us three more incommensurable goods to add to our list.

2. The second reason to reject the assimilation is that it is perfectly possible (although not always necessary) to make appropriate trade-offs between doing what's useful, doing what's pleasant, and doing what's fitting, as when one forgoes the pleasure of hilarity for the sake of due sobriety, or makes an effort to "lighten up" a bit when one grows boorish over one's agenda or one's moral views.[10] Such trade-offs aren't happily assimilated to the "common scale" metaphor, but, then, outside the mechanisms of commodities trading operated by means of markets and universal exchange values, it's hard to see what would be.[11]

3. Finally, considerations drawn from the three regions of the good enter into action in different ways: the pleasant concerns absorption in a present engagement, the useful concerns things done for the sake of attaining further, future ends, and befitting concerns things done because it is fitting that such-and-such person should do them. Although we nowadays recognize many incommensurable goods, we see them entering into the explanation of action in *exactly the same way*. They are expressive of our convictions about what matters, say, or they are the goods that frame our self-understanding, or they are the goods whose pursuit is crucial to our practical identities as fellow legislators in a Kingdom of Ends, friends, physicians, guns for hire, surfers, and so on, or they are the goods the pursuit of which is directed by such norms as we take to

be binding on us. In short, all involve thought about how it befits such-and-such a person to live.

Notice that, from the much-touted first-person perspective, very little of the daily reproduction of an individual through her purposive action and of the forms of social life in and by which she sustains herself is grounded in her settled view about how it befits her to live. It is not even clear to me that the person who *does* have a befitting-style desirability characterization to offer on behalf of such things as her choice in personal check designs, her willingness to go to the movies on Saturday, her interest in having some geraniums on the window sill, or her habit of rolling the cuffs of mated socks together before depositing them in a drawer is an appropriate ideal for a theory of practical reason. There are people who are like this. Sometimes it is the result of a secular spiritual quest and the best response to them is "Let a thousand flowers bloom!" Sometimes, it is the result of a view requiring that the reasons for acting always be very deep—the grounds for the conviction are themselves philosophical, and are not at issue in ordinary action for just anyone. More often, people who feel a deep need to be always already ultimately justified have suffered psychological injuries—one wants to say to them "Calm down!" and then "How did you come to think that you must have something very grand to offer on behalf of everything you do?" (My objection to treating the latter sort of person as a figure of excellence in reason is *ad hominem,* but as Elijah Millgram points out, when what is at issue is whether a particular sort of character is worth having or cultivating, the *ad hominem* objection is to the point.)[12]

Ordinarily, if things are going tolerably well in one's life, occasions that require reflection about how it befits one to live are rare. This is, I realize, entirely at odds with the contemporary thought that there is always an explanation for any sound action to be found in befitting-style terms. Of course, very few contemporary practical philosophers hold that the relation between how it befits me to live and tying my shoes has to be foremost in my mind if I am to have a reason to tie my shoes. The more subtle position is that I could, if asked, find a place for shoe-tying in thought about how I should live.[13]

The difficulty with these alternatives to the threefold division, however, is that the threefold division is about explaining intentional action *as such.* If the only way I could get us from shoe-tying to thought about how it befits me to live is by giving an elaborate account that I make up in my desperation not to seem shallow, then we may get a good story out of me (we may even get one quickly if I am creative and wise in the ways of moral philosophy), but we will not get the *point* of my shoe-tying.

The problem with my big story is not that I haven't thought it all out in advance of an episode of shoe-tying. If you ask me why I draw one loop through the other, I will say, "Because that's how you tie shoes." This isn't a thing I will have rehearsed in thought before stooping to tie my shoes either. But shoe-tying skills are *in* me, and I exercise these powers in tying up my laces. More important, the *desirability* of what I do in manipulating the laces links up to a thing I have in view directly: namely, my *end*, namely shoe-tying. I may have nothing much in mind when I move to tie my shoes. But if you stopped me and asked me why I was fussing with the laces, I could say: in order to tie my shoes. *Ex hypothesi*, I have *no* befitting-style consideration in view. Not even potentially with respect to this episode of lace manipulation. That's the problem. The possibility of producing a multivolume treatise on the good of keeping one's laces tied securely cannot enter into explaining a *single* instance of intentional shoe-tying *qua* intentional shoe-tying if no one has ever tied her shoes *from* and *for the sake of* the considerations set forth in the learned tomes. Compare: there are many things to be said on behalf of quitting smoking. If I quit in order to annoy my roommate and on account of my insight that she will both miss my smoking and feel unable in good conscience to seduce me into lighting up again, then the many things that can be said in favor of quitting *cannot* be said on behalf of *me* and what *I* did and why *I* did it. I quit because I took malicious glee in finding a way to annoy her without leaving her grounds for complaint.

Contemporary thought about incommensurable goods involves befitting-style practical considerations. Befitting-style practical considerations need not inform all intentional action. As such, even though there are very many incommensurable goods, we could not turn to the literature about them to understand the threefold division. At best, we would find a variety of sources of practical considerations in the discussions, and a strong tendency to treat these on the model of the befitting.

The threefold division is unlike contemporary thought about incommensurability. And this may initially leave us at a loss. But the threefold division looks much less mysterious if we think about intentional action, and on at least some readings of Aquinas's apparently convoluted account of volition, appetition, and intellection in action, the starting place is in an analysis of a completed rational act.[14]

Recall that the division is about three places where the point of doing something might enter into explaining what one does. Recall that this division is *not* arbitrary. If the end is pursued for the sake of attaining another, future end, it is good in the sense useful. If the end is pursued for its own sake as part of realizing long-term commitments in action, then it is good in the sense fitting. If the end is pursued for the sake of prolonged enjoyment in attaining it, then it is good in the sense pleasant. The useful and befitting styles of practical consideration are alike in that they direct one to *attain* one's end (in order to attain another end, or else because attaining the end is fitting). The pleasant-style practical consideration instead directs one to *savor* the activity. The pleasant and the befitting are alike in that both have us doing a thing for its own sake. But the three do different work in explaining an action by showing how it is desirable.

A Morals Clause

I have discussed the distinction between the threefold division and some contemporary work on goods. I have argued that some pleasures are not expressive of specific human good (but that actions done from and for the sake of such pleasures are desirable in the sense pleasant). I have sketched something of Foot's argument that whether or not a good *a* is choice-worthy in the sense useful will depend on what one wants *a* for. I have argued that the befitting-style desirability characterizations that *do* hook up to thought about human good don't exhaust the whole range of things one might do in connection with one's role or occupation. I have argued that we cannot assimilate the threefold division to work on incommensurable goods. And, most important, I have argued that while thought about the threefold division enables critical assessment of intentional action, we need to know what kind of action an agent intends in order to assess the act.

And here the ethical objection I gave in Chapter 2 might arise again in slightly altered form, "How is it that twiddling one's thumbs or doodling fall outside the range of this threefold division of good, but vicious acts make it in? In what sense are acts aptly described as instances of murder, rape, or betrayal, even *apparently* desirable?"

In this section, I will again respond to this objection, continuing to walk the line between secular work and Thomism.

I agree that vicious acts are bad insofar as vicious. Vicious people often know well enough that they act immorally when they act from vice. We don't suppose, for instance, envious people acting from envy don't know what is ethically sound—they can, for example, point to it in others' actions and say, "She's soooo good!" in an unkind tone of voice. In general, vicious people are often the quickest to demand that we observe the strictest standards of justice in dealing with them, rightly calculating that such considerations weigh with us.

But, I also think that one might be able to discuss some vicious acts in terms of all three regions of practical good: if the acts succeed in attaining their ends, then the means taken were useful; the acts might be sources of pleasure for the vicious agent; and (and here comes the sticking point for some contemporary ethicists) the acts might befit the vicious agent. There is, I think, no question that bad people sometimes have fun being bad. There is, I think, no question that some bad people are highly skilled, even creative, in their badness. But I want also to insist that *in the absence of substantive ethical views that set limits on the kinds of things that could be said to be fitting occupations for a human being,* the individual bad person acting ill in a way that does not cost him much, by his lights, may likewise be doing things that befit him, given the effects of vice on his will.[15]

Thomistic ethics provides a kind of theory for this, together with a substantive ethical view that sets the terms for true, befitting-style desirability characterizations. The substantive ethical view is theological. Secular ethics is not. Secular ethicists agree that vicious acts are bad, and many of them want further to see such acts as contrary to reason. But there is no widespread agreement about why or how vicious acts are contrary to reason. Neither is there the kind of theoretical work on badness that renders acute the problem of explaining the irrationality of vice. Theoretical work that makes onerous the burden of explaining how reason and ethical action are inextricably bound up together is work that takes seriously the *goods* at issue in vicious action, together with the thought that befitting-style desirability characterizations are geared to the agent's sense of what matters in life.

Formally, befitting style practical considerations concern the place of an intentional action in a larger scheme of things, an established pattern of some sort that the agent means to have shape her life. One feature of befitting-style practical considerations is that in light of them it becomes possible to distinguish acting well from faring well. On some views— Aquinas's, for example, or David Gauthier's—this may amount to no more than a distinction between acting for the sake of short-term advantage and acting for the sake of long-term interests (the latter counts as acting well, the former, merely acting with an eye toward here and now faring well).[16] Another, related feature of befitting-style practical considerations is that they show the place of a pursuit in a pattern of some kind (it is for the sake of realizing the pattern that one does some things, and omits to do others, where the omissions usually include forgoing pursuit of short-term benefits). As patterning principles, befitting-style practical considerations typically give rise to many actions of different types and are in principle inexhaustible in a single action or course. As principles that might give rise to many actions of different sorts, they determine patterns that might be realized in more than one way in a life. Such considerations are nonlocal and interminable.

It is true that ethical and moral considerations belong to befitting-style practical considerations. But as a way to explain and understand intentional action as such, there is no obvious ethical restriction on what one might find offered up under this rubric. Not only are there ethically bad actions, there are ethically bad *patterns* in life. And, like ethically splendid patterns, the ethically bad ones discussed at length by Aquinas center on genuinely good things, such as a sense of one's own worth, wealth, good food, sex, and the avoidance of subtle and sophisticated forms of human suffering. If one of us is acting from and for the sake of an ethically bad patterning principle, then what she does from and for the sake of her unethical patterning principle can bear all the marks of befitting-style desirability. She may even have *worked* to cultivate vice for the sake of pursuit of desirable things.

A capital vice can organize whole regions of one's moral personality, branching out not only into various actions, but also into subsidiary vices that strengthen a vicious man's larger vice in practice. I discussed envy in the last chapter. I turn to avarice here.

In arguing that avarice has the status of a capital vice, Aquinas notes:

[To avarice Gregory] assigns seven daughters, which are treachery, fraud, deceit, perjury, restlessness, violence, obduracy in regard to mercy. The distinction of these can be understood in the following way. For two characteristics pertain to avarice, one of which is to be excessive in retaining, and in furtherance of this, obduracy in regard to mercy or inhumanity arises from avarice, namely, because the avaricious man hardens his heart so that he will not out of compassion come to the aid of anyone at the expense of his possessions. The other characteristic pertaining to avarice is to be excessive in taking, and according to this avarice can be considered first as it is in the avaricious person's heart, and his restlessness arises from avarice because avarice brings a man unnecessary anxieties and cares, for the greedy person is not satisfied with money. . . . [S]econdly, avarice can be considered as it is in the execution of the work, and thus in acquiring other people's goods sometimes force is used and so there is violence, and sometimes deceit, which if done by word will be falsehood in word alone by which one person deceives another for gain; however in word confirmed by oath it will be perjury; but if the deceit be committed by deed, then as regards the things themselves it will be fraud, and as regards the persons treachery.[17]

A capital vice, like a cardinal virtue, lends a distinctive pattern to one's character and ends. It is an ordering principle, in the strong, generative sense of "principle" favored by medieval metaphysicians. Avarice ordinarily gives birth to and sustains her seven daughters. These in turn aid in the excessive acquisition and maintenance of wealth.

Note the use of "excessive." It occurs in the account of each capital vice and is given the same sense each time. Pursuit of wealth is only *vicious* inasmuch as it is *inordinate*, and it is inordinate "according as it is pursued contrary to the order of divine law."[18] That is, there are theological criteria for determining whether someone is *overly* attached to, for example, amassing a fortune. It is much harder to come up with criteria for excessive pursuit of wealth in circumstances where it is routinely assumed that reasonable preferences for control of wealth are inherently insatiable (as in much neoclassical economic theory).

Avarice and her daughters together shape the pursuits of a greedy man. The operation of any such vice can bear all the formal hallmarks of a befitting-style patterning item. Avarice both adds significant stress to one's existence and may require giving up doing some things one had wanted to do (for example, spend time with one's children, raise dahlias) for the sake of devising and executing elaborate stratagems meant to induce others to part with their goods in a way that increases one's own holdings (there is a distinction between acting well and faring well here). Avarice gives rise to many actions. It is not exhaustible in a single action or course. One cultivates subsidiary vices for its sake. What unites avaricious character development and the many things one does from greed is that they have their source in avarice. And so on. Formally, at least, how we thought about the befitting shows some of what we do in a favorable light—insofar as it accords with a pattern we have worked to put in place in our affairs (centered on something in itself desirable)—need not be restricted to patterns that are likely to earn gold stars in a system of moral bookkeeping. "It befits a man of the world to forgo the quiet pleasures of family life and gardening for the sake of amassing a fortune" might be what the greedy man says when asked why he seems willing to have his children and flowers tended by employees.

Anscombe makes this point using a Nazi example in her discussion of how it befits one to live. She stresses the formal character of such considerations, and how there is nothing in the formal features that especially sides with ethically sound ends:

> In the present state of philosophy, it seems necessary to choose an example which is not obscured by the fact that moral approbation on the part of the writer or reader is called into play; for such approbation is in fact irrelevant to the logical features of practical reasoning; but if it is evoked, it may seem to play a significant part. The Nazis, being pretty well universally execrated, seem to provide us with suitable material. Let us suppose some Nazis caught in a trap in which they are sure to be killed. They have a compound full of Jewish children near them. One of them selects a site and starts setting up a mortar. Why this site?— Any site with such-and-such characteristics will do, and this has them. Why set up a mortar?—It is the best way of killing off the Jewish children. Why kill the Jewish children?—It befits a Nazi, if he must die, to spend his last hour exterminating Jews. (I am a Nazi, this is my last hour, here are some Jews.) Here we have arrived at a desirability characterization which makes an end of the questions "What for?"[19]

We have reached the end of the question because we have reached the end of what can be said on behalf of the *intentional action* in question (choosing a site and setting up a mortar in order to kill children) in terms of *why* the Nazi is doing *what* he is doing, and the desirability (good) of doing *that*. Any further question about why, say, one ought to be a Nazi changes the topic away from what is in his will and what informs his act. Desirability characterizations attach to what one *does*, what one *did*, or what one *proposes to do*. By staying with the man's avowed position as a Nazi facing death, the discussion stays with what he is doing in his capacity as a Nazi facing death who intends to do what a Nazi *as such* should do under those circumstances. Again, the kind of pattern at issue is one that usually can be realized in many ways. In this vein, imagining setting out to dissuade the Nazi from murdering the children, Anscombe writes:

> [One of us might say]: "Yes, that befits a Nazi, but equally so does such-and-such: why not do something falling under *this* description instead, namely '. . .'"[20]

The attempt to stay his hand relies on the formal character of his principle.

A theory about reason in action has to apply generally to actions done for reasons, hence to ethically laudable, ethically deplorable, and ethically neutral actions that have a point. The threefold division of good is a division in kinds of desirability characterizations that can be accurately offered on behalf of what people in fact do or omit to do. The division into regions is formal. Notoriously, formal characterizations rarely set limits on the contents of the items that meet them. But from the point of view of developing a secular understanding of the senses in which intentional action can have a point, it is a *strength* that there can be many different befitting-style practical considerations that organize pursuit of goods and meet the formal requirements. Not everything people do, not even everything people do because they *rightly* take it that it suits people of their sort to do them, is ethically laudable.

In Sum

In Chapter 2, I gave a sketch of the threefold division of good and the formal sorting system it provides for practical considerations. Is the reason for acting local and terminable—that is, does it show the pursuit to be useful, given a determinate further end? Is it nonlocal and interminable—that is, would it underwrite doing many and various things over a longish course? does it show why you forgo short-term advantage for the sake of long-term interest? is it expressive of a pattern in your affairs that you have worked to put in place and realize in action? Or is the practical consideration at issue local and interminable—does it attach to doing this very sort of thing now, apart from concern with attaining further ends and possibly quite apart from the larger shape of your life (if there is a grand scheme of things in your life)?

We do not have this way of approaching questions about how pursuits are explained and justified in terms of their points. Instead, we have instrumental versus noninstrumental reasons for acting, which is usually understood as a distinction in the psychological sources of the practical considerations in question. This is, I take it, why arguments about whether "instrumental" considerations are proper reasons for acting at all often take the form of arguments about whether or how desires underwrite doing things, and what must be in place if they are to have the power to do so.

Notice, here, that it is not clear what sort of distinction is at issue in the distinction between desire-based practical considerations and non-desire-based practical considerations, *unless* it is a pale imitation of the kind of thing that is actually given some theoretical punch in the threefold division's distinction between useful-style/pleasant-style and befitting-style practical considerations. For surely what we want from our talk of desire-based reasons and non-desire-based reasons is ways of treating the difference between acting with a view to here and now faring well and acting well in light of some larger concern, ways of thinking about how whole regions of one's life might be organized with an eye toward realizing some pattern versus ways of completing tasks that may or may not accord with a larger scheme of things, ways of working through the differences between doing something because it is fun and doing something because it is useful or fitting that one should do it, and so on. I hope, at least, that we aren't really *that* concerned with the detail of individual psychology. If we were, one would expect us to study closely the work of our social scientific and clinical colleagues who actually make the secrets of the human heart their research topic and stock in trade. We are interested in the rational support for action, and how that support might show the rational structure in the living of a human life. For these purposes, our instrumental-versus-noninstrumental idea is not good enough. We can see that it is not good enough because it is easy to argue against instrumentalism and hard to shake the conviction that calculative views of practical reason can be somehow taken for granted by theorists of practical reason.

In chapters 4–6, I take up each region of the threefold division of practical good in an attempt to motivate two claims: first, that the threefold division is an extremely useful way of thinking about reason in action; second, that the threefold division shows the sense in which calculative reasons for acting might be the core of something deserving the title "the default theory of practical reason."

I begin by discussing the pleasant and befitting regions of good. For Aquinas, both have the character of ends in the sense of stopping-places for intentional action. In acting from and for the sake of pleasure, I urge, one's end is prolonging the enjoyment of the present activity. This will be a kind of interpretation of Aquinas's suggestion that when one acts from and for pleasure, one seeks rest in the thing desired, an interpretation that treats pleasure as a source of ends.

I treat some acts done from and for the sake of fit as means to or parts of realizing a pattern one means to have shape some portion of one's life. These kinds of considerations are fairly straightforwardly calculative. But I allow that there are *radically* interminable befitting-style practical considerations. I give a nonmoral example of how these might operate, largely to avoid clouding the formal issue with unnecessary baggage. As Anscombe has reminded us, "moralism . . . is bad for thinking."[21] Precisely *because* considerations of pleasure and some radically noncalculative considerations of how it befits one to live are less obviously bound up with determinate further future ends, their action-guiding role is more questionable than the action-guiding role of straightforward calculative considerations. I discuss this point at some length in connection with each of these two regions of practical good.

Finally, I turn to the useful, arguing that without useful-style practical considerations, we lose our grip on practical reason entirely. Chapters 4–6 are meant to motivate the amended fourth thesis:

Let *A* and *B* be actions of different types. One has reason to *A* only if one takes it that *A*-ing is a means to (or part of) attaining (or making it possible to attain) a further end, *B*-ing, and one wants to *B* (for no particular reason or because *B*-ing is pleasant, useful, or fitting).

4

Pleasure

Every so often he swears to start a finer life.
But when night comes with its own counsels,
its compromises, and its promises;
but when night comes with its own vigor
of the body, craving and seeking, he returns,
forlorn, to the same fatal joy.

—Cavafy

Give me now libidinous joys only,
Give me the drench of my passions, give me life coarse and rank,
To-day I go consort with Nature's darlings, to-night too,
I am for those who believe in loose delights, I share the
mid-night orgies of young men,
I dance with the dancers and drink with the drinkers.

—Walt Whitman

A life devoid of pleasure might be scarcely worth living in the eyes of those who can choose how to live; nevertheless, pursuit of pleasure can breed shameful conduct, corruption, debauchery, or profligacy—these venerable commonplaces used to frame philosophical work on pleasure.

It is a problem for ethics when an essential ingredient in a good life is systematically linked to alarming failures of self-governance.[1] Crudely, responses to the difficulty by the ancient philosophers whose views are still widely disseminated involved arguments that one must at least *think* that one is doing well in order to enjoy oneself, and that *actually* doing well (living an ethically sound life) thereby offers the most stable enjoyments, together with arguments that childish or shameful pleasures were (a) apt to be ruinous or, at least, fleeting, and (b) mostly sought in ignorance of the superior enjoyments of living well.[2] Ancient philosophers concerned with how one should live regarded outright sybaritic hedonism as a serious contender—perhaps because having access to luxury was widely regarded as having access to great goods; at any rate, because people seem naturally to prefer comfort to discomfort and to linger over positive pleasure (three opinions that seem somehow still apt).

Aquinas followed Augustine in insisting that the best pleasures were the pleasures of beatitude, a theological variant on the view that pleasure, properly engaged, is no enemy to ethical self-governance. The kind of move in question finds more modern echoes in John Stuart Mill's insistence that there is a distinction to be drawn between higher and lower pleasures, and that the higher are better. Whitman's libidinous joys are at the lower end of the Millian scale. Cavafy's fatal joy is near the bottom. The pleasure of reading poetry—perhaps even the pleasure of reading Whitman or Cavafy, but certainly of reading poetry that turns one's attention to edifying thoughts—was, for Mill, a paradigmatic example of higher pleasure.

It is less common to find philosophers discussing pleasure now than it used to be. But then, my efforts throughout this book are not so much *contrary* to more recent philosophical treatments of my topics as they are *other* than these.[3] The justification for my direction remains entirely contemporary, however. Taking *some* other route seems to me necessary if we are to understand our own idea that calculative pictures of practical reason have special claim on our attention. The route I am taking in rehabilitating (and, in part, remodeling) Aquinas's remark about the threefold division of good is the one I have found illuminating. My task is to show that the three regions are regions of good, and that the useful is the primary region. Getting pleasure to serve as a region of good requires getting pleasure to serve as a practical consideration that can figure in a desirability characterization for action (offered as a final response to Anscombe's question "Why are you A-ing?") and showing that pleasure-based reason-explanations are distinctive.

In defending the old-fashioned thought that the pleasant *is* a distinctive region of practical good, I do not incorporate the theological framework that ordains pleasure to the ends of the uncreated good. Nor do I insist that the pleasures belonging for the most part to the intellect and gentler feelings are the genuinely good pleasures. The distinction between higher and lower pleasures is not, I think, so easily drawn. Often, it seems more a thinly disguised class distinction rather than a view about pleasure, and smuggling moral satisfaction in on the "high" end seems a secular version of the doctrine that God has arranged it so that the best pleasure is reserved for the best souls. More important, championing the pleasures of intellectual, aesthetic, or ethical occupations over *all* others makes it hard to convince anyone uncorrupted by theory that your topic is pleasure.

Whether our focus is on the pallid pleasures of abstract contemplation, the thrill of morally satisfying reading, the darker business of debauchery, or the loose delights of sense appetite's pursuits, there is something about pleasure that is potentially at odds with ethics and potentially an enemy to efficiency. I take it as obvious that actions done from and for the sake of pleasure need not be good in the sense useful (as anyone who has ever left off necessary work for fun knows perfectly well). And since getting caught up in pleasure can lead you to put off doing what you think you should more generally, pleasure is not necessarily tied to befitting-style practical considerations. Nevertheless, the *pleasure* of doing this or that is sometimes the *point* of doing this or that. That is, pleasure is not alien to reason-based explanation of intentional action.[4]

If the useful covers terminable practical considerations and, hence, the actions informed by them, and the befitting orders a life, what role is there for pleasure to play in ethics or action theory? Once you have both actions and a way of lining them up like ducks in a principled row, what's left? Aquinas says that what remains is "that which terminates the movement of appetite in the form of rest in the thing desired":

> Why are you standing out there [A-ing]? It's getting cold.
> I'm watching the fog roll in over that ridge [i.e., in order to B].
> I wouldn't have thought that meteorology was your topic [i.e., why do you want to B?].
> I like watching the fog [i.e., B-ing is pleasant].
> It does this every day [i.e., you do not usually B].
> And today I am enjoying the spectacle; stop fretting [i.e., just now I am in the mood to B; don't interrupt me].

This, then, is the place of pleasure.

In this chapter, I set out to explain this region of practical good, beginning with a brief discussion of how pursuit of pleasure might get its reputation as a source of trouble in the will. I use this account both to distinguish pleasure from feelings, and to expand on my earlier characterization of pleasure-based reasons for acting. Next, I develop a loosely Thomistic account of pleasure. In doing so, I hope to show that allowing that one's reason for pursuing some primary ends is the pleasure involved need do no violence to a calculative account of reasons for acting. But the link between pleasure and action is less clear than the link between considerations of use and action. I say how near the end of the chapter. Throughout, again, my aim is to show that the pleasant is a distinctive region of practical good by showing that considerations of pleasure shed distinctive light on the point of some intentional action.

Pleasure and Danger

The thought that pursuit of pleasure, especially of sensual pleasure, breeds failures of self-governance is not entirely alien to modern philosophy. Modern philosophers frequently treat sensuality as arational. The tacit modern explanation for traditional philosophical alarm over pleasure becomes that pursuit of bodily pleasure is pursuit of an experience alien to reason. That is why a seeker of sensual pleasure is apt to exhibit tendencies to ungoverned excess (for example, to drunkenness or to luxurious sloth). Modern sensibility suggests, for example, that there are many ways to relax—massage, mineral baths, a nap in the hammock—that the happy contentment and sense of bodily well-being brought about by any of these is the *pleasure* and the things one does for its sake are the *means* to getting that kind of good feeling. This is *not* what is at issue in explaining actions done from pleasure: there is no need to treat pleasure separately from things that serve further ends if "pleasure" is merely a rubric covering all the kinds of experience that you happen to like.

Consider: there might be several ways of getting an erotic experience of type *E*, but the pleasure of good anonymous interaction that gives rise to *e* will be different from the pleasure of good companionate interaction that gives rise to *e* or good mixed group interaction that gives rise to *e*, all of which will in turn be different (no matter how vivid one's imagination) from good solitary engagements giving rise to *e*. That all these scenes involve an *e*-experience should not obscure this point—why pay or risk the unknown for what you can get by yourself for free? why seek privacy when you have a partner? Basically, if all you are after is giving yourself an *e*-experience (if, for instance, you can imagine taking the preceding questions as relevant to your practical deliberations), then there is no need to postulate pleasure as the source of what you do in those contexts where you seek an *e*-experience. You have a determinate end: namely, providing yourself with *e*. Your practical problem is simply to figure out how best to attain it, relative to other things on the agenda, and so your deliberation rests in considerations about what will be useful, given that you want to have an *e*-experience.

Here, Gilbert Ryle's summary of the two sorts of things that are treated together as aspects of pleasure is in some ways apt:

> "Pleasure" . . . is sometimes used to denote special kinds of moods, such as elation, joy and amusement. It is accordingly used to complete the description of certain feelings, such as flutters, glows and thrills. But there is another sense in which we say that a person who is so absorbed in some activity, such as golf or argument, that he is reluctant to stop, or even think of anything else, is "taking pleasure in" or "enjoying" doing what he is doing, though he is in no degree convulsed or beside himself, and though he is not, therefore, experiencing any particular feelings.[5]

Ryle is at pains to distinguish pleasure from the flutters and the glows. Such feelings, after all, can be unpleasant. More important, if what you are after is a feeling of some sort, then your practical consideration is local and terminable.[6] Enjoying what one is doing, which is my topic, is not like this.[7]

According to the secular threefold division, considerations of pleasure attach to the present action without necessarily assigning it a place in a larger scheme of things and without necessarily treating it as a means to or part of attaining a further end. By these lights, it is *not* that acting from and for pleasure allows subrational nature to erupt onto the scene of rational action, thereby undoing well-laid plans. Coming down with flu undoes well-laid plans, but we don't think it involves some fault in rational will. The trouble with pleasure is *not* that it is an irrational force that can shape action. Rather, the *kind* of rational force at issue in acting for pleasure is potentially disorderly. Considerations of pleasure direct one to *prolong* the present action. Acts done from and for pleasure involve an agent "so absorbed in some activity, such as golf or argument, that he is reluctant to stop," as Ryle puts it. In brief, pleasure is the interminable termination for rational appetite (in Thomistic parlance). More bluntly, it is the stopping-place for action that says, "Don't stop!" This very feature makes it especially easy to get carried away by pursuits that are primarily good in the sense pleasant.

Small wonder, then, that practical philosophers used to find pleasure worrisome! Local, interminable practical considerations would not obviously supply answers to questions about how one ought to live; they are too tightly bound to present action for that. By a similar token, that they are interminable sets them apart from considerations of use. Excellence in acting from and for the sake of the useful is, simply, taking sound and efficient means to one's ends. If I am engaged in conversation in order to convey information, the point is to communicate well, to formulate points clearly, explain, stay on track, and so on. If I am conversing from and for pleasure, the point is to savor the talk, enjoy the company, and so forth—sharp points may be no more than jokes, we may drift from topic to topic, and may never come to any particularly impressive conclusions.

Distinctions

There are, of course, useful-style considerations of pleasure, and one might, of course, have a view of how it befits one to live that suggests that pleasure must have a place in a good life. *Useful*-style considerations of pleasure direct one to do this or that *in order to* put oneself in the way of enjoying oneself (just as useful-style concern with others' pleasure directs one to create occasions for their enjoyment—as near as I can tell, there is no principled difference between trying to put others in the way of enjoying themselves and trying to put oneself in the way of enjoying oneself). Befitting-style considerations of pleasure, on the other hand, direct one to put oneself in the way of delight at least sometimes. Considerations of pleasure, however, lead one to make a present good that is one's own—enjoyment—last.

On this view pleasure is the active enjoyment of a present good. Not all actions that bring pleasure are done *from* pleasure, however, and not every action that is done from pleasure is done solely *for* pleasure.

Incidental pleasure first. Sometimes, I take pleasure in what I do, but do not do it from or for the sake of pleasure. For example, I might enjoy arguing, but sometimes, at least, I argue in order to support a point, not merely for the fun of arguing. When I seek to win a point, we do not need to point to the pleasure to see the good of arguing, that is, we don't need to postulate pleasure as a special *rational source* of action. I argue in order to drive home my conclusion. I will keep at it even if it is no fun at all. Likewise, I do not seek to prolong a pleasant disputation when I can win quickly and my purpose is simply to win the argument.

In acting *from* pleasure I am carried along by what I am doing and will tend to work to prolong the pleasant task while I can. Sometimes, however, the task over which I linger from pleasure is not done solely for pleasure. For example, it might happen that some afternoon when I am writing checks to creditors (because one ought to pay one's debts, or because bill-paying furthers my other ends), I find myself having fun. I take extra pains over slowly filling in the blanks on the checks, calculating my balance after each debit in a tidy hand, relishing addressing the envelopes and positioning the stamps with precision and care. Magically, I am doing the parts of bill-paying from pleasure. I manage to sustain it, say, for hours and hours. I may never again have this kind of delight in bill-paying; I suppose it could happen that I never again enjoy *anything* so much as I enjoy bill-paying on one unusual Sunday afternoon. But I sat down in order to pay bills not in the hope of amusing myself, and, *ex hypothesi,* I ought to keep at it until I am done even if the pleasure flees while there are still some debts to pay. Nothing in this will in any way diminish the suggestion that I lingered over my task *from* pleasure, that my pleasure was in paying bills. While the pleasure here is incidental, there is something for the pleasure to explain that is absent in the case where I finish a fun argument cleanly and quickly—namely, how it is that a task that usually takes me forty minutes took all afternoon when I met with neither obstacles nor interruptions, and when savoring the work itself was otherwise beside the point.

Pleasure finds its way into the threefold division of good both in cases where an incidental pleasure is prolonged, and in order to show the point of acting with no further end in view, from and for the sake of the pleasure.

Pleasure in Action

What pleasure adds to our account of practical good is the desirability of B-ing with no further end in view, where each part of B-ing or repetition of the B-ing is to be explained by the pleasure of B-ing. I might garden in order to grow food for winter (useful gardening, gardening with a further end in view). I might garden because I have become convinced that organic gardening belongs to knowing one's proper place in our world (befitting gardening, however misguided). Or, I might garden because I enjoy gardening (pleasant gardening, gardening from and for the sake of pleasure). In the latter case, when I garden *sub specie boni,* the *bonum* in question is pleasure. Gardening from and for pleasure involves hard work, and only incidentally brings delicious sensations. If one asks the gardener drenched in sweat, shoveling piles of compost as she gardens from and for pleasure, "But why did you pick such a grubby, difficult hobby?" she will respond, "I just *love* gardening." That is the kind of thing at issue here: actions undertaken with no further end in view which happen to suit the agent. If I garden solely from and for the sake of pleasure, then the armloads of flowers and baskets of vegetables I get from my efforts are a *fringe benefit,* the harvest is *incidental* to the gardening (amateur horticulturists of the sort I have in mind often give away the fruits of labor casually), the point of gardening is the pleasure I take in gardening. As such, this is the kind of case that paradigmatically cries out for a special explanation.

Aquinas's special explanation is in terms of the good of pleasure. He takes the form of his thought about pleasure from Aristotle, and much of the content from Augustine. The definition of perfect pleasure in Aquinas is unimpeded delight in the *operatio* of a connatural habit. The definition is deeply Aristotelian. Such problems as have haunted contemporary commentary on Aristotle on pleasure, however, do not appear to trouble Aquinas—for example, Aquinas seems not to wonder whether pleasure is identical with pleasant action or separate from it, a question that emerges in reading Book VII of the *Nicomachean Ethics* alongside Book X. As near as I can tell, this is partly because, for Aquinas, while I take pleasure *in* doing what it suits me to do (the pleasure is *intrinsic* to the act), that A-ing is, for me, on some occasion, pleasant is itself *contingent* on my state of mind and body, and on the circumstance of the act. The pleasure in A-ing is the source of what I do in A-ing from pleasure. In this sense, the pleasure is intrinsic to what I do. That I can take pleasure in A-ing *now,* however, is contingent on other things and if those things change, the pleasure will flee. So the pleasure involves the *fit* between agent, circumstance, and act. In this sense, although the pleasure is not separable from the action done from and for its sake, it is nevertheless not identical with the act. Keeping the happy coincidence of agent, act, and circumstances going becomes the earthly version of rest in the present good.[8]

Taking Apart the Thomistic Definition of Pleasure

Aquinas defines perfect pleasure as the unimpeded *operatio* of a habit that is itself in harmony with one's nature.[9] I explore this definition bit-by-bit, working by way of examples. Pleasure, like all three sorts of good in Aquinas, has the character of an aim. Once we are clear on what pleasure is, and what sort of explanation of action it gives, we will be in a position to show how an agent acting *from* pleasure can aim at (that is, act *for*) pleasure.

Habitual action is the exercise of acquired or developed powers. For a strict Thomist, the account of habits that are in harmony with one's nature involves a lot of theology. The secular, modern account of connatural habit centers on so-called ego-syntonic practical capacities and responses to the world. Ego-syntonic engagement is most readily grasped as what remains when we subtract the sort of engagements that prompt one to wonder, "What's wrong with me? This isn't like me." Consider, as an example of the pleasant exercise of connatural habit, Gustave Flaubert's description of deliberately handing his life over to natural processes:

> At every stage of my life I have shirked facing my problems . . . and I shall die at eighty before having formed any opinion concerning myself or, perhaps, without writing anything that would have shown me what I could do. . . . However, I worry very little about this; I live like a plant, filling myself with sun and light, with colors and fresh air. I keep eating; so to speak; afterwards the digesting will have to be done, then the shitting; and the shit had better be good! That's the important thing.[10]

Living like a plant is precisely not living with an eye toward larger pursuits, and "shitting" is not a metaphor for putting what one acquires inadvertently through vegetative lassitude to some higher purpose.[11] There is considerable skill involved in this sort of pleasure. One must keep the press of business at bay and refuse to assign leisure to any higher good. Flaubert's reversion to the vegetative, and subsequent rise to merely animal life is, in this sense, an excellent example of habitual action undertaken from and for pleasure. Aquinas would tend to chalk it up to habitual exercise of natural powers, but one suspects high cultivation in Flaubert's turn toward the light.

In order for a practical engagement to be, in the relevant sense, desirable insofar as pleasant, it must be part of an agent's (growing) practical repertoire: she must be able to do the thing well enough already to enjoy doing it,[12] or else be in a position to delight in the gradual increase of her skills while learning. Some people need to be able to do things very well in order to do them from and for pleasure. Others place no such demand on themselves. I suspect that, for most of us, it varies: we can enjoy a casual stroll without focusing on movement in some demanding way, but anything short of excellence in some other arena is unacceptable. Flaubert's Egyptian interlude may have involved a high, modern form of the art of idleness.

It is harder to scry the exercise of power and habit in less rarefied examples, however. Consider simple comfort taken from the nearness of another warm body; consider having a long cool drink on a hot day or making one's way toward the lighted window at night having been lost in the storm; consider climbing into a clean, comfortable bed after a long day's work with the prospect of a good sleep ahead—surely delight in these involves no clear exercise of one's powers! If I understand him, Aquinas offers a complex response to this kind of point.[13]

Some human habits are partly from nature. The mark of such a habit is that its end is given by nature and its exercise does not alter its basic character. If it is natural for humans to rest comfortably entwined with one another, then it will be natural to seek this. If we adults have it in us to seek the simple nearness of another human being, and to linger beside someone just for the joy of it, then the close proximity of another person will itself be a present good that can be enjoyed. In the human infant, movement toward the warm body will count as a *prehabitual* exercise of innate tendencies to move toward what sustains the organism, tendencies belonging to sense appetite—these inclinations are, for Aquinas, "formative natural habits [that] precede even the habit itself."[14] In the adult, however, the delight involves at least understanding the kind of good at issue in a simple embrace and the power to seek or shun the nearness of another. Susceptibility to this low-key sort of rational direction is, Aquinas insists, essential to the powers that comprise various habits.[15] Animals who can neither learn to refrain from doing one sort of thing nor to take up doing another sort of thing are, accordingly, treated by Aquinas as incapable of developing habits.[16] So there is at least the power to do or refrain from doing something pleasurable in the realm of habit. This all by itself lifts even the mature human's most soundly corporeal pleasures—say, the pleasure of a good shit—above the lowly business of mollusk life. The power to grasp the kind of good thing one seeks and to delay gratification moves pleasure into the sphere of *habitus* for Aquinas. Now, what of perfect pleasure?

"Perfect" carries the homely Latin sense of completion, of a whole made up of all of its parts. The parts here are not parts of an action, as I indicated above in pointing out that Aquinas does not worry whether pleasure is the same as or different from the act it explains. They are rather parts of a nexus of agent, act, and circumstance such that the agent is carried along by her act in its context, and her absorption in what she is up to is what she seeks to sustain in seeking to sustain pleasure. When the nexus is successfully sustained, the pleasure is complete, and, in this sense, perfect.

The distinction between perfect and imperfect pleasures does various kinds of work for Aquinas, some of them highly dubious. The first sort concerns the presence of pain or desire. For Aquinas, one kind of imperfect pleasure comes of satisfying the urges of sense appetite. In acts done *from* pleasure, the pleasure puts appetite to rest, in possession of its good, as the clamoring of sense appetite quiets when I eat the luscious dish I ordered. Given that I want a pick-me-up, ordering tiramisu is useful. I eat tiramisu for pleasure, however, relishing the good at hand and savoring each bite. Eating tasty dishes in this way is an exercise of my powers—not the kind of exercise connected to perfect pleasure for Aquinas, but an exercise nevertheless. For Aquinas, this sort of pleasure is imperfect because we cannot always get what we want (hence, acting from sense appetite is sometimes painful) and because sense appetite keeps cropping up as long as we are bound to this mortal coil. Neither "imperfection" should be admitted as such in a secular view. Nothing requires that I find my tiramisu even faintly unsatisfying.

The relevant sort of imperfect pleasure for a secular view will occur when one cannot shake the sense that an engagement is inadequate in some way even though one takes it up expecting pleasure and continues it because it is, after all, pleasant. Real pleasure can nevertheless come bound up with a sense of imperfection. Suppose, for example, that I delight in the embrace of one lover without entirely being able to shake off the haunting absence of another. The memory obtrudes without spoiling things entirely, but in such a way that things don't feel quite right. My pleasure is imperfect.

The other sort of imperfect Thomistic pleasure comes when one is learning how to do something. One as yet lacks the requisite skill to do the thing without thinking about it, but there is delight in the gradual increase of one's powers. A secular view can take this kind of imperfection on board as is.

In perfect pleasure, the will is content: there is neither desire to be otherwise engaged nor pain. Suppose, for example, that the pleasure I take in singing is such that, while I am singing, I am happily un-self-conscious, engaged and at peace. Suppose also that I am not especially pained if I lack opportunities to sing, nor do I experience cravings to sing, nor do I find myself moved to sing until I am hoarse. Periodically, when I am alone, I burst into song when I feel like singing, but I scarcely notice it if a week goes by without such a vocal episode. My delight in singing ought to count not only as a perfect pleasure on a secular view (as, indeed, will any kind of delight that one would chalk up to simple enjoyment of one's own life), but also as a perfect Thomistic pleasure.

Unfortunately, St. Thomas held that no earthly pleasure could have this status. He uses the distinction between perfect and imperfect to argue that the best pleasure will be the most perfect pleasure, and the only candidate for this will be endless delight in contemplating the presence of God in Paradise. In comparison, all earthly pleasures are less than perfect. Everlasting joy in beatific vision will be complete, immutable, constant, bliss.

Aquinas was, as I have mentioned, a calculative theorist. Nevertheless, the thought that considerations of pleasure are interminable is not alien to him. Part of the force of the perfect–imperfect distinction for Aquinas, I take it, together with his insistence that all the pleasures of mortal life are imperfect, is to point to the failure of fit between an interminable practical consideration and the fact that worldly pleasures stop. Night falls and the gardener goes indoors. Morning nears and the lovers drift off to sleep. One finishes reading the novel. The credits roll on the screen. In a sense, then, the pleasures of mortal life become faint promises of the endless delight of beatitude, and part of the work of practical reason in pleasant action becomes holding steady with an eye on this promise. The interminability of the consideration (together with the finitude of worldly pleasures) points one toward otherworldly pleasures.

Even here, however, Aquinas makes an indirectly illuminating point for secular work. One thing he means to discuss is ecstasy, which might seem like the highest grade of pleasure. But (a) ecstasy takes one considerably beyond delight in the exercise of one's powers, and (b) the worldly experience of ecstasy, far more than simple enjoyment of the business of one's life, is finite. When one is swept up in a moment of ecstasy, one's own powers fade and the experience opens onto something rather different. Whatever *this* difference amounts to, worldly experiences of ecstasy have precious little durability. For both of these reasons, my hunch is that worldly ecstasy is better treated by analogy to very strong sensation than as belonging to the pleasant region of practical good.[17] What one has in view in taking some drugs or seeking out e-experiences or engaging in elaborate rituals meant to induce spiritual visions and the like is a determinate, future end. The end in question in seeking bliss is not sustained exercise of one's powers in circumstances conducive to what one is doing. Rather, it is the experience of being flooded by feeling. Perfect pleasure, in the view I am urging, becomes not ecstasy, but absorption in what one is doing.

Continuing, then, with our definition, we come to *operatio,* which is generally translated as activity. As the word is used here, an activity, unlike ordinary action, remains *with the agent*—Aquinas's examples include contemplation and sensing. (The similarity to contemporary views about pleasure is most striking here: you and I might both enjoy the concert, but my pleasure is mine and your pleasure is yours; compare: my pain remains mine, however much you commiserate or however deeply you condole.) What *operatio* covers is, in this sense, the positive phenomenological side of active enjoyment—the subjective aspect of acts done from and for pleasure. This may, but need not, include delicious sensations.

Unimpeded pleasure is the un-self-conscious enjoyment of doing what one knows how to do without the distracting influence of one's own incompetence, of pressing concerns, of ambivalence, or of alien pleasures. It has a contemporary echo in discussion of "flow." When whatever one is doing is going smoothly and well such that one doesn't have to, say, think about *how* to do it (even if the doing of it itself involves thinking about some other topic), the experience is of what has lately been described as "being in the flow."[18] Unimpeded pleasure is very like flow.

Because pleasant things are done for their own sakes, the pleasure of them is the principal thing that might be said on their behalf, the principal good under whose aspect they are pursued. And perfect pleasure (discarding the otherworldly association of this phrase in Aquinas) is the pleasure of the very kind of active engagement in question—of making love, say, or swimming, or chatting with a friend—for the very agent taking part in these, and under the very circumstances that conduce to enjoying what she is up to. This is how pleasure clings to present action. Moreover, the pleasure continues throughout the course of doing what is pleasant from pleasure: we explain why I take the next spoonful of ice cream by pointing out that eating ice cream is pleasant, which is how we explained taking the last spoonful of ice cream (the first spoonful by contrast, might be explained by noting that I start in on some ice cream in order to put myself in the way of pleasant eating, and have turned to ice cream with some idea that I will enjoy eating it). That is, the pleasure coincides with and undergirds the whole of any pleasant engagement explaining each part of what I do for the sake of pleasure.

Pleasure and Practical Reason

In acting from and for pleasure, the delight is *in* the doing of an action of some kind *while* doing it. Although pleasures are intrinsic to the kinds of action one does from pleasure, *which* sort of thing will be, for one of us, pleasant at some point in life is contingent, just as tiring of the thing in question or losing one's taste for it will be contingent. If I am swimming because I enjoy it, then I am a good enough swimmer to be able to swim just for fun; swimming happens to suit me now, and, from my point of view, there is nothing more to be said on behalf of what I'm doing in the water. When I exercise my powers for the joy of it, the kind of desirability characterization for my action becomes "I am B-ing because it is in my power to B and I am here and now finding B-ing delightful in such-and-such respects." That is, B-ing is, for me, *in general,* a natural end—an exercise of some of my powers associated with cultivated sense appetite, cognitive sensitivity, or acquired skill—and, *here and now,* of all the many things I might be doing or learning how to do, B-ing is what I happen to feel like doing.[19]

The sense in which such considerations are interminable can perhaps best be grasped by contrasting this view of pleasure with a more Millian view. On Mill's view, pleasure arises as an *effect* of what one is doing. One's act gives rise to pleasure—ideally, it gives rise to pleasure incidentally or in passing. On the view I urge, on the other hand, pleasure is as much a *cause* of action as an effect of it. One is carried along *by* what one is doing at present rather than getting a good result as one goes along. The combined locality and endlessness of the sort of practical source at issue distinguishes it from ordinary calculative considerations. Millian pleasure, even Millian pleasure that we take from what we're doing as we go along, is a straightforward end-in-the-sense-stopping-place: although Mill believed that you cannot aim at pleasure, he held that a life devoid of pleasure was a bad life, and that if you had some control over the circumstances of your life and were miserable, you had good reason to cultivate your capacities for enjoyment.[20] You will have succeeded just in case you have a more pleasant experience of your life.

The opposite of Millian pleasure, accordingly, is pain. The opposite of pleasure on the loosely Thomistic picture I have sketched is more like a nexus of agent, act, and circumstance that is miserable in a way that may involve all kinds of pains, but is no mere sum of physical discomforts, and may likewise be experienced as interminable. The obvious examples are extreme—life in Nazi concentration camps, life as a slave in colonial San Domingo. If strictly Thomistic pleasure is an intimation of paradise, its opposite is an intimation of damnation—in the symbolic economy of Christianity, the opposite of worldly pleasure is a partial, worldly taste of hell. More personal extreme cases might include life in the grip of grievous loss (the deaths of one's children or of one's partner, the sudden and unexpected loss of friends, employment, and the like through one's own misconduct). And less extreme cases might be found in days when nothing goes right.[21]

On my view, when all goes right, pleasure is a source of secondary ends: namely, those ends pursued in order to *sustain* the pleasant engagement with B-ing. One As in order to B. One As repeatedly, or slowly, or some such in order to sustain the engagement with B-ing. One does other things (locks the door, dismisses a companion, seeks company, plays music, what have you) in order to B in peace. The end is to keep a good thing going. The good is the pleasure one takes in B-ing.

There are all kinds of stories about how primary ends I pursue from pleasure get into me in the first place. I am born with undeveloped capacities for some of them, perhaps, others wind up in me through good or bad parenting, and others develop as I make my way in the world, developing tastes, acquiring skills, finding avenues for active engagement that suit me temperamentally, or pique my interest, or some such. These stories explain how doing something becomes potentially pleasant for me, but they do not attach to my doing a particular kind of thing under particular circumstances at a particular time. The *end* of pleasant engagement as such is the end of sustaining the nexus of agent, action, and circumstance in order to prolong this glad coincidence. This is how considerations of pleasure as such give rise to ends, that is, how pleasure is a source of action rather than merely a consequence of it.

The work of calculative practical reason is in taking sound means to one's ends. The work of practical reason in action done from pleasure is indirectly calculative. Because actions done from pleasure are done for their own sakes rather than for the sake of attaining further ends, and because the art of pleasure is the art of being able to *persevere* in the enjoyment, such "oughts" as attend considerations of pleasure are closely associated with *continuing* to do the kind of thing in question for the sake of enjoyment. In acting *from* pleasure you act *in order to* prolong your "delight in possession of the present good." Errors of practical judgment, accordingly, will involve:

1. *Misjudging the character of what you are doing* (say, by trying to combine kinds of potentially pleasant activities that cannot be done at the same time). Example: Although I can sing or swim from and for pleasure, it will count as a violation of the Thomistic pleasure principle if I try to sing midswim.

2. *Misjudging your powers or the use to which you put them* such that what you are doing is too easy or too hard for you to enjoy. Example: In order for there to be pleasure in puzzle-working, the fit between puzzle and solver must be such that the solver hits little stumbling blocks along the way to solving the puzzle. One cannot delight in puzzles that are too easy to solve. Likewise, working a puzzle is rarely pleasant if the puzzle is too hard. If I misjudge the extent of my powers or the difficulty of the puzzle, I will wrongly continue working, thinking I stand to enjoy what I am doing, and find myself disappointed or frustrated instead.

3. *Rushing or otherwise failing to attend to what you are doing in the right sort of way to make what you are doing last.* Example: In order

fully to enjoy eating delicious food one wants to draw out the meal, to eat slowly, say, and attend to tastes and smells and textures singly and in combination. One can ruin one's own pleasure in eating if one eats too fast or too much.

4. *Failing to control the circumstances in the way necessary to promote sustained B-ing.* Example: If two friends find themselves immersed in a pleasant, confidential conversation in a place where they are likely to be approached by other people, they will do well to move to a less trafficked place; you cannot have open conversation if you have to leave off talking frequently in order to exchange casual pleasantries with other people.

Here we get some low-level "oughts" (if one wants to B for the pleasure of B-ing, then one ought to seek circumstances conducive to B-ing and one ought *not* to rush through B-ing, nor to continue B-ing when it turns out that B-ing is too hard or too easy, nor to combine incompatible actions or otherwise impede B-ing). By the lights of the threefold division, these *govern* actions done from and for pleasure.

What these "oughts" display is, again, part of what is ethically alarming about pleasure. Aquinas takes it as fairly obvious that some forms of weakness of will involve getting drawn along by the pleasure of what one is doing until one has outrun one's own sense of the boundaries of conduct. Anyone who ever has gone too far in this sense may find that the pleasure in whatever she was doing was like a thing urging her forward. When the pleasure flees, when some form of circumspection or sobriety obtrudes, she can find herself suddenly needing to repair damages of one sort or another. If I am right in thinking this is a familiar form of weakness of will, then it is a form that takes its force from the combined locality and interminability of considerations of pleasure. The relevant sort of weakness arises because the pleasure in the act that went too far was precisely the sort of thing one seeks to build and sustain in acts done from pleasure. For all that, this sort of trouble will count as a kind of *failure* of practical reason with respect to considerations of pleasure (although one might get so far worked up that one scarcely notices the failure until well after the fact). What one did created circumstances in which the very pleasure one was working to sustain fell prey to one's own overindulgence.

Pleasure is both a primary end and a source of secondary ends because it directs us to *sustain* the nexus of agent, act, and circumstance conducive to enjoyment in acts done from and for pleasure. This is how calculative practical reason is exercised in acts done from and for pleasure. The work of calculative practical reason in acting from and for pleasure, however, is less direct than the work of calculative practical reason in taking means to other ends. I will try to make this point clearer by turning to a more dreary topic: *unpleasant* attachment to present acts, namely, neurotic obsession.

One of the striking things about *interminable* practical considerations is how hard it is to be certain whether *anyone* ever acts from and for their sake. The status of interminable practical considerations (some befitting-style considerations and considerations of pleasure) as explanatory reasons for acting is more tenuous than the status of useful-style practical considerations (where it is enough to see whether an agent is taking reasonable means to her avowed ends). By drawing a formal parallel between obsessive acts and acts done from and for pleasure, I hope to underscore this point.

In my view, the status of considerations of pleasure and fit as reasons for acting depends on their relation to calculative practical reason. I have just discussed the sense in which the pleasant region of good is a source of ends (material for calculative reason). Practical justification in these terms remains primarily calculative even though considerations of pleasure operate at a slight remove from ordinary calculative practical considerations. The formal similarity between obsession and pleasure will illustrate the difficulty in taking considerations of pleasure at face value as explanatory reasons. Because of my focus on intentional action (as the topic of work on practical reason), I take it that a practical consideration that is not operating as an explanatory reason for an act is at best a *potential* justificatory reason, one as yet idle.

Obsession and Pleasure

As is the case with any of our three regions of good, it is possible to explain some actions in terms of considerations that have the formal qualities of the region in question, but that do not match the agent's sense of the point of her act. I touched on this topic in Chapter 3 by complaining about a tendency to suppose that all intentional actions could be supported by befitting-style desirability characterizations: even if it was possible to produce a multivolume account of the place of an action of some kind in the living of a good human life (a befitting-style treatise), if no one ever did an act of the relevant kind from or for the sake of the considerations set forth in the learned tome, then, *ex hypothesi,* the treatise could not supply an answer to the reasons-for-acting-seeking question "Why?" and hence could not supply a desirability characterization for *any* action of the relevant type. But the problem with getting an account of interminable reasons for acting is deeper than the trouble I outlined in Chapter 3. Pleasure is our case in point.

Formally, the distinctive features of pleasant-style practical considerations—that they are local and interminable—also will attach to various sources for acting that fall outside the purview of one's privileged sense of the point of what one is doing. Although I might have highly developed psychological diagnostic powers, and although I might use these to explain some of the things I do in terms of pathological attachment to present action, the kind of explanation of my conduct that I can give through self-observation and diagnostic skill is not interestingly different from the kind of explanation another person could give of my behavior. My psychoanalyst or physician, for instance, might be better able than I to explain some of what I do, couched in terms of local and interminable prompts to action.

Consider, for example, Sigmund Freud's remark about obsessive actions:

> Neurotic ceremonials consist in making small adjustments to particular everyday actions, small additions or restrictions or arrangements, which have always to be carried out in the same, or in a methodically varied manner. These activities give the impression of being mere formalities, and they seem quite meaningless to us. Nor do they appear otherwise to the patient himself; yet he is incapable of giving them up, for any deviation from the ceremonial is visited by intolerable anxiety, which obliges him to make his omission good. Just as trivial as the ceremonial actions themselves are the occasions and activities which are embellished, encumbered and in any case prolonged by the ceremonial—for instance, dressing and undressing, going to bed or satisfying bodily needs.[22]

Freud explains the roots of obsessive action as a kind of prompt to action that attaches to the doing of particular kinds of deeds, a prompt that appears majestically detached from both the larger scheme of the obsessive person's life (to this extent, "meaningless") and also from the determinate ends of the kinds of activities in question—the business at hand is always *prolonged* by the obsessive ceremony, that is, prevented from arriving at its destination efficiently. So, like considerations of pleasure, prompts to obsessive acts need have no clear tie to befitting-style desirability characterizations, nor to thought about what is useful, given that one means, say, to get dressed or to go to bed. And, like considerations of pleasure, the need to go through some determinate quasi ritual in the course of the business of everyday life attaches to the doing of those very things in a way that involves prolonging the business at hand: the present act, the everyday activity. The kind of activity itself (like any kind of activity—I will discuss this at some length in considering useful-style desirability characterizations) will have some calculative articulation. But the obsessive repetition of the ritual elements is at odds with completing the business at hand, and the agent can see this as well as his analyst can.

The formal isomorphism between some neurotic acts and acts done from and for pleasure is close enough to suggest that there is not always a hard, fast line between the two. For instance, it may seem as though pleasure is directly at issue in ceremonial acts after all: by performing his routine, the obsessive man seeks to avoid painful anxiety and find comfort. Avoidance of pain may not be identical with pursuit of pleasure, but pleasure and pain-avoidance are often linked; at the very least, sometimes pain is at odds with pleasure. Notice, however, that the reason Freud has had ample occasion to consider obsessive actions is that neurotic obsession is a *presenting problem* for psychotherapy. While the obsessive person cannot be comfortable unless he goes through the requisite motions, he is seeking help because he is likewise disturbed *by* his own need to perform his ceremonies. He can't comfortably *not* perform the rituals, but neither does his need to perform them suffice, in his view, to show them in a favorable light.

It is hard to say how many of one's pleasures might strike one as pathological on reflection. To some extent, whether one does a thing from pleasure or from some psychological unease may come down to the messy business of the first-person perspective. In acts done from and for the pleasure of them, one is *satisfied* with what one is doing. In some private rituals, and in many activities that begin to look dubious because one comes to sense in them the mark of bad ideology, say, or the echo of bad parenting or trauma, one can come to feel compromised by one's own interest in doing the thing in question.

Considerations of pleasure are meant to show the point of doing some of what one does. "Because it's pleasant" or "Because I enjoy it" operate as desirability characterizations for the actions in question. In this sense, although, like various neurotic acts and daily rituals, considerations of pleasure may well lead nowhere and have no very tight connection to one's considered views about what matters in life, these things alone are *not* supposed to prevent considerations of pleasure from showing the point of action. The kind of anxiety reduction managed by ordinary neurotic acts, if identified as such by the agent, is different. One does such acts in order to avoid discomfort, not from and for pleasure. Rest in the thing desired is not the same as anxiously staving off the undesirable. Nevertheless, in general, one can lose the capacity for rest in the thing desired if the desire itself comes to seem compromising.

Actions I can undertake from and for pleasure may cease to be even potentially enjoyable for me on reflection, which raises one curious feature of interminable practical considerations versus straightforwardly useful ones: *that A-ing is a means to or part of B-ing* (for a suitably skilled and cognitively equipped agent under circumstances of some sort) has considerable practical stability. Calculative practical considerations are not only fairly easy to discuss and assess but have remarkable durability (consider, for example, the fact that one often can use traditional techniques to attain ends long after innovations have altered standard practice). *That B-ing* will remain potentially pleasant for someone under some circumstances, or will continue to strike an agent as fitting quite apart from his interest in attaining any further end, is much less certain.

Pleasure and Fit

Here, it could be objected, the close fit between practical repertoire and pleasure, together with the sense that befitting-style considerations and pleasant-style ones seem similarly unstable, make it seem as though considerations of pleasure are considerations of how it befits such-and-such a person to live after all. Indeed, pleasure may have a necessary place in human life generally, and what makes pleasure a reason for acting may be that pleasure is good in the sense fitting.[23]

Notice, however, that whether one holds that a good life is at least sometimes pleasant, what pleasure explains is not the *place* of this or that kind of action in the larger scheme of one's life. Actions done from pleasure are done on the basis of what one is in the mood to do *now*. The fact that I often enjoy gardening (I am a gardener; gardening is, for me, fitting) gives me reason to expect I'll enjoy it today; but if I get out there, seeking a pleasant afternoon, and am miserable, I can't explain why I stick with it by pointing to *pleasure*. Stubbornness, maybe. Hope for a mood swing, maybe. But not pleasure. If, on the other hand, I am right and gardening is fun today, then there is something for pleasure to explain: namely, why I continue gardening this afternoon and am drawn from task to task, absorbed in the business at hand. The sort of person I am, the sort of being I am, the sort of things I have up my sleeve to do when I'm bored—these things can explain how a kind of action becomes, for me, a likely source of pleasure. *That* I hold that a life devoid of pleasure is a bad life explains why I try to put myself in the way of having some fun now and then. But what pleasure explains is a kind of fit between my mood, my circumstances, what I'm doing, and how these come together such that I am absorbed in what I do. Pleasure clings to the present action, and explains such things as why I gather all my tools (A) before I start on a particularly difficult bit of garden work that is best done quickly and efficiently. I risk ruining my own late afternoon in the garden by damaging my prized peony if I set about trying to divide it without all my equipment ready to hand. This is the distinctive contribution that considerations of pleasure make to reason-based explanation of human action. Our low-level "oughts" are meant to show how considerations of pleasure engage practical reason. They are not the "oughts" of fit. They are the "oughts" of rest in the thing desired.

By providing a distinctive sort of practical consideration with a distinctive sort of work to do in explaining action and a distinctive set of rational constraints, pleasure qualifies as a separable region of practical good on the view I am advocating. It is clearly not a region with necessary allegiance to morality. But then, neither is the useful, nor, for that matter, the whole of the befitting.

It could be objected, of course, that pleasure is *no* kind of reason for acting *at all* apart from an understanding of the place of hedonic concern in living a good life. This objection repeats the conviction that there must always be a befitting-style account of the place of an action in a life if the act is to count as an exercise of practical reason. It is my great hope that, at some point in this book, this objection will begin to appear a flat statement of philosophical prejudice. It is to the befitting that I turn next.

5

Fit

It is possible to get carried away by some part of what you are doing, and afterwards be very sorry that this happened. Sometimes this is because you meant to do several things and lost track (that is, you were inefficient) and now you face the dreary task of playing catch up. Other times, however, it's not that you didn't complete as many tasks as you had wanted. You have done plenty—more than you had planned, more even than you had thought yourself capable of doing in a single evening. In the bright light of the morning after, you find yourself wishing that you had been vastly *less* efficient than you were. You survey the damage, blinking, filled with regret. Or perhaps it was like this: you were not carried away at all. You did *exactly* what you set out to do, and succeeded brilliantly by dint of sober calculation and concentrated effort. Surveying your accomplishments, you hate yourself.

The Befitting

Traditionally, one of the things explained by pointing to considerations of how it befits one to live is the kind of regret or remorse that comes when you did very well, by the lights of your proximate ends, or in terms of sustaining a pleasant engagement, and you wish you hadn't. What you did may have been good in the sense pleasant or good in the sense useful, but was not a fit thing for you to have done. What would have been fitting would have been, you think, to have refused to pursue the end in question, or, if you needed to attain it, to find another way. What would have been fitting would have been to forgo that pleasure, or at least to rein it in a bit. We explain what you did by pointing to the pleasure in it or how it helped you to get what you wanted to get. We explain your regret by pointing out that, by your lights, what you did was unsuitable for you to do. In light of the threefold division, your actions were bad in the sense unsuitable, unbecoming, unseemly, unfit. They were out of sync with some larger scheme of things you mean to have order the relevant portion of your affairs.

The befitting is, in effect, the region of broad, patterning principles in adult human life. Practical considerations that find their home in this region concern the place of an intentional action in a pattern of some sort that the agent means to have shape some portion of her life such that actions favored by the patterning principle are ones she finds in some way suitable, fitting, appropriate, or, sometimes, required. The pattern is generally one that can be realized in more than one way. Befitting-style desirability characterizations can be given in support of doing some things, omitting to do others, and sometimes also for rejecting some means one might have taken to an end had it not been that those means were, by the lights of the patterning principle at issue, questionable or impermissible. Formally, these practical considerations are nonlocal (that is, they attach to largish stretches of one's life, possibly even to the whole of one's maturity, and can be realized by various different kinds of acts) and, like considerations of pleasure, interminable.

Just as the point of acts done from and for the sake of the pleasure in doing them is not to extinguish the pleasure, but rather to make it last, acts done from and for the sake of befitting-style practical considerations are not about being once and for all *done* with the befitting-style consideration at issue. They instead express, maintain, and enact one's sense of some larger scheme of things in one's life. One often gives a befitting-style desirability characterization for action with reference to the kind of pattern at issue: for example, "I'm telling you this because I'm your friend," "Citizens ought to B," "I have to B; my children are depending on me."

The item(s) responsible for giving an adult's life this kind of shape may be variously described, but will have a wider sphere of influence than a disposition to do A under circumstances $c_1 \ldots c_n$, or a norm concerning how one is supposed to go about doing this or that kind of thing. As I use the terms, "norms" and behavioral "dispositions" concern actions of specific types. It has become common of late for philosophers to use both "norm" and "disposition" more widely than I do. I adhere to a slightly outdated locution in order to keep a distinction in place between ordering principles that involve, say, not standing nearer than fifteen inches to a stranger when I converse with her (a nice, robust sort of norm that is in me to the extent that I am disposed to maintain culturally appropriate conversational distance between myself and those of my interlocutors with whom I have no special intimacy), and something on the order of virtues like prudence, justice, fortitude, and temperance. At the very least there is this sort of difference between norms and dispositions on the one side and virtues, vices, morality, and the like on the other: dispositions incline me to do specific kinds of things under specific sorts of circumstances and norms establish standards of correctness or adequacy in doing them; virtues, vices, and such practical considerations as Kantian duty, on the other hand, unite and give rise to many *different* kinds of intentional actions and deliberate omissions, explain some constraints on deliberation, can be in me as sources of action even if I sometimes fail to do as I think fit, and explain my regret or remorse when I fail to do what I take it I should do. These patterning principles have a much broader scope than norms or dispositions, even though norms and dispositions can figure in shaping what I do from and for the sake of my sense of how it befits me to live.

I have already gone into some detail about befitting-style practical considerations. I have pointed out that they need not be ethically praiseworthy, that, indeed, shorn of a substantive account of the human good, practical considerations concerning how best to express, enact, or cultivate an old-fashioned capital vice can be a source of befitting-style desirability characterizations.

I have also pointed out that not all stories that ethicists have told about the befitting are in any interesting sense connected with reason in action. With a little imagination, any ethicist worth her salt can cook up a large and impressive befitting-style account of the good of keeping one's shoes tied, or buying a raspberry-colored beret, or taking one of indefinitely many possible, equally efficient routes to some destination, or, or, or. But if no one ever acts from and for the sake of these considerations, then they will not figure as desirability characterizations of intentional action. They are not—*ex hypothesi,* not even *potentially,* for anyone save the creative ethicist—answers to the reasons-for-acting-seeking question "Why?" As such, far from justifying intentional action, they merely illustrate a befitting-style way of thinking about what gets done or got done.

The threefold division, as I am using it, is a division in kinds of desirability characterizations that might be given in response to the relevant question "Why?" There are many stories one can tell about what people do that are *not* the stuff of desirability characterizations. These stories are not the topic here. I turn to some of them in Chapter 8. For now, I mark that, in order to figure in showing the *point* of an intentional act *as such*, a befitting-style practical consideration offered in support of some action has to be one *for the sake of* which some agent acted on some occasion. That is how it might crop up *as* a desirability characterization for the act. Nevertheless, for the purposes of this chapter, I rather loosen the reins on this point and allow for an especially theoretically savvy group of agents to be in charge of producing befitting-style accounts of what they are up to. We are in the befitting region of good. Things get a bit heady here, and one does a disservice to the region if one ignores the responses of the deeply reflective people. Some of the accounts of how it befits one to live that I look at involve a lot of theory. I treat the theory itself as a source of desirability characterizations for the things that at least some people do. To this end, I give detailed treatment of Jack Spicer's discussions of how it befits a poet to conduct himself, and a less detailed treatment of Peter Geach's discussion of virtues.

Now, in order to be more than incidental to the agent and the action, even a very sophisticated befitting-style desirability characterization of the sort one can extract from Geach or Spicer has also to be a practical consideration *from* which the agent acted. Compare: in the Chapter 4 I pointed out that it was possible to enjoy what one was doing, and possible that the circumstances of the action were such that one acted in part from pleasure, even though one wasn't acting solely for pleasure. In this connection, I imagined suddenly finding myself relishing the activity of paying bills and drawing out the process. In the example, I lingered over my task from pleasure. I did not pay bills solely for pleasure, however, which is why I would have kept at it until all my bills were paid had the activity become tiresome. I would have finished more quickly, that's all. In this chapter, I consider such things as cultivating virtue for its usefulness and arranging one's life for the sake of poetry, imagining that people might act entirely *from and for* such considerations.

My tasks in this chapter are two. The first is to distinguish patterning principles that are merely interminable in practice from radically interminable ones. My second is, in each case, to discuss the sense in which one might be said to act from (rather than merely in accordance with) a patterning principle.

My aim in this book, again, is to motivate the sense that calculative pictures of practical reason have special claim on our attention. Calculative pictures of practical reason are end-based. It is in the service of motivating a calculative picture that I think it necessary first off to explain what *interminable* practical considerations are like. My strategy is to argue that once we understand what interminable considerations are like, and once we understand how calculative considerations figure in informing intentional action, we will be better able to see why calculative pictures of practical reason have some standing as "default" theories of reason in action. It would beg very many questions, and leave still more unanswered, to make any such argument without bothering to discuss interminable practical considerations.

There are two senses in which a befitting-style practical consideration might be interminable. Some considerations about what suitable or fitting for such-and-such an agent to do are interminable *in practice*. Others are *radically* interminable. Both kinds branch out into many different kinds of action or course. Neither sort can be exhausted in a single action. Both involve patterns that can be realized in more than one way. The ends supplied by both can be understood as means to or parts of realizing a pattern in practice. The distinction between them is just this: a befitting-style consideration that is merely *interminable in practice* takes its force from its calculative relation to attaining further ends (for example, cultivating capital vice is a means to securing worldly goods; the support for vicious patterning principles, for determining one's will to vice, comes from the desirability of controlling worldly goods and the way in which viciousness serves this end). A befitting-style consideration is *radically interminable* if the only ends it generates and serves are internal to the principle in question (for example, if I pursue art for art's sake alone, then the whole order lent to my life by aesthetic concerns is only intelligible as an aesthetic order pursued for the sake of its aesthetic merit). A deeply noncalculative theory of practical reason will generally hold that some radically interminable practical consideration supplies reasons for an agent to do something quite apart from her private interest in the ends internal to the pattern.

I begin with an account of desirability characterizations that are merely interminable in practice and then move on to discuss the radically interminable ones. I devote a lot of space to the former in part because my description of the radically interminable ones is made out in contrast with these. That is, while an account of radically interminable befitting-style practical considerations will sometimes focus on nominally identical sources of order in human life as have strictly calculative accounts—for example, both calculative and noncalculative theorists have given accounts of specific virtues as patterning forces in practice—the noncalculative theorist will give a distinctively open-ended treatment of his material. He will insist that an agent acting from a radically interminable patterning principle acts from and for the sake of that principle alone. The principle baptizes a man's actions with befitting-style desirability directly, not because arranging his affairs in a fitting way serves some other purpose or makes it possible for him to attain some other ends. Moreover, as I mentioned, a deeply noncalculative theorist of practical reason will insist that we are rationally required to work to realize some sorts of radically interminable patterns in our lives (moral patterns, usually). Because these principles serve no further ends, they cannot be grounded in an appeal to our private ends, desires, projects, plans, character traits, or what have you. The support that they lend to action is, to that extent, *not* end-based, which is to say, noncalculative.

There is no mystery about how one acts from and for the sake of a calculative consideration: one takes steps in order to attain one's intended end. The terminus of the pursuit, and what is done in order to attain it, jointly set parameters on the plausibility of crediting the agent with the end she claims to have in claiming that what she is doing is good in the sense useful. The problem of ascertaining whether a man acts from a radically interminable consideration, on the other hand, is notoriously difficult, precisely because there is no further end to look to in determining whether his claims are sincere and true. There is no further end to look to because the pattern is enacted solely for its own sake.

In my discussion of acts done from the other sort of interminable practical consideration, pleasure, the difficulty was partly revealed this way: some neurotic acts are triggered by prompts that have both of the formal hallmarks of considerations of pleasure. Obsessive attachment to little rituals, for instance, is both local and not about attaining the end associated with the business at hand, but rather serves to prolong the doing of things that reach their end when the business at hand finally is done. I hinted that many of one's pleasures could look neurotic (or otherwise pathological) from a slightly altered perspective. That is partly because there is *nothing* to point to but an ego-syntonic attempt to sustain some nexus of agent, act, and circumstance in pointing to how considerations of pleasure explain intentional action by giving the point of what gets done. Ego-syntonicity is dramatically unstable for many of us moderns. What seems entirely in accord with and expressive of my sense of myself one day can look like an effect of psychological damage or bad ideology the next. Accordingly, what I explain now, and happily, by pointing to my pleasure can metamorphose rather rapidly into a thing about me or my world that I think stands in need of correction—not a good (pleasure) at all, but rather a problematic attachment to doing various kinds of things that reads as a symptom of my having internalized something bad (misogyny, say, or heterosexism, or the echoes of childhood trauma). I said that in determining whether an act was done from pleasure, we needed to rely on "the messy business of the first-person perspective." But the difficulty in the pleasure-based understanding of action is part of a more general problem in determining whether someone acts from an interminable consideration that has no calculative link to attaining *further* ends. For people even moderately willing to entertain self-critical introspective ideas, assurance that one acts from *desirable* interminable sources is wobbly.

The question of whether some of what one does is done from and for the sake of a radically interminable befitting-style principle has an even longer history of seeming slippery indeed, because the first-person perspective here may be useless. No one was more convinced about how hard it was to know of oneself or of others that an act was done from a morally praiseworthy, radically interminable principle than Kant. His version of this trouble showed itself as a problem in ascertaining whether one had acted *from* (rather than merely in accordance with) duty: "I am willing to allow that most of our actions may accord with duty; but if we look more closely at our scheming and striving, we everywhere come across the dear self, which is always turning up; and it is on this that the purpose of our actions is based—not on the strict command of duty."[1]

Kant's idea is that acts that seem to have their source in something radically interminable—that is to say, a motive cut free from the agent's own private ends or enjoyments (namely, duty)—will look like the fruits of flatly self-interested calculation to anyone who looks hard enough. I do not take up Kant's concern directly in this chapter. It is, in various ways, more acute than mine.[2] Instead, I begin by saying what account of interminable befitting-style considerations *can* be based in a broadly calculative view about reason in action.

Patterning Principles in Sophisticated Calculative Reason

As I suggested in my initial sketch of the threefold division, the current philosophical popularity of the idea that a practically rational life is shaped by some sort of considered life plan gives us a version of ultimate end talk for secular work: the ultimate end consists in realizing the plan. That is, some patterning principles are themselves endlike. Acting from and for the sake of such considerations involves an advanced form of calculative reason.

In *practice,* the business of sophisticated calculative reason can be both nonlocal and interminable. Suppose, for example, that I have taken to heart the suggestion that you can never be too thin or too rich. Say that I (quite possibly correctly) assume that it befits middle-class women who want good things to be avid in their pursuit of a sleek body and a strong portfolio (attaining these two ends positions middle-class women to command many other goods—that is, the grounding for so patterning my life is itself calculative). The resulting rigors may keep me busy to the end of my days and will, at any rate, keep me alert to opportunities of various kinds, and lead me to omit to do various things I might otherwise enjoy or want to do. Each practical interest can be realized in more than one way (by jogging one day, strength training another, for example). I likewise will be led to constrain my choice of means to my ends with an eye toward wealth and slenderness. Conflicts in my primary aims will doubtless arise—for instance, at dinner parties where one must put in an appearance to get in on some especially promising investment, but where one will be expected to eat fattening food. Such conflicts are handled by scheduling and trade-offs.

What I have in me, what drives me and gives me some guidelines to use in sorting through what I will do some day, some week, some month, some year, is, formally, a pair of calculative concerns that bear a calculative relation to many other ends. Some of what I do is desirable in the sense useful for cultivating my body. Some of what I do is desirable in the sense useful for cultivating my fortune. And my concrete plans will take shape in light of these calculative constraints. That is, my twin ends—sleekness and high-end solvency—give rise to many actions and lend some shape to my life. Moreover, they are things *for* and *from* which I do many things and omit to do many more, they constrain my choice in means, and they set some of the terms in which some aspects of my circumstances are salient to my deliberations. Likewise, we can explain my self-loathing when I overeat, or my regret in not getting in on a good deal, by, again, appealing to the thin-and-rich principle. In this sense, endlike patterning principles answer to some of the explanatory concerns addressed by the befitting division of good. In practice, they are both nonlocal and interminable. But the point is to position myself to enjoy the goods that life in the middle classes has to offer. If it turns out that fat, poor women are best able to control the things I most want, then my reason for enacting the thin-and-rich principle will vanish.

Such patterning principles are, then, extended calculative principles. They have calculative grounding and they lend calculative order to one's affairs. While I may never be done with the business of maintaining, expressing, and realizing my ambitions (they are, in practice, interminable), *what* these direct me to do, day in and day out, is attend to how I might secure some bodily or financial benefit by my actions (they are, in principle, terminating) and *why* I want to do this is because it serves other ends more generally (the ambition itself has calculative grounding). Moreover, the question about whether I have a calculative patterning principle of the sort I claim in me, whether I am succeeding in acting from such concerns, is partly settled by seeing what I do, what I thereby accomplish, and whether, given my stated aims, I took reasonable measures to ensure success. Just as you can assess whether I am setting out to bake a cake in some reasonable fashion by seeing if what I do produces cake (or would have, had nothing interfered with the process), so too if I start out, physically sound, from some position in the middle classes, you can tell whether I am setting out to be thin and rich in some reasonable fashion by seeing if my dress size goes down and my assets grow (or would have, had nothing interfered with the ventures I undertook to those ends). What the many ends I want to attain for the sake of realizing my ambition share (the patterning force that unites them) lies within the scope of the means–end, part–whole relation that sets the terms for determining what is good in the sense useful. In this sense, what I have is more like two self-selected recurrent ends (slimness, wealth) that crop up, again and again, in a way that shapes my life, than a radically interminable patterning principle.

Most recurrent ends are not in this way self-selected. Recurrent ends usually have to do with the daily reproduction of individual and social life in a way that falls to people generally (even though the detail of how any of us goes about the business of life varies tremendously). Consider, as an example of a common recurrent end, sleeping. One is never entirely done with the business of sleeping in the sense that, again and again, getting some sleep crops up as an end, and one may need to go to some trouble to ensure that one has places to sleep—places where, say, the special vulnerability that comes of being unconscious will be bearable, and where one will be warm enough or cool enough to stand a good chance of waking again. In this sense, the need to sleep is in practice interminable, although the character of the end in question is in principle straightforwardly terminating, and the reason to make room for sleeping in life is that it serves to preserve the individual. You continue to need sleep while you live. But your need is satisfied *by* sleeping. It is possible to build such an account of patterns in life by treating recurrent ends as forming a complex whole end the parts of which must be attained regularly enough to keep one going.

The calculative character of some patterning principles is even clearer in the case of the self-chosen whole-life plan: I have established a lot of goals (more than two, anyway). Many of these may take a long time to accomplish and involve me in many concrete actions. I attain the end (realize the plan) by attaining the goals that inform it. And this way of shaping my life may, under pressure, lead to an existence that would be crippled by the loss of my calendar book. What unites the many things I do into a kind of pattern is, again, the plan. The reason to realize the plan is that it expresses my interests, allows me to develop and exercise my powers, gives me access to the things I want to get, and so on.

While I cannot imagine a view about the excellent exercise of calculative practical reason that takes no account of the recurrent ends associated with the daily reproduction of the living individual, I see no reason why a calculative theorist would have to fall in with current fashion in insisting that people must have personal life plans in order to have practical reason in them. For one thing, the philosophical passion for planning is of recent enough vintage and distinct enough social location to suggest that it is a bit of managerial and professional local color, not a first principle of practical reason. It would be a more stunning discovery than any of us *should* want to make if it turned out that practically rational lives first were lived by adult males with mercantile or bourgeois ambitions.

The world has to be arranged so that a man can count on a lot from people if he wills to realize a private, personally satisfying whole-life plan. The employees of firms on which he relies, for instance, must not go about organizing general strikes. His clothiers must have a source of clothing and a place in which to conduct business. The financial institutions must operate well enough. His car mechanic must not hit him with a wrench every time he is annoying. The makers of agenda books, pens, and other forms of scheduling hardware must keep making them. And so on. An enormous amount of human activity goes into making possible the conceiving and executing of a contemporary sort of personally rewarding, planned life. Very little of it is done by people who are conducting similarly rewarding planned lives. And this is no mere contingent truth. Not everyone can be management. For similar reasons, not everyone can occupy his life in consulting or advising or marketing or playing markets or devoting himself to the gentler pursuits of leisure. Somewhere, somehow another sort of labor has to happen if the well-planned private life is to be possible.

Practical reason, on the other hand, is not supposed to have a distinctive class location or geopolitical sphere of exercise. As such, no credible philosophical account of practical reason can base itself on the organizing principles of only the lives of those whose existence is parasitic on the multiply differently organized lives of others. For this reason, it seems to me safer to stick with the business of "naturally" recurrent ends in seeking calculative order in human affairs.

Calculative Practical Reason and Fit

It is sometimes thought that a calculative theorist of reason in action can get no purchase on desirability characterizations that aim to show the place of an intentional action in a larger scheme of things. The sort of work that befitting-style practical considerations do in explaining actions, omissions, regret, and the role of such traits as virtues in lending shape and stability to the living of a life are not supposed to be the stuff of calculative practical reason. This isn't quite right.

Armed with access to talk of recurrent ends and other calculative organizing principles, a theorist can capture quite a lot about order in human affairs, and can compass many ways of shaping pursuits over time. She can explain some forms of end management through scheduling and trade-offs. She can account for some of what an agent omits to do by pointing to how doing it would disorder his life. She even can make a kind of distinction between acting well and faring well, interpreted as a distinction between acting with an eye toward faring well overall and acting with an eye toward the pleasures of the moment or the press of a proximate end. She can account for the species of regret and remorse that are rooted in a sense that one has been rash, burnt bridges, let good things slip away, been gratuitously (that is, to no end) harsh or unkind, lost track, gone overboard, and so on. In this sense, she can get quite a lot without adverting to radically interminable befitting-style practical considerations.

She can even get a kind of account of the place of practices whose existence in the larger scheme of human social life is presupposed in the having of some ends—for example, by pointing out that extracting promises makes it possible to count on others to do things you want when you have no reason to expect that they would otherwise take an interest in doing your will, and that even being able to *imagine* extracting a promise to this end requires that the practice be there to rely on.[3] And this is how a calculative theorist will cope with traditional patterning principles like virtues as well. The virtue, fidelity, becomes the thing in us that is correlated with the practice of promising, for instance.

Accounts of the virtues that rest in the thought that one will need some courage and temperance to overcome the temptations of irascible and concupiscible appetite, prudence for calculative foresight, and justice for right relations with one's fellows (as Aquinas argues one does)[4] provide, in the relevant sense, calculative support for cultivating virtue. Here is one such account of the significance of the four cardinal virtues given by Peter Geach:

> [W]e can see the need of the four cardinal virtues to men: these virtues are needed for any large-scale worthy enterprise, just as health and sanity are needed. We need prudence or practical wisdom for any large-scale planning. We need justice to secure cooperation and mutual trust among men, without which our lives would be nasty, brutish, and short. We need temperance in order not to be deflected from our long-term and large-scale goals by seeking short-term satisfactions. And we need courage to persevere in the face of setbacks, weariness, difficulties, and dangers.[5]

Geach stresses large-scale enterprise and long-term planning in his account, in part because these are the sorts of settings in which it becomes most readily apparent that cultivating virtue may deposit an ordering force in one's affairs that could turn out to be individually ruinous, however socially necessary. He continues:

> Men need virtues as bees need stings. An individual bee may perish by stinging, all the same bees need stings; an individual man may perish by being brave or just, all the same men need courage and justice.[6]

The ideas here are not hard. Having some justified expectation of security in the company of others, and some qualities of character that give one grounds to trust that one will carry through with one's own pursuits and do one's part in joint efforts, is part of the stuff of participation in any successful social enterprise. (At least, these belong to any joint enterprise whose success was not merely a matter of dumb luck.) The virtues are qualities that stabilize pursuits from within, as it were, and become the grounds for the requisite trust. In this sense, cultivation of cardinal virtue is a means to, or part of, doing one's part in social life and enjoying the fruits thereof. The account of the place of virtue in human life is calculative: it is for the sake of attaining characteristic ends that people as such need virtues.

In order for such an account to be plausible, it must be the case that there are fairly well-understood combinations of kinds of agent, circumstance, and act that display one or more of the four virtues in question. The virtues are taking their support from how they help us do things. If you cannot make clear how planning, say, is made possible by prudence, how being able to expect others to do their part in a cooperative venture depends on their having some portion of justice in them, and how courage and temperance keep people at the tasks they are committed to seeing through, you won't be able to get this sort of account off the ground. There can be borderline cases and questions about whether some act displayed the relevant virtue. We can ask whether someone refrains from indulging in loose delights now and then from temperance or from cowardice, for example. But there cannot be much of a wobble in the central cases.

Task-based accounts of virtue argue that people will need some virtues in order for it to be reasonable to expect that they will be able to do and get what they want and need. Obviously, not every member of an organized social group must have the virtues that contribute to attaining socially necessary ends in order for those ends to be attained. Obviously some regimes, and the social groups they govern, have acquired considerable advantage through spectacular feats of collective badness. Geach is licensed to restrict his attention to large-scale *worthy* enterprises because he has in view a substantive account of human good by the lights of which the sources of community spirit required for collective evil won't count as virtue. Geach's precursor, Aquinas, likewise would not have regarded the individual traits that enable collective badness as virtues. His argument for this restriction was theological.[7] But spectacular feats of collective badness (for example, the European conquests of Africa and the Americas), like the less historically prominent feats of collective goodness, depend for their success on the group members' willingness to come together and cooperate in shared tasks, to make some individual sacrifices for the sake of collective success, to have it in them to do their parts even when they don't much feel like it, and so on. Task-based accounts of virtue see the point of the virtues in their use to social life. Where some forms of social life are at issue, one rather wishes that the members of many groups had been *less* willing to devote individual effort to accomplishing group tasks than they in fact were.

This is not to say that there haven't been modern secular efforts to argue that the traits that enable members of a group to do their bit for, say, genocide, are not in fact virtues. There have. Philippa Foot marks both the tension and the restriction in kinds of ends that might be said to be pursued from virtue this way:

> Hardly anyone is ready to say that a man who murdered his wife to get her out of the way would be acting courageously or doing a courageous act as long as he was sensible of the risk he ran. They are more likely to use expressions such as 'an act of courage' where the example is slightly different, and the evil distant from the action concerned, as when, for instance, a man does something to save his own life or the lives of his companions in the course of some wicked enterprise, such as an unjust war. But . . . why should the presence of immediate good ends and the remoteness of bad ones make any difference if the goodness and badness of action does not come into the definition of courage?[8]

It is, Foot concludes, a topic requiring further research on the part of secular theorists who see virtues as essentially bound up with doing acts necessary to human life. The inspiration for such projects will, one imagines, center on the idea that collective unjust acts are *not*, in the relevant sense, needful in human life, that, in this way, employment of the virtuous citizen in collective acts of injustice is a misuse of individual good character and, perhaps, that if the individuals in fact have the kind of character in question, they might go to the trouble to consider whether the large-scale enterprise in question is needful in human life, whether they would do better to protest the whole business than to do their part in it.

Partly because of the problem of spectacularly bad collective enterprises, my instinct would be to step back from "large-scale enterprises" in seeking calculative grounding for virtue and look to things like what is needed for childbearing and the care and education of children. For, whereas many groups of people merely find themselves caught up in large-scale enterprises (only rarely as beneficiaries), no sustainable social group survives unless it makes provisions for future generations (or else, as is true of some religious communities, unless it can rely on other groups to do so). In order to have, care for, and educate children, a group needs to make provisions for attaining recurrent ends (some members need a measure of prudence), some grounds to trust in the willingness of at least some of members to engage in cooperative tasks even when they don't especially feel like doing their parts (the group needs some relations of justice among adult members), and quite possibly a bit of restraint and a willingness to defend those who cannot protect themselves (some members need something of temperance and courage). If such an account can be given, then the virtues become means to or parts of attaining shared ends, and the calculative relation between end and virtues is what grounds virtue.

The whole of any such account will rest with thought about what is needful in variously configured forms of human social life. But this rather flat-footed calculative earthiness is not all by itself a strike against the theorist in question. As I mentioned in the Introduction, justifying practices and the like by pointing out that they are means to or parts of attaining ends that the participants can be presumed to share is breathtakingly common in practical philosophy.

Of course, a calculative theorist will only get to make this sort of argument if the relevant constituency in fact *has* those shared ends made attainable by cultivation of virtue, and some members are willing to cultivate virtue on that account. It is in light of shared ends that it can be calculatively sensible to cultivate traits that are sometimes individually disastrous. That has *always* been the sticking point with such accounts, even if they are not (as Geach's is not), desire-based, instrumentalist accounts.

One can also provide calculative support for determining one's will to vice. Here, the accounts rely on individual gain, rather than what is needful for collective enterprises like war and childrearing. Consider that moment of vicious resolve when Lady Macbeth bids:

> Come, you spirits
> That tend on mortal thoughts, unsex me here,
> And fill me from the crown to the toe top-full
> Of direst cruelty. Make thick my blood;
> Stop up th'access and passage to remorse,
> That no compunctious visitings of nature
> Shake my purpose nor keep peace between
> Th'effect and it.[9]

The Lady's determination to cruelty and callousness is called for in order to see her through helping to murder a benefactor for gain. It goes badly in the long run, of course. But plenty of real people seem at times to have got just what they sought by cultivating vicious patterning principles in order to be better equipped to accomplish their purposes. Vices, after all, aim at securing worldly goods. That is their calculative structure. It is unsurprising that the vicious thereby often enjoy worldly advantage.

Now, because there is such a thing as sophisticated calculative reason in action, merely pointing to the fact that the befitting patterns one's pursuits, allows one to distinguish acting well from faring well, sets limits on means that may be taken to ends, accounts for agent regret and remorse, explains some omissions, shows how various disparate actions are drawn together into a pattern of some sort, stresses that a different set of actions might equally well have realized the pattern, and so forth is not enough to distinguish the befitting from the useful. The merely-interminable-in-practice-befitting operates at a distance from ordinary calculative concern with attaining proximate ends, but this distance is itself traversed by the exercise of calculative practical reason.

What a calculative theorist cannot account for is a claim that radically interminable befitting-style practical considerations, ones that are not merely interminable in practice, provide a source of reasons for action quite apart from having any calculative relation an agent's other ends, needs, plans, tastes, and so on. It is to radically interminable patterning principles that I now turn.

Radically Interminable Considerations of How It Befits One to Live

Noncalculative accounts of patterning principles make *no* reference, not even indirectly, to tasks or ends made possible or attainable by the patterning principle in question. The ends pursued in the course of shaping one's life to the demands of a radically interminable practical consideration are pursued *solely* for their own sakes.

One way of putting this is that the ends or constraints set up by a radically interminable patterning principle are *internal* or *intrinsic* to the pattern at issue. For example, one cultivates a radically interminable moral patterning principle in order to be moral. Patterning principles that are merely interminable in practice, on the other hand, help agents to attain *further* ends. If agents do not seek to attain those further ends, then the support for cultivating the pattern at issue is eroded. This does not mean that such patterning principles are necessarily self-interested. But it does mean that the support for the principle comes from the ends that it helps people to attain. Consider, for example, praiseworthy promise-keeping in an account like Geach's. In his view, the ends of justice are not pursued for self-interested reasons (keeping a promise might sometimes be personally ruinous, and is virtually always a matter of doing one's word when other things one could do instead would be more useful, or pleasanter, than promise-keeping). Still, what marks the region of justice corresponding to fidelity as *virtuous* is that such institutions as the practice of promising aid people in cooperative ventures. The *collective* usefulness of the practice gives calculative grounding to the corresponding individual virtue. Contrast a life partly patterned by this sort of fidelity with a life that is shaped by cutting-edge pursuits. The genuine hipster, unlike the mere poseur, is cutting-edge solely for the sake of the cutting-edge. To do as the hip do for the sake of one's social standing, or in order to gain membership in some group, is enough to disqualify one from counting as hip. The *radical* interminability of such considerations as pattern the pursuits of inadvertent trendsetters (and of virtuous or moral people on some noncalculative accounts of these) is such that one works to enact, maintain, and express the patterning principle in question *solely* for its own sake and *not,* not even indirectly, because it serves any purpose beyond those done from and for the sake of the noncalculative principles in question. A radically interminable pattern is not cultivated on account of *any* other ends to be attained and supports only the very ends whose immediate source is *in* the noncalculative patterning principle itself, a pattern generally tied to something one values, to a role, to excellence in some standard area of human endeavor, to one's standing as a being/person of a certain sort, or what have you. The form of such desirability characterizations is something on the order of, "I am *B*-ing because it befits an *F* to *B*," where the agent is, or aspires to be, an *F.*

In describing the difference between calculative and noncalculative accounts of reasons for acting, I noted:

> Noncalculative theorists insist that there can be reasons for an agent to *B* quite apart from her plans, projects, particular attachments, character, skills, habits, or further ends; the calculative theorist denies this.

In effect, noncalculative theorists will tend to concentrate on radically interminable principles in accounting for reason in action, and will insist that some of these set standards of conduct even for people who do not self-identify as *F*s. The other sorts of principles take their action-guiding force from aspects of the individual's existing practical repertoire, further ends, character, and the like *via* the calculative relation obtaining between realizing the pattern and attaining further ends.

For example, accounts of virtue or morality that insist that neither takes its support from the ends made attainable by moral or virtuous conduct—that one acts virtuously or morally *solely* for the sake of the virtuous or moral standing of the conduct in question, insofar as, say, morality and virtue are directly and perfectly expressive of the highest good—provide radically interminable accounts of moral and virtuous patterning principles. The radically interminable reason that one keeps the promise is because promise-keeping is morally required. The reason one does what morality requires is that the ends of morality, pursued *from* and *on account of* their moral standing, are supremely good. The reason these pursuits are supremely good is that their goodness is *not* conditional on how they help any rational beings attain other ends. That is, on such views, part of the point of moral conduct is that a moral life is shaped by radically interminable befitting-style practical considerations. Otherwise, it is thought, morality will be only contingently good in roughly the way that means are contingently good—good given that they are useful to attaining ends. Lose the ends and you lose the calculative support of the means. The idea is, further, that an agent with no private stakes in acting well who (unsurprisingly) fails to heed the call to virtuous or dutiful conduct thereby displays irrationality. That is how a noncalculative account of moral or virtuous reasons for acting comes apart from calculative accounts.

I have already mentioned that Kant, who is the source of the most difficult arguments to the effect that the moral order in human affairs is radically interminable, had grave doubts about whether one could know for certain, of oneself or others, that one ever acted solely from and for the sake of morality. Part of the trouble with determining this is that self-interest (that is, the unblinking exercise of egoistic calculative reason) might favor exactly the same pursuits as does morality. In order to illustrate the radically interminable character of the motive of duty (a patterning principle of sorts), Kant tended to favor cases where self-interest and morality were as starkly opposed as possible. It is in cases where there is outright opposition between duty and egoistic calculation, and the agent follows the dictates of morality, that it is easiest to suppose that an agent acts solely from and for the sake of morality. Morality, in turn, is supposed to be in a man in such a way that, if necessary, he will strive and strain to produce moral order in his affairs. But it wasn't just self-interest that could sully a man's conduct on Kant's view. Flatly egoistic conduct will not count as virtuous on Geach's view either. Where an account like Geach's and an account like Kant's come apart is in Geach's thought that the standing of virtuous conduct is, ultimately, rooted in how virtuous conduct is needful in human affairs, even though acts of courage or justice might prove lethal to the brave or just person. Virtue is not favored by egoistic practical considerations on Geach's view, but it *is* favored by calculative considerations. Kant held that *any* such account of morality failed to capture what was distinctive and important about moral order in human life.

I think it very likely that people sometimes act from radically interminable befitting-style practical considerations. I leave radically interminable accounts of ethical and moral patterning principles to the side, however, and with them, claims that some radically interminable considerations of fitness apply to agents who take no special interest in the considerations in question. My chief interest lies in explaining what radically interminable patterning principles are like (quite apart from their alleged standing as sources of special, necessary reasons for acting), and one need not rush into the middle of hotly disputed topics in moral philosophy and the history of ideas in order to find vivid, true-life accounts of radically interminable practical principles. I turn to a fairly detailed aesthetic example in order to illustrate how a radically interminable practical principle might operate. One might have drawn such an example from any standard region of human endeavor where the goods at issue are internal to the region and where people who shape their lives to the region's demands understand themselves as somehow thereby in service to impersonal, impartial good. Academics who regard themselves as "pure scholars," for instance, might understand their work as in the service of impartial truth, rather than as a means to some further end. My example is an account of how it befits a poet to conduct himself, offered in snippets of dialogue and excerpts of prose by the poet Jack Spicer. Spicer was a bookish poet, a serious linguist, and something of a theorist of practical poetics. He describes how that which a writer can do for the sake of letting poetry happen lends a radically interminable order to the pursuits of a practicing poet.

Life from and for Poetry

On Spicer's view, poetry, properly understood, is not a straightforward representation of the real. Nor is it an expression of the writer's vision, thoughts, or feelings, recollected and made over according to the demands of poetic form. It is not even a distillation of such strands of thought and culture as the writer has acquired over the years by dint of education and training. The writer sets out instead to play host to poetry, and good poetry produces a specifically linguistic realm of experience. What we get in poetry, then, is a distinctive employment of language from and for the sake of a specifically poetic linguistic end. This is the kind of territory where one starts looking for radically interminable practical principles—notice that the ends in question, ends associated with poetry, are pursued from and for the sake of a kind of experience intrinsic to poetry. Crudely, one might express the practical consideration as "Poetry for poetry's sake!" More precisely, it is poetry for the sake of the distinctively poetical dimension of experience.[10]

Spicer came to these conclusions about poetry slowly, and began putting them into practice about the time he began writing serial poems in a form he called "books." The first such book was *After Lorca*. Written after Garcia Lorca's death, it consists of an introduction that purports to have been penned posthumously by Lorca, Spicer's letters to the dead poet, and poems that are sometimes translations of Lorca's work given a peculiar twist of one sort or another, sometimes Lorcaesque poems by Spicer, sometimes a mix. The use of "After" in the title is a complex pun: Lorca is dead, Spicer's serial poem has parts made after the fashion of Lorca, while Spicer pursues Lorca (that is, goes after him erotically) in letters and verse, "Lorca's" introduction suggests that the love in unrequited, and so on. In correspondence with Lorca, Spicer writes:

> We have both tried to be independent of images (you from the start and I only when I grew old enough to tire of trying to make things connect), to make things visible rather than to make pictures of them (phantasia non imaginari). How easy it is in erotic musings or in the truer imagination of a dream to invent a beautiful boy. How difficult to take a boy in a blue bathing suit that I have watched as casually as a tree and to make him visible in a poem as a tree is visible, not as an image or a picture but as something alive—caught forever in the structure of words. Live moons, live lemons, live boys in bathing suits. The poem is a collage of the real.[11]

"Collage of the real" is an early and relatively tame description of Spicer's sense of how poetry operates. The relevant real exists *only* in the poetry, and the collage is arranged and assembled by forces that have precious little to do with the writer's extrapoetic ends, character, experiences, sense of himself, powers, education, and craft. The engagement with Lorca, for example, is staged as a kind of incomplete possession by Lorca's ghost, and Lorca's ghost, in turn, is treated as a thing animated in no obvious way by the antifascist political engagements that left Lorca a casualty of the Spanish Civil War, Lorca's struggles with Catholicism, or any such personal details of the dead poet's life, save, possibly, something of his homosexuality. Spicer's final letter to Lorca begins:

> Dear Lorca,
>   This is the last letter. The connection between us, which has been fading away with the summer, is now finally broken. I turn in anger and dissatisfaction to the things of my life and you return, a disembodied but contagious spirit, to the printed page. It is over, this intimate

connection with the ghost of Garcia Lorca, and I wonder now how it was ever able to happen.

It was a game, I shout to myself. A game. There are no angels, ghosts, or even shadows. It was a game made out of summer and freedom and a need for poetry that would be more than the expression of my hatreds and desires. It was a game like Yeats's spooks or Blake's sexless seraphim.

Yet it was there. The poems are there, the memory not of a vision but a kind of casual friendship with an undramatic ghost who occasionally looked through my eyes and whispered to me, not really more important than my other friends, but now achieving a different level of reality by being missing. Today, alone by myself, it is like having lost a pair of eyes and a lover.

What is real, I suppose, will endure. Poe's mechanical chessplayer was not the less miraculous for having a man inside it, and when the man departed, the games it had played were no less beautiful.[12]

What is real is the poetry. The nods to Edgar Poe's avowed allegiance to mechanics as principles of poetic composition, and to the esoteric systems of William Blake and William Butler Yeats, underscore Spicer's sense that poetic production is less a matter of self-expression than something experienced as taking dictation from a source that is not itself another person (as Lorca's ghost is not the spirit of the dead *person*). It didn't much matter to Spicer how one described this source, or, rather, Spicer was wary of seeking to describe it.

As is often the case when one sets out to articulate the content of a radically interminable practical principle, Spicer's efforts to say what poetry is and what it does and how pursuit of it twists around the lives of practicing poets is, to put it mildly, strained. For all that, he offers concrete advice to practicing poets. That is, poetics is a source of ends pursued from and for the sake of poetry.

In the latter connection, consider the conversation among Spicer, poet and editor James Reid, and violinist Harry Adaskin, transcribed from Spicer's lecture about a poem he was then in the process of writing:

> JR: I was going to ask you, do you have any idea right at this moment where your poem's going to go? I mean, do you have any ideas in your own mind, or any feelings?
>
> JS: I try not to.
>
> JR: Your mind is a blank?

JS: No, it isn't, unfortunately. It's trying to be a blank. And trying to be a blank is utterly different from being a blank. Again, this guy who was talking about [the similarity between Jesuit meditative exercises and poetic activity] was absolutely dead right, on course, on the thing. The point is that you can't really make your mind a blank. You can't really get to receiving God, which St. Ignatius wanted, or receiving poems, or doing anything. You can't. It's impossible. There's this utter animal spirit which is coming out and saying, well, gee, I can lay this person if I write this line, and all sorts of things like that. It's just impossible to make your mind a blank. You just do as well as you can, just like you're playing a horn or playing a violin or playing a piano. You try your best to make your mind a blank, but you don't. I'm sure of that. [Turning to Harry Adaskin:] Well, when you're playing, what happens? Can you completely get yourself out of it?

HA: You have described it perfectly. I don't see how I could add anything to that. It's exactly true. It's the best and most accurate description of the production of art that I have ever heard.[13]

Spicer has this to say about writing poetry:

> The trick naturally is . . . not to search for the perfect poem but to let your way of writing of the moment go along its own paths, explore and retreat but never be fully realized (confined) within the boundaries of one poem. . . . There is [such a thing as good or bad poetry] but not in relation to the single poem. There is really no single poem.
>
> That is why all my stuff from the past . . . looks foul to me. The poems belong nowhere. They are one night stands filled (the best of them) with their own emotions, but pointing nowhere, as meaningless as sex in a Turkish bath. It was not my anger or frustration that got in the way of my poetry but the fact that I viewed each anger and each frustration as unique—something to be converted into poetry as one would exchange foreign money.[14]

Spicer presents considerations of poetry as patterning principles for a lot of what poets do. The desirability characterizations in question will be of the form "It befits a poet to A." What it befits a poet to do is radically interminable. Notice, first off, that marrying the tasks of poetry to *any* other ends (seduction, for instance, or expression of emotions, or thoughts) works *against* the poetry, on this view. Notice that even the attempt to write complete, self-contained *poems* is alien to the spirit of poetry. What it befits a poet to do is "completely get yourself out of it," where "it" is the poetic process, pursued for the sake of poetry, a process that can, of course, involve many distinct and otherwise disparate sorts of act.

I have already mentioned that Spicer thought of poetry as a kind of impersonal dictation from a depersonalized source. The first step for a writer beginning in this way to engage poetry involves paying attention to an unusual success: "[A]fter you've written poems for a while and struggled with them and everything else, a poem comes through in just about one-eighth of the time that a poem usually does."[15] The use of "comes through" is telling. The process Spicer is describing is one in which most of what a poet brings to the tasks of poetry (including craft, scholarship, command of languages, sensitivity, personal experience, and so on) are at best "furniture" that gets moved around by the poetic process. What the process of poetry-by-dictation is about is, in a sense, getting out of the way of the poem coming through so that "it" arranges the furniture.

The second step in the dictation process comes when the poet

> finds out that these [dictated] poems say just exactly the opposite of what he wants himself, *per se* poet, to say. Like if you want to say something about your beloved's eyebrows and the poem says the eyes should fall out, and you don't really want the eyes to fall out or have even any vague connection. Or you're trying to write a poem on Vietnam and you write a poem about skating in Vermont. These things, again, begin to show you just exactly where the road of dictation leads. Just like when you wrote the first poem which came easily and yet was a good poem, a poem beyond you.[16]

In the third stage, the writer begins putting the principles of poetry into practice deliberately when

> you start seeing whether you can clear your mind away from the things that are you, the things that you want, and everything else. Sometimes it's a twelve-hour struggle to get a ten-line poem, not changing a single word of it as you're writing, but just as it goes along, trying to distinguish between you and the poem.[17]

This involves, among other things, writing poetry without knowing where it is going, without directing the process as though it was in the service of some specific end, without attempting to express yourself, keeping "your ideas closed and your mind open."[18] Indeed, if one intends to write poetry, one should work to keep even one's own judgment as far away as possible from one's work: "[T]ry to keep as much of yourself as possible out of the poem. And whenever there's a line that you like particularly well, which expresses just how you're feeling this particular moment, which seems just lovely, then be so goddamn suspicious of it that you wait for two or three hours before you put it down on paper."[19]

The work of practical reason in acting from and for the sake of poetry is rather like the work of practical reason in some other highly disciplined pursuits. It involves guarding against the intrusion of some impulses and of self-interest. Spicer links it to a virtue of sorts, patience:

> You have to interfere with yourself. You have to, as much as possible, empty yourself for this. And that's not noninterference. I mean, it's almost an athletic thing . . . the business of being able *not* to do something, especially things which are so important to you, are you, takes a tremendous amount of patience. And it doesn't take humility, since I've never seen a humble poet.[20]

A great deal of a poet's life might revolve around, and be tuned to the requirements of, this sort of process. And there are many ways in which the requisite discipline might show itself. Spicer gives every indication of thinking that poetry by dictation (however varied episodes of dictation might be) *is* the poetic process. The poetic ends served by letting poetry come through, on this view, are by no means confined to the business of so-called language poetry, or any other such recent genre. Instead, the deliberate handiwork of any writer almost invariably ruins the poem and makes it less than a bit of real poetry. He thinks this even of the work of exceptionally self-conscious, controlled poets:

> Say Pope, for example, he would seem to be a person who kept his own identity all the way through. You take the great things of Pope's, *The Rape of the Lock,* for example. There are some things which come through that you just would swear that this little hunchback who was interested in politics could not have written, and that must have scared the hell out of him. And this is the kind of wit that only a ghost could make. "Why has man not a microscopic eye? / For this good reason / Man is not a fly."
>
> I really do think that it's probably true for all the arts, but I think that

it is true for poetry, that anyone who's doing more than just dabbling on the surface, trying to write diaries essentially, and so forth, has this feeling [of an Outside source of his work], and even if he tries to resist it, it's pretty hard.[21]

In response to a questioner who doubts that in all good poetry the writer serves as a *means* to poems, rather than a being whose self-expression is the *end* of poems (that is, whose thoughts, feelings, experiences, and aims are directly, self-consciously, and properly the topic of well-crafted poems), Spicer replies:

> Well, I just never have met a poet who's gone beyond just, you know, the first couple of years of poetry, who would say that. Really. Including the academic poets. . . . I don't think anyone who's a practicing poet, even a practicing bad poet, who's done it for a long enough time, would disagree with the fact that there is something from the Outside. I mean, you get this in Longinus, for christ's sake, all of these pretty square people going all the way back. Saint Thomas Aquinas says it, and you can't have anyone who's farther away from poetry than him.[22]

He's right, I think: what Spicer describes as the patterning of his pursuits *qua* practicing poet is very far from Aquinas.

The demands of poetry so described constitute a radically interminable organizing principle in the life of a practicing poet. It explains actions, omissions, principles for choosing among ends, the place of various activities in an overarching engagement with poetry, and some forms of regret and remorse. The *only* ends served by the relevant processes that make up poetic practice are the ends of poetry. The things done are done, as far as possible, solely in the service of poetry. But here we might ask: Does *poetry* itself serve other ends? Could there be a calculative ground for poetry even though the ends of poetry are contrary to self-interest? Spicer has doubts that the answer will be yes.

Pressed to say what poetry itself enables or makes possible—"I mean, when you write a poem and it scares you, and it's a good poem, therefore it's going to affect your thinking or your actions or something. And also your audience . . . because if it doesn't do something to you, what's the sense in its existence?"—Spicer replies:

> I'm not sure that there is any sense for a poem's existence. I wish I could tell you the opposite. I would say that I'm sort of agnostic in this thing one way or the other. I'm not sure. I simply know that I have to

write it like that. . . . The answer to the question of the poem is the same answer that Mallory answered to "Why do you climb Everest?" Not to get to the top, or to make an important . . . discovery but "because it's there."[23]

Again:

> I can't remember any good advice that I've gotten from one of my poems, that helped me be any happier or any better or sleep with any more people or get any more money or anything else. Poems are pretty useless for anything like that. The advice they give is just not interested. It's like somebody treating you fairly abstractly. At least, I've never had any experience with a poem that was really interested in my welfare, namely what I want, my happiness, or anything else. It's usually been the opposite way. They've kicked me in the teeth a few times, but they never really helped much.[24]

Spicer, I take it, describes in some detail a kind of system of practical considerations associated with poetry that are radically interminable. Moreover, he describes these pursuits as, for him, practically necessary ("I simply know that I have to write it like that"): the reasons for action he finds in poetry are, hence, deeply noncalculative. To be radically interminable a practical consideration must have *no* essential calculative tie to ends of any specific kinds, even the end of sustaining a nexus of agent, act, and circumstances that attaches to actions done from and for pleasure. (Spicer denies that considerations of poetry are considerations of pleasure, incidentally: "I'm not sure what poetry is for. All I am sure of is that it's not for pleasure, although it does give pleasure.")[25] While radically interminable befitting-style desirability characterizations *do* attach to attaining ends (for example, writing poetry), they do not serve principally to aid us in doing things we would otherwise undertake to do. What poets do *qua* poets, on this view, is done solely from and for the sake of poetry. Poets are people who somehow "must" pursue the ends of poetry. And what poetry does is produce a kind of experience in language that is distinctively poetic. And why should we care about that? Spicer's answer is: Who knows?

The pattern lent by radically interminable befitting-style practical considerations, rather, is put in place entirely for its own sake, because one takes it that the pattern is in itself good-in-the-sense-fitting, and not because working to so pattern one's affairs bears some calculative relation to accomplishing specific tasks of some other sort, individually or collectively. The very purity of the relevant kind of practical consideration becomes part of the reason it is very hard to tell whether anyone ever acts *from* a radically interminable befitting-style practical consideration. It could as easily become hard to say with confidence whether one so much as acts *in accordance with* the demands of some such practical considerations.

Consider, again, Spicer's account of actions in accordance with poetry. In a sense, you are alerted to having met the challenge of making room for poems to come through only when you are *surprised* by what happens: you write a poem better than any you were capable of writing, you set out to write a poem on some topic and something else entirely shows up on the page, you don't understand your own work, you can't really tell whether you were playing a game of spooks or serving as a conduit of verse resonant with the work of the dead Garcia Lorca, but the product stands alone and alien to your sense of yourself and your fantasies about Lorca. Your final service to poetry is giving it voice, not in the sense of "voice" where the term is a metaphor for authentic self-expression, but voice as sound and body, intonation and movement:

> The truth is that pure poetry bores everybody. It is even a bore to the poet. . . .—the dull horror of naked, pure poetry.
>   Live poetry is a kind of singing. It differs from prose, as song does, in its complexity of stress and intonation. Poetry demands a human voice to sing it and demands an audience to hear it. Without these it is naked, pure, and incomplete—a bore.[26]

Abstract, made when poetry arranges the furniture that is you, about the production of an experience that happens in reading and is better understood by your audience than by you, offering you very little, offering your audience some experience intrinsic to poetry (which may bring pleasure, but isn't for the pleasure it brings—the pleasures of poetry are incidental to poetic experience), and only deliberately and directly pursued when you interfere with yourself in order to get yourself out of the process—poetry, by Spicer's lights, serves as a radically interminable organizing principle in the life of a practicing poet.

It is, I take it, fairly tempting not to take Spicer at his word (although it is not easy to say just what taking him at his word would amount to).[27] He seems, however, to have conducted himself in the way he says one ought to, if one is a practicing poet.

Of course, where radically interminable patterning principles are concerned, the conduct of one who acts *from* them, and the conduct of one who merely acts *in accordance with* them, may be identical. This is one of the major differences between terminable (in practice or in practice and in principle) and interminable reasons for acting. If you take no means to your avowed end, if what you do is contrary to your end, then whatever else is going on with you, your avowed end is *not* what is determining your will to action. Whereas your sense of whether your actions are done from and for pleasure (rather than, say, neurosis), or from and for a radically interminable patterning principle, is less susceptible to affirmation or denial on the basis of what you in fact do. In this vein, the doubts expressed by audience members in the lectures are rather like a reformulated version of Kant's doubt about duty: "[I]f we look more closely at our scheming and striving, we everywhere come across the dear self, which is always turning up; and it is on this that the purpose of our actions is based—not on the strict command of poetry."

Such doubts arise wherever interminable practical principles are concerned. Setting them to one side, what matters here is that Spicer's self-described, poetic patterning principle is radically interminable and does the explanatory work of a befitting-style desirability characterization, whether or not one agrees that Spicer worked from and for the sake of poetry.

Spicer nowhere claims that *anyone* is required to be a poet. Rather, the consideration at issue is like this: if you are a poet, or aspire to be a poet, then you ought to conduct yourself in such-and-such way. What would we need to add to his account if we wanted a deeply noncalculative theory of poetic reasons for acting? Just this: an insistence that anyone who *could* be a poet will be irrational if she *refuses* to order some portion of her affairs to the ends of poetry, and that this will be so even if she takes no personal interest in developing her gifts, if she dislikes poetry, if she points out that the poetic life, on this view, will be an unhappy life with no guarantees of extrapoetic satisfaction in any quarter, and so forth. Formally, at least, that is what the "external reasons" theory of poetry would hold. Again, simply in terms of the kind of account of practical reason at issue, it will be what an external reasons theorist of morality or virtue will hold as well, generalized, presumably, to all rational agents. The content difference inclines us to sympathy with externalist theories of ethics, where an externalist theory of poetry would be absurd.

6

Use

I have gone into some detail about a radically interminable patterning principle and about pleasure. Both are sources of action. Both thereby supply desirability characterizations for the acts that they inform. Now, my claim in this book is that the real power of contemporary instrumentalism about practical reason is emanating from a very old insight about the rational structure of intentional action. The version of that insight that I am focusing on crucially involves the three senses in which action can present itself as desirable, and the conviction that useful-style desirability characterizations are the most important sort. Such considerations show an action to be desirable as a means to or part of attaining one or more further, determinate ends.

The Useful and Calculative Reason

To see why calculative reasons are the most important ones, it is vital to see that the further end they point to is, formally, a future end. Useful-style practical considerations look ahead to attaining an end that is in some way yet to come. The characteristic expression of this feature is that one *As in order to B,* and the thought that doing something is good in the sense useful applies both to relations between terms of an action *in the context of* performing that action, and also to *further* ends that take one beyond the present proceedings to the hours, days, weeks, or years ahead.

I think that the threefold division is exactly the right way to apprehend reasons for acting, that the temporal system Aquinas laid out for sorting desirability characterizations is sound. I do not argue for that view here, however; rather my task in this chapter is to begin making my case for the centrality of calculative practical reason. I start by arguing that *without* calculative reason, whatever topic might remain to theorists of practical reason is so far removed from anything one might want to discuss in connection with practical rationality as to render it mysterious why anyone bothers working on practical reason at all. The first part of my argument that the standard picture as duly taken to be standard will turn on supporting this claim. The second part will center on supporting the claim that calculative considerations, all on their own, might be enough to give us a theory of reason in action. I take up this second part in Chapter 5.

The threefold division will be central to both halves of my argument. Basically, my plea to look to *all three* of the senses in which pursuits can be desirable in thinking about practical reason should not convince a determined noncalculative theorist that calculative practical considerations have any weight on their own at all. Without finding some other way to approach the centrality-of-calculative-reason issue, we wind up facing off over questions about *ranking* sorts of practical considerations with no clear way to answer those questions and some danger that we'll descend to the level of table-thumping. I want to thump a table over the suggestion that morality or virtue might be useless, and that *this* would be a point in their favor. So much the worse for ethics, I say. Many of the philosophers I most admire want to thump a table over the suggestion that morality and virtue might be prized *solely* as means to ends. So much the worse for ethics, they say. And, for all we know, each camp might be thinking, like Jack Spicer's Percival, "If someone doesn't fight me I'll have to wear this armor / All of my life."[1]

The threefold division gives us another tack. We can think about the formal distinctions between useful-style desirability characterizations and interminable ones and ask, on this basis, why one might think that calculative practical considerations were especially important. More importantly, even if we never *will* agree about ethics, the threefold division at least might allow us to give a more precise description of the character of our dispute: it turns out to center on the place of radically interminable practical considerations in a practically rational life.

Means and Ends, Parts and Wholes

The useful is the realm of means–end or part–whole, calculative reasons for acting. The means–end relation is familiar. By "part–whole" I have in mind representation of intentional action as involving articulated movement that may or may not aim at attaining a further end.[2] For example, one walks by taking one step, then another, then another. I treat putting one foot in front of the other as *parts* of a *whole* process, walking. The steps–walking relation is the kind of thing I mean to gesture toward by "part–whole." If one is walking in order to get to the grocery store, then the whole process, walking, is a means to getting to the grocery store. If one is just out for a stroll, then the steps are taken as parts of walking, but the walking serves no further end. The sense in which steps are parts of walking is a bit like this: if you have had some terrible accident and need to re-learn how to walk, or if you are in mime school setting out to learn how to move as though you are walking without actually making any progress, you will learn step-by-step. Call the means–end or part–whole relation the *calculative relation*. What is useful in an intentional action is shown in the calculative relation that informs both action and intention. This relation is at the core of Anscombe's work on intention and informs much of Aquinas's system.

Anscombe focused on laying bare a structure in events involving intentional action by imagining stopping agents at various stages in the proceedings and asking them why they are A-ing, where A-ing is a type of intentional action. Her strategy brings out a familiar general feature of representations of intentional action as such. The answer to a question about means gives the end they serve. The answer to a question about the parts gives the whole. Because she used the asking and answering of "Why?" questions to examine the calculative relation in action, she was able to concentrate on features of action that are right out in plain view, whether or not the agent ever has bothered to think them out explicitly in great detail. The relevant species of calculative relation might be expressed by mentioning states of affairs, wants, intentions, beliefs, actions, or what have you. Indeed, the same reason for acting might be given in many different ways.[3]

What Anscombe saw has of course been appreciated in one form or another by the great fathers of practical philosophy. I take it, for example, that Kant's emphasis on maxims had something to do with emphasis on calculative representations of actions in prospect and I am inclined to go along with Anscombe in thinking that Aristotle's practical syllogism was a device meant to reveal the calculative form in action as well. The genius of the "Why?" question as a way of eliciting this structure is, perhaps, that it locates the structure in the action unambiguously first and foremost, and so defeats the temptation to hunt for it first in the content of a man's occurrent thoughts before he makes a move. It is easy to imagine that maxims and practical syllogisms are things one thinks out before doing anything (although hard to see why one would bother rehearsing a textbook example of the practical syllogism before reaching for a cloak in order to provide oneself with a covering—one could, of course, but it would be an odd way to occupy one's mind). "Why?" questions enter in when intentional action is already taking place. It is not that the answers have nothing to do with what an agent has in mind. It is just that the calculative answers focus on what the agent takes herself to be doing and to what end, and this, in turn, is critical to determining what kind of thing she means to be doing.

When discussing answers to the characteristic question "Why?" and intentional action, I sometimes focus on the form and content of *representations* of intentional action and sometimes on the calculative articulation of the actions themselves. The hinge between representation and event here is, of course, intention. Anscombe used to gesture toward this hinge by stressing that actions are intentional "under some descriptions but not others," intentional *qua A, B*, and *C* but not *qua D, E*, or *F*.[4] For example, grubbing in the garden might be intentional *qua* digging, checking the soil, and figuring out what to plant, but not *qua* getting dirt under my nails, making thudding and scratching noises, or dulling my trowel. The centrality of descriptions to thinking about what is and is not intentional in an action is such that it becomes very easy to slide back and forth between talk about the articulation or structure of intentional actions and talk about the form and content of representations of intentional action.

It is not that what happens when I act happens "under some descriptions but not others."[5] *Any* true description of what happens when I act is a description of the happening involving my action, that is, of this event in my life. But the reasons-for-acting-seeking "Why are you A-ing?"-question has application to a happening when what I do involves A-ing and is, *qua A*-ing, intentional. Reasons for acting given in response to the characteristic "Why are you A-ing?"-question are, accordingly, keyed to the embedded description, A-ing.

Anscombe concentrated on the fact that the characteristic "Why?" question can be given application for a series of linked descriptions that display the calculative form. Responses to this question can go beyond the action that first prompts the question "Why?" of course, most usually by mention of something in the future that expresses the intention *with which* the agent acts, a primary end served by what the agent does that is not just another description of what the agent is here and now doing. When Anscombe's hypothetical questioner asks "Why are you A-ing?" or "Why did you A?" or "Why are you going to A?" he forces his interlocutor to look to the calculative form. If his question is given application, then she accepts A as a description of something she is doing or did or will do intentionally, and, moreover, explains to what end she is, was, or will be A-ing, or what kind of thing one does by A-ing in such circumstances. She As in order to B. "In order to B," given in response to the characteristic question "Why?", describes what is taking place, shows how it is useful, and, thereby, gives reasons for A-ing. The reasons given are calculative reasons—the ancestors of what we call *instrumental reasons*.

The Calculative Order in Action

The calculative form revealed by answers to Anscombe's "Why?" question belongs to intentional action as such. This point is acknowledged by most of us but rarely discussed nowadays in part because not every answer one might give to a reason-seeking "Why are you A-ing?"-question mentions a further end served by what one is doing or a whole action of which what one is doing is a part. Sometimes the answer is "No particular reason." Sometimes the answer shows the place of what you are doing in a larger scheme of things, or points to the respects in which doing this very thing is pleasant. But that doesn't mean that we can do without plain calculative reasons in thinking about reason in action.

I begin arguing for this point by arguing that interminable considerations could not be the *only* responses to Anscombe's question. To show this is to show that these responses all on their own cannot give us a grip on intentional action. I make this part of my case by posing a softening-up thought experiment that turns on the supposition that there are *only* interminable considerations given as responses to the characteristic question "Why?" On this assumption the intentional action dissolves. In the course of considering an objection to this thought experiment, I give a revised version of one of Anscombe's arguments that under the assumption that there are only interminable answers to a question about reasons for acting, we lose our grip on intention as well. In a way, my thought experiment forms the backdrop to my adaptation of Anscombe's argument.

Here is the thought experiment. Consider a pedestrian example of intentional action: crossing the road. Imagine a "Why?" questioner stationed beside you at the curb. He first asks, "Why are you crossing the road?" You respond, say, "Just thought I would . . . no particular reason" or "Because it is sometimes pleasant to cross the street" or "It's my policy to cross the road at this hour"[6] or "Because it is moral/virtuous/fitting to cross the road under such-and-such circumstances." None of these replies gives a plain calculative reason for crossing the road. None suggests that some further, antecedently given end is served by crossing the road; none makes mention of an operation of which road-crossing is a part.

In effect, "Just thought I would . . . no particular reason" says that you just *are* crossing the road, that, *qua* crossing the road, there is nothing more to be said on behalf of what you are doing.[7] In effect, "Because it is sometimes pleasant to cross the road" says that you are just *in the mood* to cross the road. In effect, "It's my policy" says that you just *do* cross the road, regularly, say, or on certain days, or at a certain hour. In effect, "Because it is moral/virtuous/fitting to cross the road under such-and-such circumstances" says that one just *should* cross the road under such-and-such circumstances. None of these responses assigns road-crossing a calculative role in a process or course of action. All give interminable answers to Anscombe's question.

But now imagine that the "Why?" questioner asks, "Why are you stepping off the curb?" Suppose that you reply in the same way: "I just am" or "I'm just in the mood to" or "I just do" or "One just should." And now imagine that the questioner asks things like "Why are you shifting your weight that way?" "Why are you lifting your left foot?" "Why did you put your left foot down on the road?" That is, imagine the "Why?" question pressed back and further back into the interior of intentional actions like stepping off the curb, walking, and so on. Imagine that the questioner chimes in frame-by-frame, as though your crossing the street could be looked at like individual pages of a cartoon flip-book, or moment by moment like very short video clips. And imagine that you stick to your story about impulse or mood or policy or "ought to" each time the question is posed, steadfastly refusing the suggestion that weight-shifting, foot-raising, foot-moving, and so on play any part in a wider intentional action with a calculative form. If you are sincere, there are, I take it, two possibilities:

1. there is *no action left;* there are unrelated frozen frames, and it is a strange coincidence that they give every indication of adding up to stepping off the curb as the first stage in crossing the road; or
2. each frame offers a very short moving picture, but you wind up with (perhaps continuum-) many policies, plans, habits, impulses, good moments, and so on, and what looked like an intentional action of a familiar sort—stepping off the curb as part of crossing the road—is again an accidental by-product of brief, unrelated episodes each "willed" or undertaken in isolation from the others.

It may be that contemporary metaphysicians could countenance either way of thinking about events in general. But both are absurd in an account of intentional action and reasons for acting, *not* because there are too many parts, but rather because there is no describable whole governing the queried bits. There can be as many "parts" of an action as there can be distinct, applicable questions "Why?" since a "part" is just a (represented) stage in some activity, undertaken with or without any further end in view, such that completion of the stage is not identical with completion of the whole process. But if the "Why?" question is given application, if the questioner asks about something the agent is doing on purpose (like stepping off the curb) rather than something else the agent is "doing" (like wearing down the soles of her shoes, fading the dye in her coat by exposing it to sunlight, and so forth—*ex hypothesi,* asking about these doings will lead her to refuse the question "Why?" because the action is not intentional under those descriptions),[8] then the questions press toward the calculative form of what she is doing, and thereby toward the calculative reasons that could be offered in support of what she does.

The Look to the Future

Reasons for acting are reasons to do something. Doing something is (paradigmatically) doing something over time. Paradigmatically, again, attaining the end happens *after, as a result of,* and *because* one has taken the means to it, or is attained *by* doing parts of a whole process, where, again, doing a proper part is temporally distinct from doing the whole (this is how intentional action can have the sort of "interior" I invited us to press toward by pushing back the question "Why?"). The part–whole variant of the calculative relation in action is, admittedly, a more slippery sort of affair than the means–end variant. If one is even tolerably skilled at doing some kind of thing, one rarely sets out to match parts to whole in action consciously. But if the locution is to have some bite, it is important that attaining a part not coincide with attaining the whole: taking one step, and then another, and then another is walking, but taking any single step is not (which is why you can stop a man from walking by keeping him from taking the second step). Like proper means, proper parts are separable from the whole attained by doing them.

In both variants of the calculative relation, the end governs the means or parts. The means or parts are done *in order to* attain the end and *on account of* the agent's understanding that doing these things will lead to or make possible attaining an end of the relevant sort. That is how even part–whole representation of the calculative order in intentional action retains the temporal feature that figures prominently in the threefold division of practical good: useful-style practical considerations show what is desirable in doing this or that by pointing to a determinate future. To say that A-ing is desirable insofar as useful is to say that one As with an eye toward future B-ing, that A-ing will reach its happy conclusion in B-ing, that one As in order, subsequently, to B, or that repeatedly A-ing is useful because repeated A-ing amounts to B-ing.[9]

The calculative relation is what used to be captured in discussion of final causes: the end is the final cause of the means taken in its service or the parts done in order to do the whole. For the purposes of discussing how the useful plays a distinctive role in explaining and justifying intentional action, one might note here that the end does not exist until it is attained by doing something, that we nevertheless explain what is going on by discussing the end, and that, if the action is successful, it will be the case that *that very end* was attained by doing *those very parts* or taking *those very means*, and this is to the agent's credit. Once the agent succeeds, that is, it's possible to quantify over the end whose attainment crowns her efforts with success. This is another way to get at the sense in which useful-style desirability characterizations look to the future.

In the temporal interval between taking means or doing parts and attaining an end, Anscombe's question "Why?" can be posed over and over again by a philosophical interlocutor acting like an especially tiresome child. If we refuse to let the questioner press us toward noticing the calculative form, we refuse to acknowledge that what we do, in this case, amounts to intentionally crossing the road, or writing the word "action," or serving the ball, or making something, or, or, or. Such refusal doesn't amount to producing an especially rigorous analysis of intentional action, but rather to refusing to think about the relevant kinds of intentional action at all.

Does this mean that there could be no such things as genuinely atomic actions, actions that have no parts done with no further end in view?[10] No. Does it mean that no action is ever done because it is desirable solely for its own sake—that is just for fun, or on account of how it fits with some established, radically interminable pattern? No. It does not even mean that there could not be an atomic action desirable for its own sake. What it suggests is that atomic actions could not be the *central cases* of intentional action. Likewise, actions done solely for their own sakes with *no further end in view*—whether what is desirable in them is the pleasure of so doing or the radically interminable fit of so doing—*could not be the central cases of intentional action.*

And here the reader is likely either to agree, but think it an uninteresting point, or disagree, and think we must have taken a wrong turn somewhere along the line. I hope the point will look very interesting indeed if we reflect on the fact that the standard picture of practical reason is based on practical considerations drawn from this region of the good. I aim to show that the calculative structure of intentional action is responsible for the real power of the standard picture, on the assumption that the standard picture is the progenitor of contemporary instrumentalism about practical reason. To that extent, if one finds the contemporary philosophical wrangle over instrumentalism interesting, then I recommend considering exactly this sort of point.

The *prima facie* case in favor of the standard picture of practical reason stems from the centrality of useful-style desirability characterizations to understanding intentional action. Since a view about practical reason is a view about reason in action, since intention is our sort of concept-involving end-orientation (our form of rational appetite, how the reason *in* us can be reason *toward* action), since intentional action as such is structured by the calculative relation, and since the standard picture locates reasons for acting in that same relation, the standard picture has both feet planted at the core of an understanding of reason in and toward action. No other region of the good, *taken on its own,* has this kind of immediate link to what people do generally because no other region of the good draws its basic structure from the rational order of intentional action as such.

Still, I devote the next section to adapting one of Anscombe's arguments for the sake of responding to the reader who thinks we have got off track.

The Calculative Order in Intention

The reader who thinks we must have gone the wrong way might note that if there has been one result most sought by work on ethics and practical reason by secular Anglo–North American mainstream philosophers over the last half century, it has been arguments that every rational adult has a reason to be moral. I have placed moral reasons for acting among the many befitting-style practical considerations. Whether one agrees with the placement, many philosophers have held, following Kant, that moral reasons are radically interminable. In a sense, the pedestrian thought experiment suggests that insofar as practical reason is reason in or toward action, moral reasons *taken in isolation from* calculative reasons could not be central to the topic (more generally, that interminable reasons for acting taken in isolation from calculative reasons could not be central to the topic). I suspect that the natural response to this suggestion, if it is taken seriously, will be to suppose that where we went wrong was by getting ourselves tangled up in thought about intentional action. The opponent might put the point this way: "Look, this is all well and good if your focus is *action,* but what if your focus is on intention? or on beliefs and desires? or on the character of reason itself? Pretty much all of what you've been doing has derived from an insistence that we focus on action, but intentional action is the *result* of practical reason. Why not look to the *source?*"

I consider one such source—practical reasoning—in Chapter 7. The objection points to other suggestions about sources for reason in action, however, and in the remainder of this chapter I give grounds for dismissing some and take another up in detail.

One of the suggestions is that reason in action comes from beliefs and desires. I will not enter into the controversies surrounding the question what sorts of conditions must be met to get *from* beliefs and desires *to* doing things for reasons. I merely note that there is significant controversy on this topic, and that the conflict suggests that many conditions must be met if we are to have the right sort of guarantee that beliefs and desires *are* the "source" of intentional action, since there is always the worry of the wayward causal chain, the case where the content of the mental states matches what is done, but what is done is not done on account of, or from, the belief-desire system.[11] Any satisfactory hookup between intentional action and the belief-desire system will be one that makes the content of what gets done match up nonaccidentally with what the agent has in mind. My sense is that looking to the action will therefore do no violence to this picture of sources for rational action.

Another source might be reason itself. Discussion of reason itself— that is, Reason with a capital "R"—tends to be highly abstract. As near as I can tell, much of this work involves the thought that Reason is apprehended through reflection on its characteristic activity (for example, thinking, managing sense perception in multiple modalities). If Reason shows itself in intentional action as well—if it has, one might say, a practical employment—then it is hard to see why we wouldn't look to intentional action to "detect" the operations of Reason in practice. I suppose we could take a phrase like Kant's "A good will is not good because of what it effects or accomplishes,"[12] agree that will is the same as practical reason, and really run with that in the direction of suggesting that practical reason has no necessary link to intentional action at all. I do not mean to take such flight seriously. I mean there is no other way to "get to the source" than *via* its results—it is not as though we could stand before naked Reason and ask it to account for itself. The ordinary "results" of Reason's *practical* employment would seem to be intentional action. Kant did not say that the good will isn't the source of intentional action. He was just pointing out that sometimes the good will faces so many obstacles that it cannot accomplish what it means to do, and that it is no less good for its failure to be adequately enacted under such conditions.

Some might object that it is not intentional action, but rather willing, that shows the activity of practical reason, where "willing" has none of the characteristics associated with, say, intending. For example, some philosophers have held that a man could intelligibly be said to *will* things that it is entirely beyond his power ever to accomplish or bring about by his action, such as that the principle of his action be a universal law of nature, or that every finite, dependent rational agent be only as happy as it is good. One cannot *intend* to do what one cannot do. Apparently, however, like a dark god, one can will just about anything, provided one is consistent about it. At the very least, we want an explanation of this. We want to know why we ought to call such an episode an instance of willing rather than a lamentable descent into megalomania.[13] Things approach paradox, incidentally, if, rather than *explain* this very strange use of "will," one gestures in the direction of Kant (who is the source of the phrases) and relies on his considerable authority to carry the day. According to Kant, (a) all and only finite, dependent rational beings are addressees of imperatives (that is, by definition *not* the sort of beings that have the power to author laws of nature or dispense cosmic justice), *and* (b) such phrases figure prominently in articulations of *that very imperative* that governs the doings of finite, dependent rational beings (namely, the "ought" statement that shows how such beings are supposed to use their finite powers). In the absence of solid, widely accepted clarification on such points coming from good scholars of Kant, it seems safer to stick with intention. Whatever else one says about willing, intention ought to be among its fruits.

And here we come to the version of the objection that I mean to take seriously: Why not concentrate on intention rather than intentional action? After all, all sorts of things that are not directly shown in action can shape intention. Indeed, you can act with a view to *disguising* some of your real intentions.

I take it that what motivates the objection is the thought that interminable practical considerations, taken in isolation from the calculative order in intentional action, might be both central to understanding intention and invisible if we have our attention fixed firmly on intentional action. The idea is, in part, that an awful lot of noncalculative reason can be back behind intentional action, and that of course it won't appear that way if we look no further than the observable proceedings that were Anscombe's focus: that is, intentional actions. We need to look to intention, and all that goes into it, not merely to what of one's intentions can be read straight off from what one is doing and to what end.

I respond to this objection by working from one of Anscombe's arguments.[14] Anscombe argued for the related conclusion that we lose the concept of intention if we fail to take the calculative order in intentional action as central to understanding intention. My thought experiment relied on pressing toward the *interior* of ordinary intentional action. The following adaptation of Anscombe's argument depends on considering what happens if we refuse to look *beyond* ordinary action toward further, future ends. What is at issue in both the thought experiment and the argument I give in this section is the centrality of the calculative order, and, hence, of useful-style practical considerations, to thought about practical reason. In my thought experiment, the calculative order was crucial to understanding ordinary intentional action; here it is central to understanding intention. If you like, we are here concerned with what sort of "hinge" between representation and event is involved in the relation between action and intention. I mean my adaptation of Anscombe's argument to make trouble for anyone who wants to argue that the source of action is intention, and that the source of sound intention is *strictly* interminable practical considerations. Anscombe's argument can be reshaped into an argument that you can have as big and varied a system of interminable practical considerations as you please, but that, without the calculative order, you lose track of intention and lose your grip on whatever seemed interesting about interminable considerations as well.

To begin with, some truisms. Our topic is voluntary action, intention, and reasons for acting. Whatever one's views about freedom of the will, if one has any, there is a distinction between voluntary actions and involuntary behavior, and the distinction is such that the agent experiences herself as having choice about whether to take action where voluntary action is at issue. No one deliberates about whether to *A voluntarily*. Instead, one deliberates about whether to *A*. (I can deliberate about whether to take steps to manage or alter some of my involuntary behaviors, for example, about whether to take medication to control seizures, but the topic is still things I take it are in my power to do.) Voluntary actions are intentional under some descriptions but not others. The relevant descriptions inform both intention and act. Some aspects of an agent's intentions are shown in what she does (the portion you describe when your question "Why are you *A*-ing?" is given application, for any of indefinitely many true descriptions, *A*). Other aspects of intention are not. Reasons for acting are adduced in order to explain and justify intentional action. An agent forms intentions in light of what she takes to be the reasons for acting as she intends to act. When we criticize her actions, intentions, plans, policies, or decisions, we point to some trouble in the relation between what an agent did or proposes to do and the reasons given in support of action or action in prospect. All this, I take it, is familiar and part of what is taken for granted in contemporary discussions of practical reason. I treat all of these things as aspects of our topic in philosophical work on practical reason, and take it that they form a kind of shared field of concern, whether or not each theorist working in our area has a position on each topic. I do not mean the points I've listed to be exhaustive. They aren't.

The question is what happens if we remove the calculative order—hence useful-style desirability characterizations, hence calculative reasons for acting—from our topic. The answer is that without further, future ends served by what is done, without useful-style desirability characterizations, we will lose the sense in which action and intention are open to rational criticism. Losing the critical purchase on action and intention, in turn, will amount to losing our grip on our shared field of concern. That is my destination in this argument, the second part of my case that interminable considerations, taken *all on their own,* could *not* provide an account of practical reason.

Imagine stripping away thought about what is useful from the sources of intention. Imagine that there is no such thing as reasoning with an eye toward matching means to ends or parts to wholes in action. Imagine that criticism of action and intention, likewise, does not turn on thought about whether what an agent proposes to do displays a sound grip on the calculative relation. Imagine that there is no such thing as calculative practical reasoning at all. It is not a force that shapes intention. It is not a force that informs action. It sets no standards for praise or criticism. Its absence is complete. It is as if God pulled a plug and calculative practical reason was drained out of our field of concern.[15]

This proposal is less puzzling than it might at first appear, owing to a theoretical tendency in recent work on practical reason. I earlier described that tendency by suggesting that a schematic drawing of it might involve representation of a large human head with a lot of things going on inside it plus an external flash mark. The interior of the big head was the sphere of reason. The flash mark was the intentional action. There were many rich and tight connections between the flash mark and the contents of the head—the flash mark *expressed* something of what went on in the head, or the flash mark was rationally caused by what went on in the head, or both head and flash mark were governed by the norms and commitments that framed the agent's deliberations, or the flash mark was criticized or praised in part by reference to the psychological processes whose fruit it was, or criticized and praised through such psychological ascription as could be made on the basis of many such flash marks, including speech acts, and so on ("or" is here inclusive). For all that, the spareness of the flash mark indicated that *intentional action* was serving as an unanalyzed primitive in the theories. My pedestrian thought experiment was meant to suggest that what was missing in the flash mark was discussion of the calculative order in the action. Let intentional action *remain* unanalyzed for the purposes of this new argument. We are leaving the territory of the flash mark and approaching the territory of the big head, in order to see whether we can make sense of its operations without considering the place of calculative practical reason in them.

Getting rid of calculative reason wouldn't seem to make our topic go away. We still have voluntary, intentional actions. We still have practical reasoning, and moral psychology, and psychological state ascription and commitments and expressions of these and so on. By the lights of the threefold division, we still have two sorts of reasons for acting: radically interminable befitting-style principles and considerations of pleasure. We are operating under four suppositions:

a. voluntary actions are intentional under some descriptions but not others
b. some psychological states and processes inform intention and, hence, action
c. actions and intentions are subject to rational criticism
d. the only sorts of answers available to a reasons-for-acting-seeking question "Why are you A-ing?" (when the question is given application) are:
   d_1. "I feel like A-ing" (treat this as ambiguous between "No reason" and "Because A-ing is pleasant")
   d_2. "I am supposed to A" (allow this answer to range across all of the true radically interminable befitting-style desirability characterizations that can be given in support of the agent's A-ing under the circumstances, that is, all befitting-style desirability characterizations *except* those that have calculative grounding); these responses express the agent's reasons for A-ing and, hence, the items under consideration in determining whether the action or intention is rational

Both calculative and noncalculative theorists operate in light of the first three assumptions. Assumption (d), however, restricts our attention to *interminable* practical considerations. The responses to the reasons-for-acting-seeking question that are ruled out by (d) are all and only calculative responses. Moreover, whether we think an action or intention sound, we will not advert to the calculative order in giving practical praise or criticism or advice, not even indirectly. Calculative practical reason, recall, is gone. It is not part of *any* agent's equipment, whether what the agent is doing is going about her own business or calling others to account for theirs. What does this do to our understanding of the first three assumptions?

The first assumption directs our attention to voluntary actions and to the descriptions under which they are intentional. In my thought experiment, I argued that not all descriptions of intentional actions can get going without attending to the calculative form. Here, then, we have to be careful. Because we are excluding useful-style desirability characterizations, even if what you are doing or will do is or will be intentional under several descriptions, these descriptions cannot be *linked* after the fashion of representation of the calculative order. You shift weight to one foot *and* step off the curb *and* step onto the street *and* walk across the road *and* enter the cafe at the other side. This is true and, we may suppose, what you intend. What we cannot say is that you A, B, and C in order to cross the road, or that you cross the road in order to get to the other side, or that you intend anything that might be expressed in this idiom. Let this be our interpretation of assumption (a). It gives us a way of looking at voluntary action *apart from* calculative reason, and so of focusing our attention on whether interminable backing for it is enough to give us a grip on practical reason. Moreover, this interpretation allows us to retain action in our noncalculative theory of practical reason. We retain it this way: there can be as much *content* to action as we like; it can express as richly textured a field of the agent's psychology, commitments, practical identity, and so forth as we please; it can be subject to praise or criticism in many dimensions and from many angles; it's just that neither the content of the action nor the content of its critical assessment displays the calculative *form*.

What of (b) and (c)? Together these are meant to capture the richness of the psychological antecedents of action, as well as the thought that one can be called on to justify what one does from and for the sake of the practical considerations at issue. They focus our attention both on the processes that issue in intention and action, and on the business of justification and criticism, which is central to work on practical reason. By (d), we are assuming that the practical considerations from which intentions are formed and by which explanation, criticism, and justification are guided are themselves interminable. The two sorts of answers that we are allowing in, on the side of agent and on the side of critic, cover the two sorts of interminable practical considerations I have discussed: radically interminable patterning principles and considerations of pleasure.

And now we are in a position to assess what remains when calculative reason goes away.

The first sort of answer, (d_1), in effect says that you are A-ing because you are in the mood to A. This will be true just in case you are in fact in the mood to A, and this is, in fact, why you are A-ing. By assumption (b), you A on account of some of the psychological underpinnings of your act, perhaps together with something about your circumstances and something about A-ing that makes it pleasant for you. Allow that things on your side are in good shape: you *are* in the mood to A, and A because you are in the mood to do it. The desirability characterization is both sincere and true.

Now let's move to the critic's side. How will rational criticism get a purchase on the agent who As—wrongly we think—when she is in the mood to do so? How does assumption (c) apply in this case? Any criticism of what our agent does will involve some kind of doctrine to the effect that being in the mood to A is not reason enough for A-ing. Perhaps we think it is a sign of pathology even to be in the *mood* to A, much less to A when the mood is upon one. Or perhaps A-ing is all well and good, and there's nothing wrong with being in the mood to do it, but *now* is not the time, nor *here* the place, for A-ing. Or perhaps no one could consistently hold that A-ing was to be done under these circumstances. Or perhaps this agent couldn't *really* think that it was all right to A under these circumstances. Notice, however, that because we have left useful-style practical considerations out of the picture, our criticism will be mounted *in the absence* of any account of whether it is in the agent's interests, serves her further ends, or is useful to people generally, or some such, to avoid A-ing when in the mood to A. We can say whatever we like about the agent, her act, and her reasons for acting. What we cannot say is that what's wrong with her action is that she has miscalculated.

What is the status of our criticism? It can't be that what *we* are doing in criticizing her is saying things *in order to* prompt her to behave differently, or *in order to* get her to reconsider, or, indeed, *in order to* make anything happen. Just as *she* can't reason about what to do in order to make it possible to attain the whole or some part of her ends, *we* can't criticize her in order to attain or make it possible to attain the whole or some part of *our* ends. This form of reasoning, calculative reasoning, is precisely what has been drained out of the field of our concern. We can't praise her in order to get her to keep doing the kind of thing she's doing. We can't criticize her in order to make her stop and reconsider. She does what she does. We make our pronouncements about it. She keeps at it or stops. But we can't introduce a *calculative* link between these events, nor can we let our intentions or hers be calculatively informed.

In this sense, even if she accepts our criticism, it is not as though we have any reason to suppose that she *ought to* or *will* take steps *in order to* see to it that she does not do that again. Our agent *cannot* reason in that way (namely, about what to do *in order to* improve anything), and, by the supposition, neither can we. The "in order to" style of reasoning is what drained out of the theory of practical reason.

If we are good at making damning pronouncements, we may make the agent feel bad. Afterward there might be a change. Anything is possible. But even *systematic* alteration in her behavior *after* hearing what we think about what she's done will *not* be to her credit, *qua* rational agent. In order to give her rational credit for changing her ways, we would have to imagine that she deliberately took some steps *in order to* change. In excluding the calculative order, in excluding useful-style desirability characterizations, we have excluded the determinate, future-end-directed mode of practical reasoning. Under this assumption, criticism of an agent who does what she does because she is in the mood to do it becomes a little like calling her names.

What of the second sort of answer, the sort given in (d_2): "I am supposed to *A*"? Under our assumption, this answer, that we are allowing to range across all radically interminable befitting-style practical considerations that could be given in support of action or intention again leaves it next to impossible to get any grip on the thought that intentions and voluntary actions as such are subject to rational criticism. Again, the trouble is that, once we have excluded all calculative reasons and all calculative reasoning from our topic, "rational criticism" degenerates into something more on the order of the politer forms of invective. Even if you are *wrong* in thinking that you are supposed to *A,* we ought not to expect you to do anything in the direction of seeing to it that you do not make this error again. The direction you would look to improve yourself is to the future, and we would have to give you access to a mode of reasoning that has been excluded by hypothesis if we held that you could do anything in order that things change. Criticism, discovery of one's own faulty judgment—such things cannot, by assumption, be taken to heart in any way that would lead one to take steps in order to improve. Nor, if one's judgment is sound, could one take steps in order to ensure that one conducts oneself in the same way next time. There is no such thing as doing anything *in order that* anything else might happen. That is precisely what has been excluded.

Is anything left? Do we even have voluntary action left if we have retained interminable desirability characterizations but have lost the form of judgment central to the whole activity of practical self-correction when one errs, practical self-improvement in order to decrease the chances that one will err in the future, and the many little things that a person struggling to act well does by way of working to hold herself constant in doing as she is supposed to do? What remains when the possibility of self-directed learning, maintenance, and correction are gone?

A concept of voluntary action does remain, and, in light of assumption (d), it takes exactly the form you might expect. Voluntary actions can be commanded. Accordingly, "I am *A*-ing because I feel like *A*-ing" indicates that there is no special authority backing up the action and "I am *A*-ing because I am supposed to *A*" indicates some sort of authoritative source for *A*-ing. And this even leaves room to sort things through a bit, so that we can get a grip on how voluntary actions are intentional under some descriptions but not others (which is needed if we are to retain some hold on supposition [a]). The example in Anscombe's argument involves imagining someone's saying "Tremble!" to you in a terrible voice. You tremble in response, but you are not thereby *obeying* an order. So there is doing something because and on account of being commanded to do it, doing something just because you feel like doing it, and doing something that was commanded, but not *on account of* the command. These become the three sorts of relation that might obtain between what goes on in the big head and its practical result or expression, the flash mark.

How important is this distinction? All that remains are two sorts of desirability characterizations. These are, in effect, one that says "The buck stops here, I did it just because it was what I felt like doing" and one that points a finger upward toward some "higher" source and indicates that the A-ing was done in obedience to that. It does not much matter *which* higher source—conscience, rules of etiquette, the way of one's people, God, the suits, the officials, the advice of a psychic friend, some dictates of pure noncalculative reason, the motive of duty, your sense of what matters in life, the moral law, hipsters, the voice of one's employer or superior officer, a municipal ordinance, the norms you take to be binding on you, or whatever else has authority for you—because the distinction is otherwise completely *idle*. It is not as though, for example, you could investigate the source in order to determine whether it merited your obedience. It is not as though you could work to rein in or to cultivate your rebellious streak on account of an authoritative determination that some source of commands was or was not worthy of your obedience. It is not even as though having the remaining criterion to mark off voluntary from involuntary actions is *useful* because it is, after all, good to know which things we can, and which we cannot, make happen by giving orders to ourselves or to others. Usefulness is what *cannot* be appealed to by the suppositions. One can no more give orders in order to make things happen than one can obey orders in order to do as the authoritative source commands. So, yes, there is a distinction between voluntary and involuntary actions, and it gives us a way of talking about the fact that intentional actions are intentional under some descriptions but not others. But it is hard to see that it's a distinction that could make any difference. Instead, it is a mystery *why* anyone would have thought it important to be able to tell the difference between voluntary and involuntary actions in the first place.

Quite literally, on our four assumptions suitably interpreted to keep the calculative order out of the picture, the distinction cannot possibly do any work, cannot be put to use. And this, Anscombe concludes, is enough to show that future intention with which one acts is absolutely central to the concept of intention. In the view I have been urging, it is enough to show that useful-style practical considerations have a special place in thought about reason in action. The calculative order in doing things is crucial to work on intention generally, and it is this order that explains how and why it might be to the point to determine such things as the distinction between voluntary and involuntary action. Without considerations of what is useful, without this kind of look to the future, there's no point to the rest of it, really—no grounds for expecting anyone to change anything in order to respond to criticism, no reason to think anyone would purposefully take steps to keep doing as she should do, no reason to treat rational practical criticism as interestingly different from calling people bad names. Arguing with someone's purported reasons for acting becomes a certain form of rudeness, under assumption (d).

I take it that *these* kinds of considerations are what give the standard picture a very serious claim on our attention in thinking about practical reason. I announced at the outset of this book that I was going to urge that the sensible core of contemporary work on instrumentalism is to be found in very old thought about the rational structure of intentional action. The sort of point I have just made in adapting Anscombe's argument, together with the points in the pedestrian thought experiment, is half of why I think this. The other half has to do with how very powerful non-desire-based versions of the standard picture can be. It is finally time to turn to the standard picture.

7

The Standard Picture of Practical Reason

In the argument that I adapted from Anscombe, the only thing that we left out of our theoretical discussion of practical reason was the calculative order and, hence, useful-style desirability characterizations. Without the calculative order, questions about normative authority, practical reason, and reasons for acting went idle. The ensuing void left us with noncalculative pronouncements *about* action, but without reasons *for* acting, and, hence, without a topic for work on practical reason. In short, *no* strictly and utterly noncalculative account of practical rationality could be sufficient for understanding practical reason. That is, *no* strictly and utterly noncalculative account of practical rationality could be true. This result is the first part of my limited defense of the standard picture of practical reason.

It is through considerations about what is useful—through calculative reasons for acting—that any serious thought about criticism, praise, normative authority, and the like find their home in work on practical reason. Put somewhat differently, the mere possibility of giving interminable desirability characterizations in response to a reasons-for-acting-seeking question "But why B?" is *not* enough to provide us with noncalculative reasons for acting. Shorn of determinate future implications, shorn of any connection to what is good in the sense useful, interminable considerations do not *count* as reasons for acting. You can see that they do not count as reasons for acting because there is no point in criticizing what is done on account of them.

In order to get noncalculative pronouncements given in response to Anscombe's question to amount to reasons for acting, it is, then, important to find how they might involve some determinate future-directed employment of practical reason. Anticipating this requirement, I smuggled in the raw materials for doing so in describing both the work of practical reason in pleasure and the character of radically interminable patterning principles. To get concerns that primarily attach to present action (considerations of pleasure) to provide *reasons* for acting I credited the agent acting from and for pleasure with wanting to *prolong* the doing of the present action, and to engage in it in a way that allowed for unimpeded enjoyment. The look to the future is *in* the glance that directs one's attention to keeping the good thing going. This is how considerations of pleasure frame the work of reason in action, by directing the agent to take steps to maintain the pleasant nexus of agent, action, and circumstance.

Two things are required to give radically interminable befitting-style considerations some practical import: they must be principles that give shape to some of what the agent does and they have to give rise to the ends that they underwrite. Tradition has it that patterning principles can shape your actions in two ways: (1) the pattern is in you, as a source of some of your ends, and you act *from* and for the sake of the pattern; (2) the pattern is not in you, but you knowingly, deliberately act in *accordance* with the dictates of the patterning principle (perhaps in order to habituate yourself to the pattern). In either case, the pattern has to have some determinate practical implications, at least in central cases. Determinate practical implications include such things as prohibitions and requirements, that is, limits on ends or means that may be taken in their service. Seeing a patterning principle at work is seeing it as shaping action, omissions, plans, policies, deliberation, and the like. Part of what gives Jack Spicer's account of living from and for the sake of poetry some weight is that Spicer was a very fine poet with an excellent ear who got down to brass tacks fairly quickly in his advice to poets and whose own life was about as miserable as you'd expect, given his account of his patterning principle. Whether we buy Spicer's description of poetry and its practice, and whether—even if we buy his account—we think Spicer in fact acted from and for the sake of poetry alone, poetic practical considerations are not best understood as operating *in isolation* from calculative practical reason. Rather, they supply some of the *materials* for the exercise of calculative reason in the service of poetry.

The way to prevent interminable considerations from going idle, then, is to treat them as sources of ends or limits. This gives us the link between considerations of pleasure or fit and calculative reasons that, I have argued, *must* be there if the noncalculative ones are to be worth paying attention to.

In this sense, although I have left room for interminable considerations, it is only because they have essential links to the useful that they count as reasons for acting. Interminable considerations all on their own are not enough to give us reasons for acting. The calculative order is necessary to understanding practical reason.

Still, that there are (or may be) such things as radically interminable practical principles and practical considerations attaching to present action (pleasures) suggests that a calculative picture of practical reason may not be sufficient to account for reason in action. In this chapter, in continuing my limited defense of the standard picture, I work to argue that the standard picture *might* be sufficient for getting a grip on practical reason.

The Standard Picture

The version of the standard picture that I will be at pains to defend just is the version of the fourth thesis altered to describe reasons for acting:

> Let A and B be actions of different types. One has reason to A only if one takes it that A-ing is a means to (or part of) attaining (or making it possible to attain) a further end, B-ing, and one wants to B (for no particular reason or because B-ing is pleasant, useful, or fitting).

In short, if one has a reason for A-ing, then one acts in the service of some further end, B-ing. While B-ing, a primary end with respect to A-ing, might be secondary with respect to other ends (which is to say, may itself be pursued because it is useful), the thrust of the standard picture is that the reasons terminate in a desirability characterization for B-ing (or by noting that, under this description, there is no such desirability characterization to give). That is, there are no reasons to do anything unless one seeks to attain a determinate end.

How can the two interminable varieties of desirability consideration fit with this insistence? When one says that B-ing is desirable in the sense fitting, on this view, what one is saying is that B-ing is *part of* maintaining or realizing a significant pattern in one's affairs. When one says that what one is doing is desirable in the sense pleasant, on the other hand, one points out that, just now, one is inclined to savor the business at hand, *B*-ing, and that something of *how* one is going about *A*-ing-in-order-to-*savor-the-business-at-hand* answers to the end of *prolonging* the engagement. What pleasure and considerations of fit provide, on this account, are two sources of intentional action. That is to say, two sources of ends.

Now, treating interminable considerations as sources of ends is not the same as transforming them into plain calculative considerations. So why not just bite the bullet at this point and say that even though the meditation on looking to the future inspired by the threefold division can make it possible to see why one can take something of a calculative picture of practical reason for granted, it also shows how a calculative picture will *fail?* That is, why not just say that pleasure and radically interminable considerations of fit give the two kinds of reasons there are for primary ends, that calculative reason levers these into action, and that a complete account of practical reason therefore needs both?

In my ongoing attempt to sharpen the point of controversy between calculative and noncalculative theories of practical reason, I settled upon this:

> Noncalculative theorists insist that there can be reasons for an agent to
> *B* quite apart from her plans, projects, particular attachments, character, skills, habits, or further ends; the calculative theorist denies this.

On the view I have sketched of pleasure, pleasant-style considerations do not operate apart from various facts about the agent, hence could not supply noncalculative reasons for *B*-ing in the relevant sense. Patterning principles that are merely interminable in practice (like whole-life plans, the thin-and-rich principle, and Thomistic accounts of virtue and vice) likewise are fixed by what is in an agent's will, by what she seeks to accomplish or participate in. Hence, these do not supply noncalculative reasons for *B*-ing either. What I must argue against in order to defend the standard picture, then, is the claim that some rational considerations should shape an agent's pursuits no matter what she already means to accomplish or make possible in practice, that this is a requirement of practical reason.

My argument proceeds in stages. First, I describe the virtues of the standard picture. I do this in order to link this view of reasons to the structure of intentional action more systematically. This allows me to consider the first form of an objection to the standard picture. The standard picture treats having a determinate end in view as *necessary* for having a reason to do something. My first batch of opponents instead claim that having an end is *sufficient* for having reasons to do something, but not necessary (for if it were necessary, then there would be no so-called external reasons for acting; on my view, the standard picture will be defeated if there are such things as reasons for me to do something quite apart from my ends, character, plans, skills, and so on—that is, if there are external reasons). In the course of considering this objection, I encounter my next batch of opponents, those who argue that noncalculative practical reasoning is both essential in human life and, by definition, detached from what an agent already has it in mind to do. The bulk of this chapter is devoted to contrasting calculative practical reasoning from the other sort. Finally, I consider whether the calculative order in intentional action is enough, all on its own, to provide standards for rational criticism. My argument that it is concludes my defense of the standard picture.

The Virtues of the Standard Picture

The standard picture of reasons for acting centers on the calculative relation between means and end, parts and whole, and the way this relation informs intentional action. I think that the best thing about the standard picture is that *intentional action as such, and paradigmatically, is informed by the calculative relation and so any ordinary intentional action is a candidate for calculative reasons explanation.*[1]

Whenever someone deliberately does something over time, it ought to be possible

a. to represent her doings as having an intended means–end or part–whole *form,*
b. to see her course as the sort of thing that *could have been chosen* through calculative practical reasoning,[2]
c. to identify her primary end in action (the whole activity in which she wants to engage or the further end served by her action), to identify the *parts* of what she does by pointing to the *whole* activity in which they have their place or the character of the *means* she takes by pointing to the further *end* they are meant to serve,

    d. to treat attaining the primary end as a criterion of *success* for her
       action, and

    e. to use the form and content of her action or course as a basis for
       identifying *as such* any *interruptions* or *obstacles* that she might en-
       counter.

This, in turn, is how the standard picture can lever a truth about representation of intentional actions into some normative requirements on
action. The normativity comes in through the calculative form *via* convention (or creative but reasonable calculation) about means and ends,
parts and wholes in action. If I leave out the leavening agent when baking cake, then I have made an error in baking and no longer am entitled
to confidence that the result ought to be the sort of cake I mean to make.
Winding up with strangely sweet, gummy flatbread is in this case failing.
It is clear that it counts as an error, hence, as criticizable, because I intended to produce a cake and had available a recipe for making cake. (If
I had no recipe, and was not enough of a baker to wing it, then I had no
business setting out to make cake to begin with.) While such assessments are agent-relative in the sense that "having" calculative reasons
for *A*-ing (adding baking powder) depends on (among other things)
wanting to *B* (bake a cake), and not everyone will want to *B*, such things
as whether the means were well-chosen, whether one attained *B* using
the means or in the manner by which one meant to attain it, and so on
are not purely "subjective" or "agent-relative" matters at all. This is
how such considerations meet the Williams criterion for having to do
with good. The calculative form of intentional action provides a general
framework for explaining and assessing intentional action as such. The
good at issue here is good-in-the-sense-useful.

My opponents may raise many objections at this point. For example,
they may object to the phrase "sources of ends" as a description of how
interminable considerations can be practical. Many will prefer to say
that the first exercise of practical reason is in *setting* ends, that what lifts
us above the lowly shrew is not just that we can apparently want anything, but rather that it is up to us to determine our directions in life by
setting ends in accordance with our considered views about what matters. I later cope with this objection in an argument about practical
reasoning. Presumably, if we are going to count *end-setting* or *intention-
formation* or *end-adoption* or some other such "activity" as the primary

exercise of practical reason, it will be because the ends are set or adopted, decisions made, intentions formed as a result of reasoning. Merely taking it into one's head to do a thing ought not count as the primary exercise of practical reason, after all.

The most basic objection will insist that I have got things turned the wrong way around, that having a determinate future end is *sufficient* grounds for rational action, but is not *necessary*. I turn to this objection first.

Sufficiency and Necessity

The usual way that some theorists interested in noncalculative practical matters treat the point that intentional action has a calculative form relevant to thought about reasons for acting is *via* some such phrase as Kant's "Whoever wills the end, wills (so far as reason has decisive influence on his action) the means which are indispensably necessary and in his power,"[3] interpreting this sentence to mean that willing an end provides a *sufficient* condition for willing the means to that end, not, however, that willing an end is necessary for having reasons to act. If it were not necessary, after all, then there might be reasons that were not keyed to what an agent means to do, to make happen, or to make possible. If, for all that, willing an end was sufficient for having reasons to do things, then we could retain the thought that the calculative order shapes action and intention without losing the sense that there are deeply noncalculative reasons for acting. That is how this move fits into an argument against the standard picture.

Kant's phrase, a statement of the hypothetical imperative, is about reasons for acting and Kant accepts the thought that reasons for acting connect action to the good. The kind of good at issue in the hypothetical imperative is *bonitas pragmatica* or *bonitas problematica*,[4] both of which involve useful-style desirability. The sense in which the hypothetical imperative involves a perspective from which the good at issue can be recognized by more than one agent is that it binds all addressees of imperatives. Drawing on this sentence, contemporary noncalculative theorists may suggest that "if one is determined to B and takes it that A-ing is the means to, or a part of B-ing, then one has reason to A," that is, they will concede that having a primary end is a *sufficient* condition for having a reason to A, but not that wanting to attain a primary end is a necessary condition.[5] They then focus on the kinds of noncalculative constraints that must be met if the agent is to will an end in accordance with Reason.

There are problems with this approach, problems signaled by the surprising absence of attention paid to the modal at the heart of Kant's claim (I mean surprising given the frequency with which the passage has been quoted).[6] Although the passage is usually quoted with reference to calculative reasons for acting generally, why would we suppose that we ever had discovered the "*indispensably necessary* means" to attaining an end?[7] Well, if the means that "lie within [a man's] power" are sufficiently constrained—say, if he and his buddy are handcuffed to a bomb that will go off in two minutes, and one of them must pick the handcuff lock if they are to free themselves, and the only object available for lock-picking is a bit of wire protruding from one man's shoulder (which got stuck there during an earlier brush with mortality) that he must yank free with his teeth and drop into his buddy's palm if the buddy (who has the requisite locksmith skill) is to pick the lock, and the man stuck with wire is determined that the two of them will free themselves, then his only choice is to yank the wire out, and so on—then he confronts indispensably necessary means to his end.[8]

Sufficiently hobbled agents with sufficiently urgent ends can face necessary means. Sufficiently unimaginative, stubborn, or lazy agents who only attend to one way of attaining an end may likewise face necessary means (because of their own psychological limitations, not because they are otherwise in dire straits). These cases involve contingent necessity. I suppose that sufficiently picky agents with sufficiently fussy ends might find that their practical problems admit of unique solutions *noncontingently,* because of the character of what they mean to do. But what is remarkable about cases where some means are in some sense necessary to attaining a given end is how *rare* they are in human life, which may be why calculative rational choice theorists who represent the solution to a formal choice problem as a *line* (rather than a point on a line) do not find themselves pressed to defend the suggestion that *infinitely* many courses will solve the problem equally well. Kant's remark has the ring of truth, but *not* because it applies directly to all calculative practical considerations. It doesn't.[9]

Kant's truth concerned imperatives, and casting a practical "argument" in the imperatival mood does tend to obscure the more usual availability of many means to a given end.[10] Anscombe made the point by considering a syllogism on the order of "Do whatever is conducive to avoiding a car crash / Such-and-such is conducive to avoiding a car crash / Ergo: do such-and-such" rehearsed while driving a car. She commented:

> [S]omeone professing to accept the premises will be inconsistent if, when nothing intervenes to prevent him, he fails to act on the particular order with which the argument ends. But this syllogism suffers from the disadvantage that the first, universal, premise is an insane one, which no one could accept for a minute if he thought out what it meant. For there are usually a hundred different and incompatible things conducive to not having a car crash; such as, perhaps, driving into the private gateway immediately on your left and abandoning your car there, and driving into the private gateway immediately on your right and abandoning the car there.[11]

The point is general: Do whatever in your power is conducive to B-ing/ A-ing is in your power and conducive to B-ing/C-ing is in your power and conducive to B-ing/A-ing is incompatible with C-ing/Ergo . . . ? Its upshot is this: under normal conditions, wanting to B cannot provide a sufficient condition for (committing yourself to) doing anything in particular aptly characterized as *an action of the type A-ing*. There is even a little wiggle room for our two men handcuffed to the bomb: the man stuck with wire could a seize the wire with his teeth from more than one position, bracing himself this way or that, or he could release it into his buddy's palm at one of several verbal signals, on the count of three, say, or when the buddy shouts, "Now!"

Suppose we were to get rid of the "indispensable necessity" clause and instead try "If one wants to B, then one has reason to do something or other acceptable to one and within one's powers that one believes will make possible attaining the whole or some part of one's primary end, B-ing."[12] The restriction to acceptable means is crucial to the sufficiency claim.[13] Obviously, the mere fact that I understand that something I can do *will* help me attain an end is not enough to give me even a *prima facie* reason to do it. For instance, I have just bought a chef's knife. I have it in a bag. I want a seat on the bus, but all seats are taken. Threatening a child who has a seat with the knife may be one way to get a seat, and I may know that I could do this, but I do not take it that this establishes even a *prima facie* reason to threaten the child with a knife. Once the restriction is in place, and once we have removed the troublesome necessity clause, there is something to the sufficiency claim.

The sufficiency claim concerns wanting. Kant's remark concerns willing, rather than wanting, and willing is special for Kant, but for most of us it is surely rather close to intending. I am implicitly treating wanting *to B* as a species of wanting isomorphic with intending. Both take as their objects ends that it is in one's power to attain, for instance, and are more naturally expressed by "_ing *to A*" than "_ing *that p*." Further, while there may be a little gap between wanting to *A* and intending to *A*, the latter will be the more usual form, since, at the point we can ascribe a want shaped just like an intention, the lack of full-blown intention will admit of some special explanation—for example, one may not be up to doing the thing ("I want to stand in line and buy my ticket and ride the Demon roller coaster and be able to say I've done it, but . . ."), or there might be something one *can* do toward getting what one wants that isn't enough to put one's end within reach (for example, one buys lottery tickets *wanting* to win, but not *intending* to win). Finally and most importantly, "because I intend to *B*" and "because I want to *B*" and "in order to *B*" all give the *same* reason for *A*-ing.[14] For this reason, I am treating wanting to *A*-in-order-to-*B* as the form of wanting relevant to the standard picture. Anscombe simply restricted use of "want" to this kind of wanting: "The wanting that interests us is neither wishing nor hoping nor the feeling of desire, and cannot be said to exist in the man who does nothing towards getting what he wants."[15] More recently, David Velleman made a similar claim about the proper use of "desire" in work on practical reason.[16] I am not requiring that we resolutely abstain from using the words "want," "desire," or "prefer" except when "intend" would do almost as well, but I am urging that we take seriously the suggestion that one way of using the terms—or, if you like, one species of wanting—has special relevance to work on practical reason. This wanting takes as its object attainable ends. It is directed at actions that are intentional under a series of linked representations informed by the calculative relation. Concentrating on calculative wanting gives a boost to the hunch that the calculative relation must somehow be basic to reasons for acting because understanding the contents of this sort of want and understanding what kind of representation of events is at issue in representation of intentional action *both* turn on looking to the calculative form.

But now, consider the version of the sufficiency claim that is not absurd. If one wants to B, then one has reason to do something or other acceptable to one and within one's powers that one believes will make possible attaining the whole or some part of one's primary end, B-ing. And here, let's think about *what* one has reason to do. Suppose that several things come to mind. Or suppose that nothing does. In either case, one has to figure out what to do. And here we confront a source of action and intention that has been discussed extensively in recent work: practical deliberation. Many new theorists of practical reason devote themselves to investigating the character of practical reasoning. And the closer one looks at the content of episodes of practical reasoning, the more improbable the standard picture looks.

For example, many of my opponents hold that sound practical deliberation can lead you to change your ends in such a way that you go from wanting, say, primarily to C to wanting instead to B, or from having no determinate primary end in view to settling on B-ing as a worthy pursuit. This is a problem for my account because the role of *any* sort of practical deliberation on my view will be to take you from wanting to B to doing something in order to make possible the whole or some part of B-ing. And *that* will require coming up with acceptable means to or parts of doing something that can be correctly described as B-ing, whether B-ing has its source an indeterminate principle that exerts interminable influence on your will (like "doing as it befits a practicing poet to do"), or is an end that has just cropped up under the circumstances (like "getting free before the bomb goes off"). The idiom that belongs to thought about what is useful, that is, comes into play once one has something to do in view. But, on the face of it, at least, not all reasons for acting take shape in the course of finding means to antecedently given ends. Some reasoning seems to be about *getting* determinate ends rather than figuring out how to attain the ones you've already got. And this looks like trouble.

Practical Reasoning

In my account of the standard picture, I have stressed cases where one has an end in view, even if that end is given by some noncalculative pattern or the pleasure one takes in what one is here and now doing. The threefold division of good is a division in desirability characterizations, which are offered on behalf of what one does, of what one did, or of what one intends to do. Desirability characterizations, that is, attach to proceedings with a means–end or part–whole form, to intentional actions. And this all by itself may seem question-begging, because it directs our attention to what the agent has in mind to do without being overly particular about how she got it into her head to do that. Figuring out what to pursue is not always anywhere near as easy as figuring out how to do what you anyway want to do. After all, what if you have no idea what to seek? What if you have some general thoughts about what you want to get, but do not know what will *count* as getting it under such-and-such circumstances even when the circumstances seem to offer some prospect of yielding some benefit? What if the circumstances you face are so unlike others you have faced that you must put aside business as usual to see both what matters here and how to go about getting it?

If we are in any of these sorts of trouble, it is of no help to know that any course of action we pursue will have the kind of articulation envisaged in the standard picture, and that the calculative relation will be a source of some reasons for doing what we do. Not all the work of figuring out what to do or pursue in such circumstances is a matter of calculation. But figuring these things out *is* practical reasoning. *Ex hypothesi,* the sort of figuring involved when we do not know what to pursue is noncalculative. And won't noncalculative reasoning produce noncalculative *reasons* for doing the things we decide to do? *Strictly* noncalculative reasons that provide reasoned support for primary ends? And isn't the fact that we do not come into the world with our dance cards full, or even with a clear vision of what we might want out of life, all by itself enough to show that the standard picture will almost inevitably give out just where we need our powers of practical reason the most?

Recently, there has been a lot of philosophical attention paid to thought processes that are (a) directed at what one should do or how one should live, and (b) not about matching means to antecedently given ends. This work stresses the significance of practical deliberation as a source of reasons for acting. Call pictures of practical rationality that center on practical reasoning *deliberative accounts of practical reason.*

According to deliberative accounts of practical reason, what makes some consideration a reason for acting is its actual or potential role in sound practical reasoning. Calculative reasoning is about matching means *to* ends. Noncalculative deliberation is deliberation *of* ends. The latter, it seems, can find no place in a standard picture of reasons for act-ing. And yet, most reasonably thoughtful people who have some choice about what to do with themselves at some point or other find themselves engaged in deliberation of ends. And so, it seems, the standard picture is false. My response to this objection comes in stages.

To begin with, it is true that a lot of what one thinks about when thinking about an especially thorny practical problem has very little to do with matching means to ends. We sometimes begin wanting some-thing exceedingly vague—say, to get out of a rut (a practical consider-ation that gives next to no practical guidance)—and wind up wanting to go for a swim (a proper end-in-the-sense-term). We sometimes have a perfectly determinate end in view and, on reflection, wind up pursuing something else entirely with no thought that further ends govern the change. And sometimes we find ourselves facing circumstances in which no conceivable thing we might do will answer to our various views about what ought to be done. I further take it that none of these kinds of practical thinking—end-specification, shift in primary ends, or the hunt for an acceptable course in hostile circumstances—is calculative in its *content*. None of them *could* have calculative content. And one way of putting this point is by saying that all involve deliberation of ends, not means. But it is also true that the outcome of *any* successful episode of practical deliberation, calculative or noncalculative, is *new ends:* when one decides what to do, one sets out to do things that one had not in-tended to do initially.[17] The first premise of my argument in response to deliberative theories is this:

1. Both calculative and noncalculative practical reasoning is a source of new ends.

What, then, is the difference between the two, if it isn't that one gives you new ends and the other doesn't?

I suggest it is the following: in calculative deliberation, what you are after is, in some sense, already there to be found or determinate enough that you will know once you have found it (the "or" is inclusive). There are at least four different ways in which you might be trailing after some-thing that is already there or have a clear enough objective in view that your search can be guided by what you are trying to find. First, you might be hunting for a technique to attain some objective, a technique someone else already cooked up (as someone else invented a recipe for chicken that you try out at home). Much of mundane calculative practical reasoning with which many of us are familiar is in this sense technical: you ask the clerk at the hardware store how to install new washers in the kitchen faucet, you read the manual in order to learn how to set up your new equipment, you read labels to find out how to use what you've bought, you consult schedules to find out how to access public transportation, you ask more experienced people how to do this or that, and, once you have a grasp of how one does the thing in question, you think along as you follow the instructions. Here, not only does your practical task take the form of finding out how to attain an end-in-the-sense-of-stopping-place; you can rely on existing technical solutions to your problem.

The second way in which what you are after may already be there is constitutive. Sometimes, the constitutive relation is given by the artifice of human convention. For example, you are learning the rules governing the movement of chess pieces while trying to play the game. Moving your pieces legally is not a *technique* for playing chess but a positive requirement on any movement *counting* as a chess move (contrast this with learning various standard chess openings that serve as techniques for play). Constitutive learning and reasoning trace the part–whole relation, and the standard parts (in a game, the legal moves) take their character from preexisting wholes (in a game, the game). You master the two together as you set about learning to participate in a kind of activity governed in this way by convention.

The third way in which the solution to your problem is somehow there to be found concerns the natural order of things (the constitutive relation is, if you like, given by nature rather than its close second, culture). Say, for example, an accident has damaged the nerves in one of your hands and you are regaining its use, learning to compensate for the numbness by watching what you do. You are practicing picking up a ball. There aren't exactly *techniques* for grasping objects with one's hands as there are, say, for doing shadow play with one's fingers in order to produce rabbits and bears in silhouette on the nursery wall. Rather, there are many features of hands and how they move that support normal hand movement. For instance, you will be more likely to succeed in your attempts at grasping the ball if you cradle the ball between your palm and inwardly bent fingers than if you press the back of your hand against the ball and stretch your fingers back away from your palm. The physiognomy of the human hand is what one relies on (and learns about) when setting out to do on purpose things that come naturally to people with an ordinary range of feeling and movement in their hands.

A similar sort of system of constraints attends the business of technical innovation in the face of a determinate practical problem. You need to A. No one has quite figured out a procedure for A-ing, but A-ing is an end-in-the-sense-of-term. So, for instance, you need to transport a large quantity of exceedingly volatile or delicate material from one place to another. There are many packing and transport techniques available, but none answers to the exact combination of fragility and peril that shapes your predicament. You investigate combinations of packing materials and means of transport with an eye toward finding the combination that will get your stuff safely from one place to another. You may not succeed, but if you fail, this will be apparent because the end provides something like a criterion for success.

The fourth way in which something might already be there to be found occurs in straightforward "calculative" work: you want to fill in your truth table the right way to get an A on your logic homework, or you want to solve a simple engineering problem or balance your checkbook or figure out how much wood you need to buy in order to make a box of such-and-such dimensions or how much paint you need for the back porch. The sense in which what you are after is already there is demonstrative: the solution to your practical problem can be *derived* using garden varieties of demonstrative inference. What gives rational support to the answers on your homework, or your decision to use three struts in the structure, or your addition and subtraction in the checkbook column, or the amount of paint or wood you bring home for your project is not merely *that* you thought these things through. It is that your thinking was sound in light of the basic principles of arithmetic, truth-functional logic, materials science, or engineering. In short, it is not that you got *an* answer, but that your got (one of) the *right* answer(s), that supports what you do.

The thought that calculative deliberation is somehow governed by a determinate end (whereas noncalculative reasoning is *not*) means that the agent has some sort of objective in view and deliberates or calculates or does research in order to make use of those resources in some sense already *there* in order to attain that objective. A kind of creativity can crop up in this sort of thing: you want to make *a* cake, begin making yellow cake, discover you are out of vanilla extract, and decide to use a dash of some other liquor instead; you want to make a plywood box, but don't decide what sort of plywood to use until you are at the lumber yard; you want to swim twenty-four laps, and change strokes after the first twelve to give yourself a little breather before completing your swim; there are various ways to prove the theorem on the logic homework, and you take a different route from the one your study partner takes; given a pile of diverse objects and a storage locker, the job is to get as many objects into the locker as possible, and you hit upon a novel, highly efficient way of stowing your gear. But although there is room for discretion in thinking how to complete your task in each case, in none of these cases is it the fact *that* one thinks about something that *makes* what one does reasonable. Rather, it is that *one hits upon a reasonable thing to do*. And, with a little experience or worldly know-how, one often can hit upon a reasonable thing to do without much thought at all.

In calculative deliberation, standards not produced by your thinking, but somehow set in or by the practical task you face, are what determine whether your practical thinking went well or failed miserably: the fact that you worked hard producing an incorrect proof doesn't save the proof; the fact that you devised your very own plumbing strategy and applied it perfectly doesn't fix the sink; the fact that *you* think you ought to be permitted to castle after moving your king doesn't legitimate the chess move; and the fact that you would love to be able to grasp objects with the back of your hand doesn't make it reasonable to direct your rehabilitation efforts accordingly (unless you have interestingly deformed hands). How exactly to account for the various ways in which tasks and principles and the natural or conventional order of thing set limits on what can count as sound calculative deliberation is a difficult matter. But there is, at least, a rough, intuitive sort of sense to be made of the suggestion that calculative practical thinking doesn't so much *produce* reasons for acting as it *tracks* them.[18]

Practical calculation trails after truths, new means to attaining determinate ends, helpful hints from those who have gone before, and established techniques. This is, I take it, a kind of basic presupposition of a calculative picture of practical reasoning: the "reasoning" bit is just ordinary reasoning of a perfectly familiar sort, aided, say, by imagination and such creativity as is involved in finding new applications for older ways of doing things, and also by hitting upon novel techniques to solve familiar kinds of problems given a changed set of definite parameters. In short, calculative deliberation *seeks* aptness, rather than somehow *making* things apt. In this sense, *that* the reasoning occurs is not the important point. What is important is rather that the reasoning *follow* in the furrows of the true and the useful, or extend these in the direction of the plausible. This point of contrast is the starting place for my response to the deliberative theorist.

Noncalculative Practical Reasoning

In describing the contrast between calculative and noncalculative deliberation, David Wiggins wrote:

> It is absolutely plain what counts as my having adequate covering or as my having succeeded in drawing a plane figure of the prescribed kind using only a ruler and compass. The practical question here is only what means and measures will work or work best or most easily to those ends. But the standard problem in a nontechnical deliberation is quite different. In the nontechnical case I shall characteristically have an extremely vague description of what I want—a good life, a satisfying profession, an interesting holiday, an amusing evening—and the problem is not to see what will be causally efficacious in bring this about but to see what really *qualifies* as an adequate and practically realizable specification of what would satisfy this want.[19]

The view I have been laying out isn't exactly that calculative or technical practical reasoning is entirely a matter of finding "causally efficacious" means by which to attain determinate ends. This is *one* form such reasoning might take, but it could just as well trace constitutive part–whole relations, or else involve straightforward demonstrative inference, neither of which looks like causal reasoning by contemporary philosophical lights. But the point of contrast is clear enough. And this is why engaging in practical reasoning is not always necessary in the calculative case.

It would be slightly hysterical to hold a narrowly deliberative account of the nature of calculative reasons for acting, to hold that no one who had not thought things through all on her own had a reason to take established means to some definite end. There is such a thing as reinventing the wheel. Far from being a mark of practical excellence, it is a *fool-*

ish thing to do unless one's further ends are such as to merit making a study of the relevant field.

Matters are otherwise with some noncalculative practical thinking. In some noncalculative cases, one *has* to go through the thinking in order to figure out what to pursue, and what will count as solving the problem is in no sense contained in an adequate statement of the problem. Because the thinking generates not only determinate ends but also such support as there might be for pursuing them and a sense of what further end, exactly, they are meant to serve, noncalculative deliberation is not simply on the trail of something that is in some sense already there, either in the form of a preexisting technique or kind of whole activity with learnable parts, or else in the form of a problem so well-defined as to provide something like criteria for its own successful solution. The thinking bit in noncalculative practical deliberation is essential, not optional, *not* one way things might have gotten accomplished (although one could instead have simply looked something up or asked someone how to do the thing in question), but the *only* way one could wind up with a clear course. Make this the second premise in my response to the deliberative theorist:

2. Solving a calculative practical problem need not involve practical deliberation whereas sorting through a noncalculative practical problem requires engaging in practical deliberation.

Why? Consider, one of Wiggins's examples: wanting an interesting holiday. If one is going to argue that wanting an interesting holiday gives Jack a reason to book a week's stay in a Key West resort, one needs to be able to say something about Jack and something about Key West that will show why *he* might find *that* kind of holiday interesting. Indeed, Jack needs to be able to say something about himself and his destination if he takes it that wanting an interesting holiday gives him a reason for vacationing at Key West. If you ask, "But why *Key West?*" and he replies (in all sincerity), "Any holiday that takes me to an unfamiliar place is for me interesting," then he has given no reason for selecting Key West rather than some other destination (which was the aim of his deliberation, after all). His practical consideration would equally well have supported a holiday in my garden shed. He needs to have found something about Key West particularly interesting to go from wanting an interesting holiday to wanting a Key West vacation.[20] And some form of practical deliberation has to have made the difference, if only the sort that is involved in having daydreams of paradise, coming across a travel brochure about Key West, finding this place especially intriguing in light of the fantasy, and so booking a stay there.

How Jack finds his way to Key West involves a change in the state of the world of a particular sort. By hypothesis, at t, Jack has an inchoate want (another agent might have a problematic determinate end in view, or a choice between incompatible ends that cannot be resolved in light of her further ends, or views about what sorts of things she ought to do and a circumstance in which anything she does do will be at odds with some part of what she ought to do); at $t + 1$, however, our agent has new determinate ends and a sense of how to attain them. What occurred in the interval is practical deliberation. Because, according to deliberative theorists, practical deliberation is or could have been responsible for the *change in the state of the world* from bewildered or puzzled agent to newly determined agent, "practical reasoning" must be functioning in deliberative accounts as the description of some kind of event. In short, deliberative accounts of reasons-for-acting treat practical deliberation as something that comes in *episodes,* as a kind of event, and this is so even in cases where no deliberation took place, but the theorist holds that *had* sound deliberation occurred, the agent *would have* settled upon B-ing as her primary end. The hypothetical is a counterfactual. The "fact" in question is the occurrence of an episode of practical reasoning. This is the third premise of my response to the deliberative objection:

3. The practical deliberation required in order to solve a noncalculative practical problem is itself a kind of event.

Episodes of Practical Reasoning

What are the characteristics of an episode of practical deliberation? What manner of event is this? Practical deliberation is an activity *directed at* deciding what to do. As such, it can succeed (one settles on a suitable action or course of action) or fail to reach its intended destination (one worries and worries and cannot decide). It can be interrupted (as when a pot boils over while one is sitting at the table trying to decide how to handle little John's trouble at school, and one leaves off thinking about John in order to save the soup). It can be interfered with (as when you are just about to figure out how to end the war without compromising national interests and the enemy kidnaps you and drugs you and you are not able to complete your thought). It can go well or badly. It can be timely, long overdue, or wasteful.

Further, the need to stop and think about what to do next can be something that you notice and think about. Say you are pressed to make an important decision rather quickly. You can give it some thought if you are willing to postpone one of your projects, or no thought if you try to accomplish everything on time, but you can't give it as much thought as you would like. You say to yourself, "I'll be late with project P and spend the afternoon deciding whether or not to do this thing. I don't want to go on impulse with this one. It's too important."

And here comes premise four. Practical reasoning itself has the structure familiar from Anscombe's work on intentional action, and displays the features of intentional action that I outlined above in discussing the virtues of the standard picture. Sometimes, one needs to do it in order to figure out what to do or pursue. Other times not. Practical reasoning is an event with a calculative form. One wants to know what to do. One attains the end when one decides what to do. If what "comes to mind" or "goes through one's head" between setting out to figure out, for example what to plant and deciding what to plant has the sort of relevance to the garden project that it must if we are to describe as the content of gardening-directed practical reasoning—rather than, say, idle speculation or the inward rehearsal of a song that is stuck in one's head,—then this will be because the process was a means to, or part of, deciding what to do.[21] In short, the reasoning must be a means to or part of decision-making; otherwise, what's taking place isn't *practical deliberation* at all. This is my fourth premise:

> 4. The kind of event at issue in noncalculative practical deliberation operates as a means to or part of deciding what to do.

This end, the end of figuring out what to do, must be in place to guide and constrain the operation of practical reason in a *bona fide* episode of practical deliberation. *This* end is what marks one's attempt at practical deliberation as a failure if one winds up with no idea what to do. *This* end is what allows us to see that getting caught up in wondering what the neighbors are up to is a distraction from your deliberative process, that having someone snatch up the notepad where you've been working things out and refuse to give it back is an obstacle or interruption, and so on. *This* end is also what allows us to see an error in reason if you pay no attention to what you can reasonably expect to accomplish when you are deciding what to pursue. The antecedent specification of your end (namely, deciding what to do) is presupposed in our very description of your thought process as an episode of practical reasoning.

Aquinas offered various arguments to the effect that practical reasoning could not get off the ground without an antecedently specified end. Some of them would not be accepted nowadays (for instance, "A fault is never attributed to an agent, if the failure is related to something that is not the agent's end. Thus, the fault of failing to heal is imputed to the physician, but not to the builder or the grammarian.")[22] (I take it that we are happy to fault people for their primary ends—otherwise, there would not be whole schools of contemporary ethics in which the claim is made that even a scoundrel has a reason to change his ways quite apart from his view of what matters in life.) Another of Aquinas's arguments, however, is more likely to attract our interest:

> [I]f an agent did not incline toward some definite effect, all results would be a matter of indifference for him. Now, he who looks upon a manifold number of things with indifference no more succeeds in doing one of them than another. Hence, from an agent contingently indifferent to alternatives no effect follows, unless he be determined to one effect by something. So it would be impossible for him to act. Therefore, every agent tends toward some determinate effect, and this is called his end.[23]

Here, even if we do agree, we will point out that it does not occur to Aquinas that people might be routinely at a loss about what to pursue, that he imagines that people are always already up to something.[24] This is true. And it is also true that contemporary emphasis has shifted the ground of discussion for theorists of practical reason considerably. The business of setting ends for oneself has become the focus of contemporary work on practical reason. The thought nowadays is that the first business of practical deliberation is not figuring out how to attain primary ends, but rather determining which primary ends to pursue. But the literature on setting ends is literature on events of some kind— namely, what I have been calling *episodes* of practical deliberation. And guess what? These episodes have a point because they have an intended *destination.* That destination, moreover, is to be reached in the future. The look to the future is a look toward deciding what to do. Hence, reaching a decision about what to pursue is the *primary end* in light of which we can assess whether the reasoning succeeded, failed, was interrupted, hit obstacles, was sound or defective, and so on. As such, practical reasoning potentially will invite (or be part of an answer to) various of Anscombe's characteristic questions "Why?":

> Why are you sitting there staring at those bits of paper?
> I'm trying to figure out if any action is called for in the case of X.
> Why are you doing that? (E.g., Isn't it obvious? or You ought to know by now, or It's not your business, or I thought we were going to the movies!)
> I'm hoping for a promotion, and the boss will love me if I figure it out.

As Anselm Müller puts it:

> Practical thinking is, in this, rather like its typical result: acting with an intention. The action is done *with a view to* an end and *on account of* my insight that it helps to bring this end about.[25]

The practical thinker's understanding of his end guides his thinking. He can tell us what he is trying to get, and this bit of information is supposed to hang together with what he is doing, and to explain something about why he *stops* doing it when he does (paradigmatically, when he settles on a course of action).

In Sum

You cannot establish that the standard picture is false by pointing out that the *content* of some actual or possible episodes of practical reasoning will not involve explicit mention of determinate ends and the means that might be taken in their service. It is not the content of an episode of thinking that establishes the thinking as practical deliberation, after all. It is the *purpose* of the thinking that gives it this character. Notice, first off, that the content of absolutely clear-cut calculative practical reasoning can be identical to the content of a demonstrative inference: you want to do well on your logic homework and write things down to this end, and in so doing, prove a theorem in order to do well in logic class.

And second off, even if you are clueless about what to do, unless how you cope with your own bafflement amounts to doing various things in order to figure out what to do, your response to your quandary won't count as practical reasoning at all. If what you are doing counts as practical reasoning, this will be because the steps you take are taken *in order to* figure out what to do. Again, the "in order to" form of thought is the one that tracks the calculative relation in action.

Moreover, for at least some practical quandaries, some ways of determining primary ends will be better than others. For example, if I have just inherited a dilapidated house, and if I have neither any part of the builder's art nor any understanding of the local real estate market, I will do best to consult a builder and a realtor if I am trying to determine whether to keep the structure with an eye toward repairing and inhabiting it, raze it, wait to sell it, sell it now and acquire more suitable digs with the profit, or what have you. I am at a loss what to do, and have nothing in me that would put me in a good position to make a wise decision.

If I face a different kind of problem, if, for example, the decision about what to pursue is radically unconstrained, if nothing could even count as sound advice under some circumstances, then it is unclear why we wouldn't describe my "end-setting" as just plunking for something in order to get on with it. Plunking does not have a rich calculative form. But neither is it an exercise of reason.

The deep point about practical reason is that without an end, there is nothing to engage or direct practical reason, and this is so even when the end is "setting" primary or secondary ends. This, then, is my conclusion:

> Whether the content of an episode of practical deliberation makes specific mention of ends and means, the form of any episode of practical deliberation is end-governed; in noncalculative deliberation, the end is figuring out what to pursue; in calculative deliberation, the end is figuring out how to attain an end that you already seek to attain.

So the fact that we take ourselves to be practically clueless more often than Aquinas would have dreamed possible will not get rid of the standard picture because, unless how we proceed in the midst of our ambivalence and doubt is itself by means of intentional action (that is, by means of what I have been calling *episodes* of practical reasoning that themselves are informed by the calculative relation), how we proceed will amount to merely plunking for something or other, either in some grand existential sense, or else because we face circumstances rather like those that defeated Buridan's ass. In the practical deliberation case, we are still, formally, within the purview of the standard picture. In the plunking case, we have left reason behind. I conclude, then, that rather than getting rid of the standard picture, deliberative theorists are discussing the possible contents of *calculatively ordered courses* whose end is determining what to do.

While deliberative accounts of practical reason cause trouble for contemporary instrumentalism, as near as I can tell, they do not impugn the version of the standard picture I seek to defend. Rather, they provide very useful accounts about what to do when one is in doubt about how to proceed, about why it makes sense to take the path suggested by the theorist, and about how we come to be in circumstances that call for the kind of deliberation in question. They are good-in-the-sense-useful. This seems to me a reason to *praise* them, not to criticize them.

The Normative Objection

And here one might object that it is unclear that there *is* such a thing as something being good-in-the-sense-useful. I have helped myself to this locution, but I have not said in detail how the calculative order might all on its own carry the kind of normative force suggested by seeing the useful as a region of good. To argue that the standard picture deserves the status of a default picture of practical reason, it is not enough to show that interminable considerations all on their own cannot give us a theory of practical reason. I must also show that calculative reason all on its own could. This is the final stage of my limited defense of the standard picture.

I have been making an unusual suggestion about the standard picture: that its appeal is based on a truth about (representations of) intentional action. The more usual approach is to locate its power in some general psychological or metaphysical claim (say, that the faculty of desire is the only possible source for ends), to praise its ethical neutrality, or else to claim that adherence to the standard picture is required by due piety toward technical social science.[26] I have also, implicitly, suggested that such psychological "realism" as the standard picture can claim concerns the kind of wanting that mimics the calculative articulation of intentional action. My aim in doing so has been in part to account for the widespread hunch that calculative theories of practical reason *do not require* argumentative support, and in part to *provide arguments* in favor of one such account, the standard picture of reasons for acting. I now respond to an objection about taking the standard picture as a picture of reason in action, rather than just a point about the basic structure of purposiveness. This objection allows that intentional action as such has a means–end/part–whole articulation, but denies that anything of importance for work on practical reason hangs on this. We can formulate the challenge posed by it variously. It questions whether useful-style responses to Anscombe's "Why?" question count as desirability characterizations, say, or whether calculative reasons really are reasons for acting at all, or whether the useful is a region of good, or whether the calculative order in intentional action should be seen as bearing reason into action. Call it the *normative objection*.

Whenever we nowadays discuss calculative practical reason, we tend to talk in terms of *groups* of primary ends or *series* of choices, not in terms of the simple, organized processes Anscombe treated under the heading "*intentional actions.*" So, for example, in order to explain why *A*-ing is a better means to *B*-ing than *C*-ing for Jim, one tends to discuss the relation between *C*-ing, *A*-ing, and other things Jim means to do. But this suggests that the rationality of deciding to *A* (rather than *C*) in order to *B* only comes into focus against a backdrop involving many other practical considerations (for example, Jim's interest in *D*-ing later on). The threat is that it will turn out that intentional actions are not in and of themselves rational or irrational. They may be more or less successful, but they will only show themselves rational or irrational in light of some other sort of practical consideration. If there is a genuine principle of practical reason somewhere in the vicinity of the calculative form of intentional action, then this principle will have to be of the sort that could guide action. We will want to see whether it ever could be *violated* before dignifying its observance with terms of praise like "*rational.*"[27] (I have assumed throughout this essay that rational standing is deeply linked to practical criticism, and that a reason for acting is, as such, a potential object for criticism.)

Now, I could complain about the "do *A* rather than *C*" construe of the object of rational assessment in action that seems forced upon us by this objection. If we start out by denying that the calculative relation between A-ing and B-ing could rationalize A-ing (given that one wants to B and recognizes the calculative relation between A-ing and B-ing), then it is unsurprising that the calculative principle does not look like a genuine principle of practical reason. But neither is it at all clear that interminable practical consideration—the sorts usually expressed with phrases like "for the sake of," which can't be recast as "in order to"—fare any better than the calculative relation when pressed to justify A-ing *rather than* C-ing in cases where A-ing and C-ing could both be chosen for the sake of, say, poetry.[28] Further, since the version of the standard picture with which I am working asserts only that seeing a calculative relation between A-ing and B-ing is a *necessary* condition for having a reason to A (given that one wants to B, and so forth), and since repeated application of the "rather than" question drives one toward the search for the uniquely good solution to a practical problem (which is usually a search in vain), the "rather than" question is less obviously applicable to the version of the standard picture with which I have been working than it is to other versions. While I think that there is merit in these complaints, I do not rest content with them because they don't eliminate the point that if intentional action can't all on its own be irrational, then it can't all on its own be rational either (which is true).

I suspect that the term "rational" does point to some kind of pattern in one's pursuits. Seen in this light, the question becomes: Does the calculative form all by itself provide enough of a pattern in the event it informs (the intentional action) to make it possible for the pattern to be excellently executed in action or badly executed in action from the point of view of plain calculative practical reason? I think that it does.

A crude sort of irrationality can enter into the crude processes I've been discussing under the rubric "intentional actions." The irrationality to be found in crude intentional actions will enter into their calculative structure (this structure will provide the pattern that is violated in irrational intentional action). I consider three points at which calculative irrationality might show itself: (1) when the agent has taken means to a further end, that end is attained, and the agent does not thereby stop doing what she was doing in order to attain it, (2) when the agent discovers that what she is doing in order to attain an end will not work, but again keeps at it, and (3) when the agent does something in order to attain an end without having reason to suppose that what she is doing will do the trick and with good reason to suppose that what she's doing won't work. The latter is the most extreme problem and will be, in mature human agents, the most rare. What I have to offer on behalf of christening the practical problems I am about to survey as cases of "practical irrationality" is this: all exhibit failure to act in accordance with a sound grasp of the calculative order in action and so are open to calculative practical criticism, and in each case the failure is the kind of thing the agent could admit was a problem. If there was such a thing as basic calculative irrationality of a sort provided for by the informal version of the standard picture on which I have been relying, this is the form it would *have* to take. My discussion of calculative irrationality is by way of examples. One of them is familiar from Anscombe's work. One is meant to be a common kind of thing that sometimes happens. And one is a true-life adventure. All rely on the thought that the calculative form is a pattern and that successful intentional action shows a practically rational grasp of that pattern.

The first point of entry for irrationality concerns the sense in which attaining an end provides a natural stopping place for means–end action. Suppose I have mislaid my keys and think that I may have left them in my purse. I sit down, empty my purse entirely and sort through its contents carefully, then repack my purse. I am supposed to stop checking my purse for my keys. This is a basic "supposed to" of calculative practical reason. One familiar form of practical irrationality is being unable to stop doing something once you've accomplished what you set out to do. It is a mild failure: the things that you keep on doing will exhibit calculative form (I keep rechecking my purse, hunting for my keys), but the end in service of which you were doing those things is attained (I have determined that the keys are not there), you have no further end in view, and you aren't exactly having fun. Some people who have this problem describe it as a kind of neurotic tic that leads one to continue doing the things one was doing *solely* as means to attaining an end after the end is attained and, thus, after the calculative reason for doing them has vanished.[29] That is how they make trouble in an intention.

The second point where irrationality might enter into intentional action occurs when one discovers that the linkage between what one is doing and what one means to accomplish thereby is not in place.

Anscombe treats it at some length.[30] Suppose you ask me why I am pumping and I explain that I'm replenishing the water supply for the house and you point out that there is a hole in the pipe leading to the cistern, that all the water is running out, and that I cannot replenish the water supply by pumping.[31] Again, I am supposed to stop pumping. And, again, this is no mere descriptive "supposed to." While we would indeed predict that I will stop pumping on discovering the leak, we make this prediction because my reason for pumping will have vanished and I ought either to stop and repair the pipe, get someone else to fix it, find another way to replenish the water supply, or give up. If I get mad or stubborn or try to convince myself that maybe a little water is trickling through and keep pumping a minute or two more, I display a part–whole variant of can't-stop irrationality: I no longer have reason to suppose that pumping *amounts to* replenishing the water supply (which was my reason for pumping), and still I pump.

The third point of entry concerns a deeper problem with an intention. My example of it is taken from a party I attended a few years back. A man at the party was doing wonderful card magic for us and one of the guests suddenly said, "Let me!" He handed her the deck of cards, and she then proceeded to shuffle them, ask us to pick cards, and so on. It soon became clear that she had no idea how to do card magic. Finally she said, blushing, "This is irrational, huh?" And all of us nodded and laughed.[32] This form of irrationality is the kind that prompts one to ask, in annoyance or amusement, "What on earth do you think you're doing?" (at least, when one is asking what whole activity is supposed to be taking place, with the suspicion that the agent isn't managing to do the kind of thing in question and the thought that the agent knows better than to imagine he could B by A-ing—the question has other uses as a form of rudeness or to suggest that rules are being broken).

The homely examples of this kind of failure to act in accordance with one's own rational powers tend to crop up when one is alone. Sometimes, when no one else is looking, even a grown-up will set out to do something that she knows she can't actually do, if only because it would be such a pleasant surprise if she could do it. Although she is scarcely able to avoid belly flops when diving into the water, finding that she has the pool to herself for a change, she leaps from the diving board intending to do a double-twisting pike, having seen someone do one in competition and being struck at how fine it must feel to do such a thing. Afterward, she counts herself lucky that she wasn't seriously injured, and is very glad that no one else saw her contortions. Or this: feeling bored one afternoon, she thinks how pleasant it would be to have some cake, and sets about "making one" with neither a mix nor a recipe, even though she lacks not just skill at baking but any other kind of culinary expertise that might be extended in that direction, and so has no reason to suppose she stands a good chance of figuring out how to bake a cake. The result goes quietly into the good night of the rubbish, and she cleans up the kitchen before anyone arrives to ask what she was up to. In these cases, the agent knows that she lacks the skill required to do what she intends to do, but goes at it anyway, on impulse or out of boredom. One of the reasons one tends not to do such things in the presence of others is that one somehow expects to fail, and doesn't want to have to discuss how one both knew one couldn't B yet set out to B in spite of this.

In all three sorts of cases, the kind of irrationality in question makes trouble in the intention. In the more sophisticated examples involving, say, intransitive ends, we find a more subtle version of the same kind of problem.

Reasons for Acting

The noncalculative theorist holds that practical reason *requires* that one pay heed to interminable practical considerations. The calculative theorist should respond by asking "Why?" There are three sorts of interminable practical considerations that might inform action. Let's take them in turn.

Pleasure, on the standard picture, is a source of ends. In acting from and for pleasure, the agent seeks to sustain a delightful nexus of agent, action, and circumstance. There is no particular reason to do this. There may, however, be reasons to *stop:* one stops when the pleasure has flown (the reason to keep at it has vanished), or in order to end on a pleasant note *before* the pleasure has flown (for example, in order to avoid pain, to provide oneself an incentive to do the thing again soon, to make good memories, or some such), or because it is time to get on with other things. All three of the cases have calculative structure, as is obvious in the scheduling case and the case where one stops before the pleasure has flown in order to accomplish something else. In the case where pleasure flees, what has become clear on the standard picture is that it is no longer possible to sustain the nexus of person, circumstance, and action—that is, what one is doing is no longer a means to that end.

Similarly, there is no threat posed to a calculative view of practical reason by befitting-style practical considerations that are only interminable in practice, that is to say, those concerned with recurrent ends, with a self-chosen or endorsed role (like being a poet or a parent or a friend), with plans, or with securing goods like wealth or honor, and those rooted in the internalization of social practices that are collectively useful (for example, virtues on an account like Geach's, or etiquette).

The only threat to a calculative view would come from the claim that we need the guidance of a radically interminable patterning principle in setting ends. What, then, of radically interminable patterning principles, like poetry or duty (on some accounts of these)? A calculative theorist who is willing to allow that there are such things as acting from and for a radically interminable patterning principle can cope with the admission by treating the principle as some among the many sources of human ends, and suggesting that one acts to attain the ends provided by the principle just as one acts in order to attain other of one's ends. There is no special reason to do this. Rather, the reason there *is* is calculative (one does such-and-such for the sake of poetry, or because one means to do one's duty) and carries the force of end-based practical justification.

This response will not satisfy noncalculative theorists. Some additional considerations might help. Notice, first off, that *no one* seemed to feel the need to account for radically interminable patterning principles in premodern philosophy, which all by itself puts a strain on the view that they are first principles of practical reason. For whereas you need to understand what is distinctive about modern science in order to do justice to questions in philosophy of science, and perhaps in metaphysics and epistemology as well, practical reason is supposed to have been around all the while that people have been around, and in operation in roughly the same way wherever people have been.

Second, notice that, from the point of view of what gets done, the conduct of a man acting from a radically interminable patterning principle might be *identical* to the conduct of a man who, for whatever reason—personal advantage, perversity, neurosis, a strong desire to lay claim to higher ground, self-deception about the character of his own motive—merely acts in accordance with the dictates of the pattern. That is, while there might be people out there who act from and solely for the sake of realizing the demands of radically interminable principles, it is not as though what they do need be any different from what the rest of us do.

It might be objected that the rest of us *need* the pure exemplars in order to have any grip on how to live, say, poetically or dutifully. But here, as a third consideration, notice that, because for all we can tell it is merely *possible* that someone sometimes acts strictly from and for the sake of whatever radically interminable principle we have in mind, it isn't entirely clear that a world in which *no one* succeeded in so purifying his will would be a world lacking in role models for the rest of us. If we take it into our heads to pursue novel, fabulous things, or act in order to let poetry come through, or to do only as duty permits, it is possible to explain what happens by treating morality, art, and hipness as determinate, recurrent ends that lend, basically, the same kind of calculative order to our affairs as does such things as the need to sleep sometimes and to eat something now and again. That is, we can explain and justify what gets done by pointing to the agents' ends and the things done as means to or parts of attaining those. In this sense, it certainly *looks* as though we can get by without making a story about radically interminable patterning principles central to our theory of individual practical reason.

Here it might be objected that we need radically interminable principles to establish rational order in individual life *noncontingently*. How else can there be reasoned choice of final ends? First, there is no reason to suppose that final ends, even desirable final ends, could or should have a singular source. Even Kant held that we are necessarily interested in securing conditions conducive to our own happiness—an end that does not come from reason, in his view, but sets important limits on any plausible theory of human reason (large portions of Kant's corpus, for instance, are devoted to trying to square duty with a natural, necessary interest in faring well). Noncontingency need not be a matter of reason.

Second, without final ends in place to constrain some part of the operation of practical reason, it is entirely unclear what will count as successful practical reasoning. This is so even if the ends are given by social practices like promising or by principles like Spicer's poetry. Notice that, to the extent that Spicer's account made sense, it made sense because the claim was that one had to get out of the way *in order to* let poetry come through. The specific technical suggestions were suggestions about how to gauge one's success in these terms, and how to interrupt the dear self in its efforts to express itself. Without at least this much end-specification in place, we would be down to something on the order of a quasi-mystical doctrine with no obvious point of practical application. "Do what conduces to producing great literature" is so far from a bit of helpful advice as to fail to count as advice at all. Even Kant's magnificent turn on the Golden Rule at least had a bit of the Golden Rule at its core to help guide deliberation and give theorists some sense of how he was understanding the principles underlying what plain people know well enough (namely, their duty). (I take up Kant more directly, but very briefly, in Appendix C.)

Radically interminable accounts of patterns in human affairs are creatures of theory, after all (of moral theory and of some forms of aesthetic theory—for example, Russian formalism in literary analysis, Spicer's practical poetics). Whether the accounts in question are accounts *of* principles of conduct is, I think, still an open question. Moreover, *no* such account about individual practical reason has secured widespread agreement on the part of contemporary, secular practical philosophers. Instead, often as not, what we find in contemporary work are stories about how allowing a radically interminable practical principle to shape your affairs is a means to or part of attaining some important end. And we don't even agree about *those* stories. The standard picture, on the other hand, is lodged squarely in territory that no clear-headed practical philosopher can afford to ignore.

That is how a calculative theorist ought to respond to a noncalculative theorist, I think.

Further, I am convinced that the version of the standard picture that I have treated at length is *rightly* viewed as a default theory of practical reason. I see no sign that any of the secular theorists of practical reason who has been arguing against instrumentalism recently has taken the calculative order in intention and action seriously enough to do more than tilt at straw men. In this sense, I think that the standard picture is untouched by contemporary assaults on instrumentalism and its treatment of (Humean or neo-Humean) desire as a component of reasons for acting.

The modern philosophical interest in providing a noncalculative theory of practical reason has centered on the need to find rational support for morality, or for some other department of the ethical. If this is what we seek, then, as I have mentioned, my doubts about noncalculative theories of practical reason are not lessened by the fact that we have mostly ignored medieval Christian moral philosophy. The medieval patristic and scholastic philosophers had it in their favor that they needed to make sense of the idea that people could be held accountable for their sins. Under the assumption that you are only held accountable for what you do when you have your wits about you (you can, of course, do all kinds of things that will tend to deprive you of full use of your faculties, and then the question becomes whether you did wrong in so disabling yourself), this meant that the Christian philosophers needed to understand the rational structure of unethical action and the reasoning behind it. We have tended to ignore accounts of the rational order in wrongdoing in contemporary, secular work on practical reason. The result is akin to trying to describe what it is like to walk when you have let one of your legs atrophy and have forgotten how it was to have the full use of both limbs—one half of the apparatus is a dull, numb thing that gets dragged along without your being able to feel the vitality it once had. As I have also mentioned, the resulting blank spot in our work does not give me confidence that we will come up with a compelling secular noncalculative theory of reason in action that does the job of demonstrating how individual wrongdoing is necessarily imperfectly rational.

Nevertheless, part of the way in which the defense of the standard picture that I have given is limited is just this: for all I know, someone will produce the strictly noncalculative argument needed to compel widespread, secular philosophical agreement that the standard picture is false, whether or not that argument provides the so-far elusive account of how every individual failure to act ethically betrays a sin against practical reason. I, for one, would owe the author of such an argument my deepest gratitude.

This concludes my diagnosis of the source of our conviction that something about instrumental reason is crucial to understanding practical rationality. It also concludes my limited defense of a standard picture of reasons for acting. I am fairly certain that the diagnosis is sound, and I supply some notes in Appendix E to the effect that something like this version of the standard picture underlies some otherwise very puzzling intuitions that drive formal work on decision and choice. In Chapter 8, I turn to ethics in light of my limited defense of the standard picture.

8

Ethics

In looking at the world *as it is,* we shall find it folly to deny that, to worldly success, a surer path is Villainy than Virtue. What the Scriptures mean by the *"leaven* of unrighteousness" is that leaven by which men *rise.*

—Edgar Poe

Throughout my defense of the standard picture I have followed current practice in supposing that the locus of thought about practical reason is in thought about individual adult human beings in full possession of their powers as agents. Throughout my sporadic engagements with ethical topics, I have gone along with the thought that providing an account of the much-sought link between practical reason and ethics is a matter of showing that the individual human who knowingly and deliberately acts unethically thereby fails to do as practical reason recommends. I have expressed serious skepticism about the possibility of producing such an account, suggesting that whatever sorts of defect may plague deliberate unethical conduct are not defects of plain practical reason. In a way, Poe's aphorism[1] expresses why I think this. Sound exercise of individual practical reason ought somehow to conduce to the individual's faring well by his own lights. While conscientious good people doubtless profit from their goodness by their own lights, this is, I suspect, because their sense of what it means for them to fare well is partly a matter of their acting well.[2]

One obvious way to produce a straightforward calculative link between acting well and faring well is to leave control of the worldly goods off the list of things that conduce to faring well, or at least to assign control of worldly goods an inferior and subordinate status, since individual pursuit of these is usually better served by vice than virtue. The principle that controls cultivation of vice is, after all, the end of acquiring substantial control over worldly goods, using the available means. By contrast, Nature does not aim to reward individual virtue with worldly goods. Once the worldly goods have taken a duly subordinate role in our account of human good, however, our readers may well accuse us of failing to give due regard to faring well in our account of acting well (or of living well, for that matter).

It is, of course, a defect in a society if it routinely rewards vice and punishes virtue, if this is somehow engineered into its basic institutional structure. But this is, I suspect, because the unit that is served by individual cultivation of virtue is first a larger social unit, a collective. And while none of us will survive past infancy if some form of collective is not in place to equip us with what we need in order to make our way in variously complex social worlds, and while viciousness succeeds just in case there are enough channels or individuals around to make it possible to control goods by vicious means that could not exist outside an elaborate social world, the essential parasitism of vice does not seem to prevent vicious people from securing worldly goods.

Part of what can be gained from reading Aquinas on human evil is a sense that it is *not* the theoretically sophisticated immoralists (figments of philosophical imagination), nor even historical moral monsters, who threaten our sense that immorality is irrational. Rather, it is an embodied practical orientation favoring worldliness.

Such an orientation may be a very quiet affair. We see it in a man who has no close friends, no attachment to good causes unless working for them is independently personally rewarding (as when, for instance, he takes vicarious pleasure in the energy and passion of others who work for them), no sense that what he does is intrinsically useful to anybody else; the man who is careful with his money and his health, enjoys fine things, and privately suspects that others who seem to burden themselves with debt or unhappiness for the sake of strangers are saps. Such a person does not really respect other people as such, and this lack may show itself in many acts of wrongdoing—in telling smallish self-serving lies, for instance, or cheating here and there whenever he is unlikely to suffer any bad consequences from doing so. He is likely to be greedy and envious. He may also be prone to the self-regarding, banked anger of resentment. He is proud of things that would not seem to merit a self-congratulatory posture. His caution seems more a species of cowardice than prudence. Such warmth as he shows the world is in the heat of a burst of temper, the flush of the prospect of private gain, or such passion as attaches to petty intrigues pursued gratuitously—at any rate, *not* the healthy glow of an open heart. Basically, the sorts of goods that one is tempted to call "goods of the spirit" do not animate this man's life, however unbearable he might find the thought that there is *anything* worth having that he can't somehow get. This man does not merely act ill now and then (although he will do when he stands to gain safely thereby). He lives ill. And if he is clever, he does so in a way that is unlikely to cost him much by his lights.

As the tone of my sketch ought to suggest, I agree that there is something wrong with this sort of person, a type of person commonly at ease in avowedly secular and rationalist contexts where great stress is placed on individual achievements and these achievements are abstract (for instance, accomplishing something that draws a lot of attention from one's fellows but does not obviously serve any larger purpose). What is wrong with the worldly man? What the calculative theorist must say, I think, is that he is unethical. What the calculative theorist cannot say, I think, is that the worldly man's lack of virtue marks him as irrational.

Ethical Considerations

In this chapter, I return to some points about ethics and the standard picture that I touched on earlier. I make an argument or two in this chapter, but my concern chiefly is to discuss the costs of embracing the version of the standard picture that I have defended. Although I suspect that people sometimes act from and for the sake of pleasure or radically interminable patterning principles, my qualms about providing an overarching systematic theory of the centrality of noncalculative considerations to practical reason place me in the same boat as an instrumentalist with respect to ethics. The structure of my remarks in this chapter involve entertaining and rejecting various suggestions about how an advocate of the standard picture might help herself to claims that individual unethical conduct is invariably irrational insofar as unethical.

Reason in the Long Run

It might be thought that an advocate of the standard picture could have more to say on behalf of ethical patterning principles than I have so far offered. It might be thought that a calculative theorist could lever her way into arguing that leading a practically rational mature human life requires that adults work to put some patterning principles into practice, that one must have some sort of overarching pattern in one's affairs on pain of irrationality. From there, considerations about overall well-being or flourishing might support, say, substantive ethical conclusions based in a calculative picture of reason in action. I do not think that the calculative theorist is entitled to make these moves.

One strength of the view I have defended is that it finds pattern enough for reason to get a grip in the singular course of action. This in turn suggests, however, that it will be hard to argue that one *must* have a larger plan in order to have reason governing one's pursuits. This places my calculative theorist at odds with many instrumentalists who rely on large systems of ends and thought about the centrality of planning in human life in order to support conclusions that calculative reason favors granting befitting-style practical considerations pride of place in rational life (befitting-style considerations that are merely interminable in practice, mind you, but befitting-style considerations nevertheless).

On the version of the standard picture that I have defended, it is unclear that anyone who thinks no more than a day ahead will display essential irrationality. There are many kinds of circumstances, for instance, where one has good reason to suppose that one's long-term interests will be exhausted in a very short while (consider Anscombe's Nazi). There are widely influential schools of thought about what is good in life that insist that unencumbered absorption in the present moment is what makes life worth living, and that worry about what will come of it at some future time is both vain and the chief source of evil. In both of these cases, the friend of long-term interest might reply that it is no objection to his view that many people think that the best way to spend the whole of one's life is by focusing on vivid appreciation of each moment or that if one is about to die, one should adjust one's plans accordingly. In the former case, there *is* a view about long-term interests—it is just that living well is living in the moment. In the latter, circumstances have simply derailed one's prospects in a way that makes it inappropriate to look to the long run.

It is harder to see how my kind of calculative theorist could respond to objections drawn from other sorts of cases, however. Consider a life lived as it comes along, with no eye toward the big picture, the sort of life Paul Bowles described in his autobiography. Near the conclusion he noted: "In my tale . . . there are no dramatic victories because there was no struggle. I hung on and waited. It seems to me that this must be what most people do."[3] There is an aura of ruefulness in this admission. But this aspect of the tone is in part, I think, because Bowles is at pains to *deny* that he has some higher principle governing his moves (his title is *Without Stopping,* by which he seems to mean without governance by an ultimate end, even of the sort involved in doing the parts of a life plan). A tone of triumph in the end might suggest that he was an advocate of the centrality of spontaneity as an organizing principle in life, and this is part of what we are *not* supposed to conclude. For all that, there is a lot of exuberance in the memoir of going here and there, spurred on mostly by chance encounters with opportunity and the odd collection of people who can come into a life not rendered closed to their influence by a definite plan. There may or may not be some other sort of problem in such a life—it is, for example, a difficult setting for child-rearing—but on its own such a life isn't obviously contrary to plain calculative reason. It is a sort of life more commonly encountered among the very poor and the very rich than among members of the North Atlantic middle classes. But my point is that the calculative relation orders intentional action and courses whether one goes at life as it comes or settles on a definite course. If the calculative relation is the source of reasons for acting, it will retain this status whether one does one thing, then another, then another, or cannot keep track of all the irons in the fire without a multiyear agenda book. This is another sense in which the standard picture retains the form of ethical neutrality claimed for instrumentalism, and at a similar cost.

To argue that a man who sees no reason to cultivate long-term projects and plans sins against reason, in my view, is to produce the prudential version of an ethical external reason statement. The most serious drawbacks of the standard picture revolve around its failure to see a legitimate place for such statements, and I turn to them in the next section, then to where this failure leaves us in some remarks about ethical skepticism.

What about External Reasons?

In sharpening the point at issue between calculative and noncalculative theorists, I settled on:

Noncalculative theorists insist that there can be reasons for an agent to B quite apart from her plans, projects, particular attachments, character, skills, habits, or further ends; the calculative theorist denies this.

That is, the version of the standard picture that I have defended involves internalism about reasons for acting in a broad sense of "internalism"—a sense related to the one that Bernard Williams has embraced. To say that Smith has a reason for A-ing on this view is to say that there is something about Smith, and something about A-ing, that makes A-ing useful to him, or fitting for him to do, or pleasant for him to linger in doing, where the latter two count as reasons just in case they bear some fairly tight relation to calculative concerns. In Williams's locution, if Smith has a reason to A, then A-ing stands in some nonaccidental relation to Smith's "subjective motivational set." The nonaccidental relation is one that Smith himself might trace in deliberating well about what to do. And there are various constraints on what would count as deliberating well. The constraints are, as Williams puts it, "by no means fully determinate and they are certainly not 'formal'," among other things because they "allow for such things as the exercise of imagination."[4] But we might add that at least some of these constraints are themselves coming from the calculative order in deliberation.

Deliberating is figuring out what to do, and how one goes about it is by taking means to, or doing parts of, sorting out the practical difficulties one faces. There is the possibility of error here in all three of the ways I discussed in Chapter 7: one can have hit upon a perfectly reasonable thing to do and keep returning and going over it all again; one can know that some path of investigation will not yield what one seeks (one can know, say, that there is no technique for doing what one wants to do), and yet keep banging one's head against a preferred brick wall; or one can understand that some solution is not really practicable and plunge ahead as though it were. Further, the path one takes, and how one makes one's way along it, can be better or worse. But what matters for my purposes is the general commitment to internalism embodied in the version of the standard picture at issue. For however broad-minded one is about how far an agent's subjective motivational set might be extended by however wide a range of ways of deciding what to do one cares to mention, it remains the case on this view that *without* some link (straightforwardly calculative or tenuous and hedged by hypotheticals and counterfactuals) between aspects of the agent's practical orientation and things about the action in question, there is no reason for him to do the thing in question at all. And this leaves my calculative theorist with no way to account for the practical force of the "ought" in an external "ought" statement.

An external "ought" statement holds that one has reason to A even if there is *no* sound deliberative route from one's subjective motivational set to a decision to A. The external reasons theorist need not hold that a formal argument could be waged in the service of altering a recalcitrant man's motivational set in the direction of getting him to A on some occasion even though A-ing under the circumstances runs against the grain of his subjective motivational set. The external reasons theorist can instead insist that something on the order of a radical and deep shift of character might be required to get a deeply recalcitrant man to change his ways in the direction of doing as he ought to do. But for all that, the external reasons theorist insists, it can be true of such a person that he ought to A, and that he therefore has a reason for A-ing, a reason that floats free of the constraints of his subjective motivational set and finds its home elsewhere (say, in a substantive account of ethical life). As John McDowell puts it, the transition from being unmoved by, say, sound ethical reasons statements to being motivated by them may be seen as "a transition *to* deliberating correctly, not one effected *by* deliberating correctly; effecting the transition may need some non-rational alteration like conversion."[5]

The kind of external reasons statement that has attracted the most attention is the ethical or moral reasons statement, addressed to someone bent on acting unethically or immorally. In this sense, like many interesting issues about reasons for acting, this one is linked to work on the question whether everyone has a reason "to be moral." This work has most often been pursued under the impact of the thought that all reasons for acting are based in desires, or that one always acts in the service of maximizing preference satisfaction, minimizing regret, or seeking satisfactory levels of preference satisfaction or regret minimization. That is, much of the work on the "Why be moral?" question revolves around contemporary instrumentalism. In this setting, the debate gives good reason to doubt instrumentalism. It does not impugn the standard picture in the same way, however.

Instrumentalism and External Reasons

In a sense, from a narrowly instrumentalist point of view, *all* ethical and moral reasons statements are "external." For example, "I am A-ing because I promised to A" is supposed to explain why you A when you would prefer *not* to A, as when you explain leaving off doing something productive or pleasant in order to keep a dull appointment. While some of us are nowadays happy to postulate further beliefs or preferences to explain why people do things they don't especially want to do under these circumstances, actually, by instrumentalists' lights, it is pretty hard to explain. It is a hard problem from an instrumentalist perspective because promises serve to get people to do things in the *absence* of any clear desire or preference to do them and in the *presence* of purposes that will be thwarted or delayed by promise-keeping. Anscombe makes the point this way:

> What ways are there for getting human beings to do things? You can make a man fall over by pushing him; you cannot usefully make his hand write a letter or mix concrete by pushing; for in general if you have to push his hand in the right way, you might as well not use him at all. You can order him to do what you want, and if you have authority he will perhaps obey you. Again, if you have power to hurt him or help him according as he disregards or obeys your orders, or if he loves you so as to accord with your requests, you have ways of getting him to do things. . . . Now getting one another to do things without the application of physical force is a necessity in human life, and that far beyond what can be secured by those other means.[6]

If I love you or fear you, then there is no need to get me to promise to do anything. You need only let me know what you would have me do, and if I can do it without unduly injuring myself, I will. I will do it for your sake if I love you. I will do it for my own sake if I fear you. Whatever the case, how things are between the two of us makes it possible for you to get me to do things. But if you instead rely on extracting promises to get me to do something, and if this technique is effective, then your strategy depends on the thought that sometimes people will keep promises when some of their purposes will be thwarted or delayed by doing their word. And as Anscombe also points out, "one constantly has such purposes."[7] Because one constantly has purposes that must be set aside in order to do what one ethically or morally ought to do, there is a sense in which, for instrumentalists, all such "ought" statements are external. Further, because the forces of love and fear, however powerful, are not generally enough to generate coordinating systems of desire adequate to the task of making possible complex, ethicopolitical cooperative social life, the externality of moral "ought" statements is a serious problem for instrumentalism. The example of promise-keeping can help explain how serious.

If the problem about promise-keeping for instrumentalists is that it involves doing things one would rather not when various ways of breaking one's promises would involve doing as one likes, if there are rarely dire consequences to breaking ordinary promises, and if people sometimes keep promises in this sort of tight corner (which is, ordinarily, ubiquitous), then, understood as a substantive thesis about the subjective conditions of action, "All action aims at maximal preference satisfaction or minimal regret" is *prima facie* false. (If "All action aims at sufficient levels of preference satisfaction or regret minimization" isn't *also* demonstrably false in light of normal-person promise-keeping, this is only because it is rather vague and may not be capable of being shown to be false by counterexample.) Additionally, if "because I promised to A" gives a *reason* for A-ing, then, again *prima facie*, "All reasons for acting are desire-based" is false. On many contemporary views about the character of moral reasons, the promise-keeper case could be extended to cover the whole field of duties and properly ethical concerns. In principle and in general, acting for the sake of moral or ethical concerns involves acting well in a way that is at odds with faring well (in the short run, at least) since there is always *something* more pleasant or profitable to do than get caught up by ethical matters (for example, catch a movie, take exercise, read, chat with a friend, nap, daydream), there are often very few dire consequences to doing as one pleases rather than doing what one ethically should do, and even if one has a positive desire to do as one morally or ethically ought to do, the proof of one's moral or ethical strength of character comes when one *hasn't* any such urge to act morally or ethically. Basically, in light of any ordinary ethical action pursued in the face of any opportunity cost and in the absence of any intention to further one's own interests by moral or ethical means, instrumentalism is *prima facie* false.

Much secular moral philosophy holds that acting *from* the relevant principles *always* involves incurring opportunity costs without any counterbalancing private gain in view. Moreover, thought about what it is to act *from*, rather than merely *in accordance with,* morality or ethics is drawn from reflection on reasonably smooth social life, the kind that is scarcely conceivable and certainly unexpected if people are incapable of forgoing private, short-term advantage for the sake of doing as they ethically or morally should. For to expect smooth social life without presupposing our capacity for ethical or moral conduct is to imagine that force, fears, and loves alone are enough to get us to behave decently with one another. And this is probably not how things are with us. It is hard enough to account for what happens in such tight-knit social circles as functioning families on the force-love-and-fear hypothesis, let alone to extend it to cover larger social organizations that manage to operate well without the lubrication of sentiment. Which is to say that, on the face of it, reasonably smooth social life cannot be theorized by instrumentalism as the nonaccidental outcome of sound individual exercises of practical reason. On a strictly instrumentalist picture of reasons for acting, moral "ought" statements are, all of them, *externalist.* Hence, on a strictly instrumentalist picture of reasons for acting, moral claims *as such* do *not* provide reasons for acting at all.

Now it may well be that reasonably smooth social life is rare. And it may well be that determination to seek private advantage provides some explanation for this, with additional explanatory resources to be found in the fact that very strong other-directed sentiment of either the loving or fearful variety is fragile, and can resolve itself into hostility or indifference under pressure. But there are some examples of reasonably smooth social interaction among strangers out there, and the smoothness owes something to the fact that those involved can coordinate their efforts even though they have no special sentimental ties, one to another. The obvious explanation is that it is possible for the participants to forgo short-term private gain for the sake of some larger principle, that is, that the participants display a capacity for moral or ethical conduct. And this capacity looks mysterious from the instrumentalist's point of view.

One obvious response to the smooth social life counterexample is to argue that instrumentalism is *true,* but that people who do what they morally or ethically ought to do when they would rather do otherwise are to that extent irrational. This response, I take it, looks to involve holding onto a theory one shouldn't want to keep in the face of a reason to let go of it (after all, one wants to theorize good social life as one fruit of human rationality). Another response is to argue that people can have desires for smooth social life that are more powerful than their desires for private gain. This is true, but gives instrumentalists no more reason to expect smooth social life than did the force-love-and-fear hypothesis, since, according to strict instrumentalism, desires are partly arational, inconstant, and so on. A third response is to argue that moral "ought" statements, if believed true, necessarily generate desires or preferences to act morally. Even if this were true (which seems unlikely), it would involve dropping the claim that desires or preferences are arational sources of reasons for acting, since beliefs are reason-governed, and the claim is that a reason-governed state can change the tides of desire. In short, reflection on ethics or morality is enough to render instrumentalism dubious. But this kind of case leaves the standard picture, and its brand of internalism, untouched.

The Standard Picture and External Reasons

Bernard Williams is not, strictly, an instrumentalist. Neither is an advocate of the standard picture. Both Williams and such an advocate can hold that there may be things in one's character that lead one to forgo short-term gain, private advantage, rewards—in short, opportunities to fare well in the short-run—for the sake of acting well in the sense of doing as it ethically or prudentially befits one to do, and that these items do *not* have the characteristics of the instrumentalists' preferences or desires. For Williams, this happens when one's subjective motivational set contains elements that side with one's long-term private interests or with ethics. In a way, my calculative theorist agrees, although I prefer that she say that one can forgo the prospect of rewards or private gain when pursuit of them conflicts with the ends constitutive of, or produced by, patterning principles. In this sense, the version of internalism about reasons for acting that Williams embraces and that my advocate of the standard picture finds herself with does not require holding that, strictly, there are no reasons to be moral or act ethically. What it *does* require, however, is that if Smith has a reason to be moral or act ethically, this will be because Smith has it in him to act from moral or ethical practical considerations. Which, in turn, entails that, even though there are moral and ethical reasons for acting, there are no true *external reasons* statements.

Williams supports this position by pointing out that reasons to act are reasons for somebody to do something, and that the "for"-ness of reasons presses us toward internalism. A reason for acting is as such potentially explanatory of what somebody deliberately does (this is in part why one way to find reasons for acting is to think about desirability characterizations that might be offered in support of having in fact *done* this or that.) If Smith could *not* be brought round to seeing himself as having a reason to tell the truth and pay his debts, and if this failure is not caused by Smith's inability to reason, then such considerations could *not* explain his doing these things. From Smith's point of view, conduct in accordance with morality might be a species of weakness of will.

While this leaves no room to account for the force of external reasons statements, the Williamsesque internalist thinks that he does not *have* to account for the legitimate force of external reasons statements. He thinks that there could be no source for such force but the place that practical considerations have in shaping individual human lives within their cultural context, that this place is what is explained by ascribing subjective motivational sets to people, and that the point is that there is no guarantee that everyone's subjective motivational set will have elements that hook onto the kinds of considerations that are, for virtuous or dutiful people, action-guiding. To insist that people who are left cold by some considerations that others find decisive nevertheless have reason to act on the basis of those considerations is, effectively, so much "bluff."[8]

John McDowell agrees that practical considerations have the standing and force they do because of the role they play in shaping human life and conduct. But he argues that Williams's account of that role trades on neo-Humean views about the subjectivity of value which in turn rely on a deeply distorted picture of the role human psychology plays in determining what we have reason to do. The apparent emptiness of external reasons statements in Williams's account, McDowell argues, comes of the fact that Williams will not allow that external reasons statements have content and force insofar as they express truths about what is valuable and, hence, choice-worthy. Because the Williamsesque internalist will not help himself to perfectly straightforward, objective truths about value, he has no way to grasp the content and force of external reasons statements.

According to McDowell, external reasons statements are about how things are, evaluatively. That a person who has no grip on the ethical does not recognize them as reason-giving is not to say that they aren't reasons statements. It is simply to say that the unethical person is operating outside the ethical order. The reasons are external to *her* because she has not been brought up inside the evaluative, reason-giving frame that is the ethical. And although there may be no way to argue an adult into perceiving values aright when she is sunk in darkness on this matter, that does not mean that there is nothing there to be seen. It just means that she is blind to the ethical in some ways. The best hope of seeing how things stand with ethical value for a person who has not been brought up from youth in such a way as to make ethical insight possible may be some sort of nonrational shift. Conversion to the ethical, for instance.

I have not taken much of a stand on questions about the metaphysics of value. But I and my calculative theorist alike are entirely willing to grant that there are objective values. We are entirely willing to grant that people who behave excellently with one another are onto some of them, and are to be credited with genuine ethical insight and wisdom. Even granting all of this is *not enough* to save external reasons statements of the sort that interest McDowell according to the standard picture. That is, robustly objective values are not enough to make it the case that externalist "ought" statements about ethical matters and the like express reasons for acting. They may well be true statements about the ethical. But, when addressed to sufficiently nasty people, they are not reasons-for-acting statements.

McDowell's use of "conversion" in this connection is telling, I think.[9] One obstacle contemporary secular Anglo–North American practical philosophers face in arguing that externalist statements express reasons for acting is partly that we have inherited an ethical tradition grounded in systems of thought and practice that crucially concern themselves with divine providence, but we have lost the license to employ the foundational theological context in making sense of the kind of "ought" that is bound up in that context. One solution to this trouble might be to seek a grounding for ethics in ancient sources, supplemented by modern metaphysics and epistemology. But the old-fashioned "ought" is not the only thing we have inherited from a western European theological past. We also have inherited volumes and volumes of work on the rational structure of human evil, produced partly in the service of extending the ancient insights about practical reason. It is true that we neglect this work almost entirely in our discussions of the reasons to be moral. But disabused of this ignorance, it becomes for us a pressing question just in what sense a mortal being who, say, has a couple of capital vices to her credit has a reason to change her ways. Recall that capital vices organize pursuit of *as such desirable things*—no problem about objective value here, notice, no quasi- or neo- or flat-out-Humean idea about projecting values, no worries about metaphysical queerness, no hesitation in thinking things intrinsically, objectively choice-worthy, but rather a nice, robust, detailed account of objective value in light of which it is possible to theorize the rational structure of human evil-doing. The trouble is that when you lift this theory out of its theological context, you lose the ability to mount a straightforwardly calculative argument to the effect that the vicious are sunk in rational error. You can retain the thought that collective life requires that there be some virtue to steady individual persons in practice. You can retain the thought that there are many good things in human life that are inconceivable outside of a reasonably well-ordered society. You can retain the thought that ethics invariably involves a look to the wider context of collective forms of life. You can retain the thought that some modes of collective social life will be destabilized from within if marked by some modes of institutionalized injustice, for example, oppression, discriminatory practices, and domination.[10] But you need also to take into account that habituating oneself to some modes of discreetly acting ill will be individually advantageous even in a well-ordered society, that siding with justice can be individually ruinous even in a well-ordered society, and so on.

McDowell's argument against Williams's internalism won't work against an advocate of the standard picture who is constructing a godless variant of Thomism. Nor will complaints about desires or passions or bad sorts of psychologism. Nor, incidentally, will arguments to the effect that divine law ethics are somehow philosophically second-rate. It does not matter what standing secular theorists give divine law ethics generally. What matters is that divine law ethicists have left us theories not just about the rational structure of morality, but about the rational structure of immorality, and the two sorts of theories *share* an account of the objective good available in mortal life and of the social character of that good. Faced with this, and agreeing with both Williams and McDowell that reasons for acting are such because of the force they have in shaping human life, I see no way to treat all true statements about what ethics or morality calls for as statements about what everyone has reason to do or pursue.

The external reasons statement is certainly *external* to the motivational set of the vicious, but it is not a statement about reasons for acting that the vicious would appreciate if only they had a grip on what was objectively good. Quite the contrary, with Aquinas, it looks to me that you couldn't pry some of the objectively good stuff of mortal life from the hands of the vicious if your life depended on it. The vicious are likely to accuse you of trying to get them to give up a bird in the hand for a *ghost* in the bush if you try. Now it is also true that without some measure of justice, prudence, courage, and restraint, human life becomes disordered, and that viciousness requires some measure of social order to operate well (for instance, you cannot perpetrate some forms of fraud unless there is an institution of contract that leads people to expect each other to do their word). In this sense, some vice is parasitic on social order. And the order in magnificently vicious life is *not* a sort that conduces to order at large. But it is equally clear that the measure of order required for a relatively stable society is not such as to preclude viciousness, and that enlightened self-interest for the vicious, while not enough to get them to do acts of justice *from* justice, seems to be enough to get them to be circumspect in their viciousness sometimes. Just as the avaricious man can harden his heart in order to prevent his losing assets to generous impulses, the calculatively rational greedy man can calculate how far to go in extracting things from others, lest their resentment grow and boil over against him. Very smart, very alert, very bad people are very hard to catch out. And I do not know how to argue that they have a reason to change their ways, beyond pointing out that some of the best things in human life are not possible for them. The obvious rejoinder is that what they get is plenty good enough.

I take it, then, that both I and my calculative theorist are left having to deny that the "ought" that shows up in a statement like "Smith ought to tell Jones the truth about x and pay the debts they have jointly incurred," where Smith is a con artist and Jones is his victim, means that Smith *has a reason* to fess up and pay the debts. Rather, Smith has a reason to lie through his teeth, take the money, and head for the hills. His reason is a straightforward, calculative reason that will be every bit as strong as his scheme is careful. What I must say instead is that Smith has an ethically bad scheme in the works and that, if it goes through as planned, Jones will suffer tremendously for it. I will also say that if there is justice in this case, then Smith will not get away with it, that Smith is a bad man, all the worse if he went to some trouble to win Jones's trust as part of the con, that what Smith is doing is vicious, that Smith is in the wrong, and so on. What I do not know how to do is give a secular account of the sense in which Smith has a reason to foil his own plan, and I do not know this because I do not know how to argue that in betraying Jones's trust, Smith sins against reason. There may be such an argument. I have just not found one that I take to be entirely compelling. And my sense is that Anscombe was right in suggesting that our conviction that the external "ought" statement must have special reason-giving force together with the trouble we have had in explaining that force owe much to the fact that the kind of statement at issue has its home in a form of life governed by thought about divine law and divine providence.[11] If this is right, however, then the mere fact that we have this form of words and employ it with a sense of conviction does not mean that we have a legitimate way of expressing ourselves in a secular context.

Very recently, drawing on work by Warren Quinn, Philippa Foot has moved aside from Anscombe's position on this point, within a framework of thought about ethics and reason that I find especially congenial. I now turn to this strategy for supporting external reasons statements.

The Foot–Quinn Approach

Warren Quinn argued that any plausible account of practical rationality had to be one in which it was clear why practical rationality was an important topic. He argued, further, that if excellence in the exercise of practical reason was no more than efficiency in voluntarily satisfying present desires (understood as Humean mental states), it would be mysterious *why* practical rationality was an important topic (Quinn's examples include a man who feels compelled to turn on radios, not in order to listen to music or for any other purpose, but just because they are there).[12] I agree with Quinn on this point, which is related to the point of the argument I adapted from Anscombe: "I just am" or "One just should" cannot be the only responses to the reasons-for-acting-seeking question "Why are you A-ing?" But the problem posed by the worldly man is *not* a problem about Humean desire-based reasons versus other sorts of reasons.

I have set up the ordinary man of the world as my "immoralist." What moves the worldly man is *not* an idiosyncratic set of desires.[13] The worldly man instead determines his will to the pursuit of control over worldly goods, and the more perfectly he does so, the more he will develop and nurture his will for the sake of that end. These are the kinds of goods often at issue in war. They are the goods at issue in capital vice, the goods one argues that a man stood to gain when one argues in court that he had a motive to commit some crime. The man who threatens the claim that immorality is irrational need be neither a warmonger nor a spectacular criminal. He can be more common and less noticeable than either of these sorts. I have described him in terms thick with the conviction that his life is less than a human life should be. But, first, these are not the terms he would use to describe himself, and second, he is not *wrong* about the goodness of wealth, sensual pleasure, honor, and the like. And the question for a calculative theorist of practical reason becomes: *What* is he missing? In what does his error consist?

Developing another suggestion by Quinn, Philippa Foot has recently argued that we will get nowhere on this topic if we start with an independent account of practical reason and then try to build up to a picture of the irrationality of immorality. If I understand her, her main thought could be translated into the Thomistic parlance I have favored this way: the as-such desirables sought by the quietly vicious man are only desirable because of the place they have in human life more generally; criticism and praise of actions and agents cannot so much as get off the ground if we do not attend to the broader context of our form of life, a context that includes both thought about our natural strengths and vulnerabilities and thought about the complexity of linguistically competent participation in public, collective social endeavors. But this in turn suggests that individual practical rationality is excellence of action and character in the wider context of the form of life. To whatever extent morality, justice, and virtue are best understood in this context, they enter into our very assessments of individual practical rationality in a way comparable to the way that an understanding of the life-forms of other animals enters into assessment of individual animals.

Foot's argument is subtle and difficult. She draws extensively on Aquinas, on Anscombe, on Geach, and on the work of Michael Thompson (work inspired by Anscombe that has been vital to my work here), as well as on Quinn's suggestive later papers. She holds both that the grounding for morality is to be found in thought about what is needed for sound collective life (she has a variant of a task-based, corrective account of the virtues, for instance), and that the person who knowingly acts ill is to that extent irrational. "Irrationality" here functions as a rubric covering all forms of systematic defect in the rational will—tendencies to act on the basis of culpably mistaken judgment about what one should do. While she holds that there are various substantive regions of human good that serve as shared sources of sound practical considerations (for instance, considerations of justice or prudence, aesthetic considerations, pleasure- or desire-based considerations), she holds that practical judgment is "all things considered" judgment about what one should do. While circumstance may deprive us of the power to do what we should do (what we *would* do, in a better world, so far as reason was, for us, decisive), it is the aim of practical judgment to lend rational order to an individual life. This order is best realized by acting well, that is, acting as it befits a member of our species to act in order fully to share in the goods that a human social life has to offer.

Foot's image of the coincidence of excellence in the exercise of practical reason (practical rationality) and the ethical is substantially informed by a vision of a good life that is fairly earthy: a life with friendship, family, the goods of cultural endeavors, pleasure, health, security, and the like. It is not, I hope, an especially controversial picture of human goods. Her treatment of systematic tendencies to unethical conduct is staged as a confrontation with Nietzsche. The aim of her essay is not so much to enter into debates about what is good (save for the encounter with Nietzsche), but rather to describe the framework in which such arguments will take place by reference to what is needful in collective human life. And while one might wish that she had devoted more space to explaining how "all things considered" judgment will square, say, considerations of justice with considerations of private advantage or aesthetic considerations (traditionally, at least, philosophers have found reason to doubt that all of these considerations, properly taken into account, will favor the same range of actions in prospect), what we have in Foot is a secular, naturalist view of the ethical very like the one I have favored coupled with a denial of internalism about reasons for acting.

Again, if I understand her, Foot's claim is that internalism *invariably* carries the baggage of an instrumentalist picture of motivation—one in which desire is at once unruly and a core component in reasons for acting such that, say, desire sets ends of action and reasons finds means to attaining those ends. I have treated such pictures of motivation as the clunking, weak progeny of a genuine, deep insight into the rational structure of (representations of) intentional action as such, which has a means–end, part–whole calculative articulation. I have denied throughout that this insight drives us toward bifurcationist moral psychology. And I have instead insisted that the sources of final ends are various, and that while we can provide interminable desirability characterizations for some of what we do, and while we can be asked to explain the sense in which it befits a man to harden his heart in order to amass a fortune, the sense in which it is pleasant to engage in consensual erotic blade play, or the sense in which it is useful to make a very dangerous climb without safety equipment, if our aim is to assess the rationality of what is done, our topic remains considerations that (potentially, at least) inform intentional action. To this extent, Foot and I agree.

We further agree, I expect, in thinking that in assessing desirability characterizations, we will have in view thought about our practical good, about what there is worth going for in some life or other, and so on. Moreover, we agree that practical rationality ought to serve the practically rational person: it ought to improve her life rather than destroy it. The difficulty that I encounter beyond this point stems directly from an encounter with Aquinas's treatment of capital vice. For even though we cannot so much as get off the ground in talking about capital vice without supposing that its characteristic acts are bad acts (just as we can't begin discussion of virtue without supposing that its characteristic acts are good acts), the task-based story about virtue locates the "tasks" in collective life. Unless the form of collective life at issue is, to some extent, well ordered—a thing that *no* individual can bring about by an act of private will—acting well (in the sense of acting ethically) and faring well need not coincide.[14] In short, succeeding in habituating oneself to virtue will not confer benefit to individuals in their lifetimes unless some portion of the social context of individual action is reasonably stable and sound.[15] Virtue instills in the virtuous person a system of incapacities to pursue advantage by some means or under some circumstances. In so doing, virtue operates, as Williams once put it, as "proof against rewards."[16]

Viciousness seeks instead to make one *amenable* to rewards (the vicious man asks, "Why would we want to guard against rewards unless doing so was a means to securing even bigger rewards?"). Vice equips a man to hold his own under brutal social conditions. It equips a man to prey on his fellows for the sake of personal gain in a better world. Basically, viciousness aims to profit the individual in ways that both virtuous and vicious people can appreciate. Moreover, it is because of the goods at issue in vicious conduct that we can see the point of habituating oneself to vice.

And the question between the standard picture and Foot's view becomes: What hangs on being able to charge the vicious man with irrationality? What hangs on it, I think, is that if the vicious man is irrational, then he ought to take steps to change his ways even though doing so will cost him a lot by his lights and even though it is likely that the effects of viciousness on his will are such as to erode his capacities to enjoy the fruits of ethical conduct. I do not think that it is possible to motivate this claim without advancing a substantive account of human good, one that makes what I am tempted to call *goods of the spirit* central to the living of any successful human life.

The devil is in the details here in more ways than one. My hunch is that Foot will face a dilemma. Either (1) she can treat any agent who is systematically deaf to the call of some interesting range of practical considerations tied up with thought about human good (considerations of justice, say, or prudential considerations, or aesthetic considerations) as "irrational" (such that most, perhaps even all, humans will turn out to have defective wills, just as an average human will display dozens of markers of genetic defect in her chromosomal material), in which case irrationality is not quite as serious a matter as one might have thought; or else (2) it will turn out that irrationality is both important and rather more rare than that, in light of a substantive view of human good. The substantive account will need not only to reinstate the deep unity in deployment of action assessment rooted in the threefold division from a thoroughly secular, naturalist point of view (showing how considerations that attach to the present act, patterning considerations, and considerations that get their force from their relation to attaining proximate ends will *not*, all things considered, conflict—at least, not in a well-ordered form of social life), but also to handle conflicts among patterning principles (the "plural and incommensurable goods" trouble, traditionally located in the way considerations of justice might oppose considerations of long-term well-being, pleasure, advantage, and so on).

Foot hopes to show inextricable ties between the questions "Why be moral?" and "Why be rational?" The latter question is obviously misguided (it asks for a reason, and one shows that one is already deep into the business of accepting reasons, that is to say, of rationality, if one asks for reasons). I do not see how the two wind up linked, largely because it strikes me that a calculative theorist who does not begin by assuming such a link can get very far indeed in theorizing reason in action. Far from it being the case that we can gain no purchase on reason in action without paying attention to the ethical, I take it that the threefold division gives us an ethically neutral, rich account of practical reason and good, one that gives ethics a place without making it central to the entire machinery. In effect, I have devoted most of this book to motivating this claim.

Foot does not think that it is possible to work one's way up to ethics from an ethically neutral conception of practical reason. I agree. But she thinks that thought about good as the constitutive aim of practical reason suggests that we cannot get an ethically neutral account of practical reason *at all,* so there can be no proper question of working one's way up to the ethical from an ethically neutral account of practical reason. I have tried to "get" an ethically neutral account of practical reason by wrenching Thomistic thought from its theological, ethical frame, and stressing the theory of vice. How it goes from here will depend on the plausibility of the mangled version of Thomism that I have produced.

Reasons to Be Moral

One could try to turn the tables and say that the ethicists' urge to find reasons for being good or acting well is misplaced—as though someone needed a reason to do what she anyway ought to do![17] One could express horror at this thought akin to the sort of horror one feels when confronted with a certain naive Christianity that seems to start from the supposition that, save for the torments of hell in prospect, all of us would *of course* roam about murdering, raping, stealing or destroying things, and generally being as bad as it is in our power to be.[18] I must say that I prefer the horror approach to the more usual "Honesty is the best policy." But I cannot imagine that high-minded revulsion will get us very far faced with the prospect that immoral actions cannot be shown invariably to be irrational by the standard picture's lights.

What may help, however, is to notice that (on a more traditional sense of the term "irrational" than Foot's) irrationality is not the only way action can fail. There are all kinds of things that can be wrong with a rational action of some type (for example, *that* it is an act of brutality, *that* it is murder, *that* it is rape, *that* it is fraud) and there are all kinds of things that might be said about a man who not only acts ill, but cultivates such habits as may be required to make acting ill the ordinary run of things in his life. As Williams points out and as I suggested in the example about Smith, any number of terms of abuse impugning the character of actions and agents, for instance, will be applicable.[19] Notice, too, that the less the action looks like a failure of reason, the more deplorable the man who performs it will be.

Consider, as an example of deeply bad conduct, torturing someone for the fun of it. On the calculative view I described, in a sense, the better the torturer is at what he does, the longer he is able to sustain his grisly pursuits for the joy of it, the more he stands convicted of having knowingly, deliberately, and unabashedly done evil. This won't come out as a failure of practical reason, but that doesn't mean that there's nothing wrong with it. Nor does it mean that people who would never do or even consider doing any such thing are somehow stupid.

Leaving the cases of atrocity to one side for the moment, it sometimes seems to me that the urgency surrounding the question "Why be moral?" and the depth of interest in tying morality to reason stems from concern that if two practical excellences—rationality and morality—are not inextricably bound up together, we will turn out to have been foolish for bothering about ethics. It is as though we live in perpetual anxiety lest some con artist who has made us his dupe should say, *sotto voce,* "Suckers!" on his way out the door, and as though we could find deep consolation at that point in the thought, "Well, but he was irrational to have done it!"

The more usual way of discussing the urgency (which Williams was surely right to point out seems less than strictly philosophical)[20] is with reference to an article of faith that, if it is rational to be moral, then surely even a fiend could be argued into being a good person, or else charged with a sin against reason. Of course, if a man's behavior is truly and reliably fiendish, and if our arguments for the inextricable tie between reason and morality are sound, then one shares Williams's perplexity over why one would think rational suasion a technique for stay-

ing his hand.[21] Surely the fiendish man's "error"—for that is what
fiendishness will turn out to be: an error in judgment of some kind—
goes all the way down to mistakes about principles rather than remaining at the more benign level of ignorance on some point of fact, and if
reason and morality are very close, it is hard to see why one would expect principles of inference to carry him along reliably when moral principles leave him cold. One will have convicted him of gross irrationality.
What sense is there to the suggestion that one's next obvious move is to
reason with him rather than, say, run away and come back prepared to
overpower him? Is the thought that we need to know that someone's reason is diseased in order to feel justified in forcibly subduing him? that
being licensed to charge someone with irrationality is more powerful
than *merely* being licensed to charge him with, say, crimes against humanity? that the latter has no *force* unless it is the same as the former? It
is hard to say. But the difficulties in answering such questions are why I
think that the urgency surrounding the question "Why be moral?" has
more to do with a worry that people will be accused of stupidity if they
try to be good than it does with a sincere conviction on the part of contemporary moral philosophers that people who routinely do bad things
can be brought round to seeing an error of judgment in their ways
through techniques of rational discussion. Either that or there are serious differences of opinion about how bad people can be, in spite of
enough documentation of utter depravity in human affairs to suggest
that the answer is very, very bad.

Whatever the case, there is a point to what the practiced torturer does
for pleasure: he enjoys injuring and maiming those who cannot defend
themselves and so has schooled himself in the art of both giving pain
and prolonging his victims' agony by, say, making sure that they do not
die too quickly. This makes what he does morally reprehensible, I would
suggest, and, insofar as one can understand taking pleasure in that sort
of exercise of power, is also what renders his habit intelligible. The fact
that one can see the point of the thing, however, does not mean that one
is likely to do it, nor does it mean that there is nothing wrong with what
the torturer does, even if he is so bad that nothing anyone could say
would convince him to stop.

But, however prominent atrocity has been in shaping the last five
hundred years or so of human history, and however frequent the occurrence of moral catastrophe, the lone moral monster who defies us to give

him an argument that will make him stop on pain of irrationality is not really our topic, I think. Lone moral monsters thrive under circumstances that they do not, themselves, produce. There is some reason to suppose that those circumstances are usually made possible by the actions and omissions of people who are not morally monstrous. They are more like my worldly man than they are like monsters.

The larger concern, I think, is the worry that if secular moral philosophy can find no rational requirement that one behave ethically, then those of us who at least try to conduct ourselves ethically with our fellows will turn out to have been fools, especially because doing so generally involves forgoing short-term gain for oneself or one's circle. Here, I think, it *is* to the point to discuss the goods of this life whose price is decent conduct. In part *because* it is within the power of a reasonably bright, reasonably strategic person to take advantage of her fellows, it matters when she does not. There is a kind of strength that shows itself in siding with the ethical in practice when it is easier to let things slide. Working on behalf of what is ethically sound when one doesn't need to in order to protect one's own hide, when doing so might damage some of one's interests, is, I think, clearly the sort of thing that humans *can* do and that it is to our credit *to* do. Moreover, some modes of intercourse with our fellows are only possible if we side with the ethical, and some joys are not available to the wicked. This style of reflection is not enough to establish that calculation how best to find happiness invariably leads one to work to be good. Rather, it suggests that if you have it in you to be good (which, presumably, people in general do), then striving to cultivate the relevant powers is not without its rewards, and these rewards are internal to the work of striving to conduct oneself ethically.

The "up" side of the kind of internalism at issue is that, just as ethical reasons for acting are reasons *for* people working from ethical patterning principles to act, the satisfactions of an ethical life are satisfactions *for* people who have it in them to so pattern their affairs. Even if you could convince a fiend by argument to give up fiendish pursuits, even if you could structure the world so that a man inclined to fiendishness could never profit by bad action (thereby removing incentives to fiendish pursuits), you could not give a fiend access to the goods of a virtuous life. Those goods are for the virtuous.

Anscombe's Argument

In arguing that interminable practical considerations taken in isolation from the calculative order could not be central to practical reason, I noted that I was basing my argument on one of Anscombe's arguments. In this appendix, I lay out how the adaptation of Anscombe's argument works.

Anscombe made her argument by supposing (a) that *intention* only occurs as it does in *intentional action* (that is, in discussion of present or past proceedings) and (b) that the only answer to the question "Why are you A-ing?", granted that the question is given application, was "I just am, that's all."[1] If I understand her, however, the argument turns on supposing that there is never a further, future end such that the agent A*s* in order to *B*. She later noted that when she wrote many of her papers on ethics and her book *Intention,* she was engaged in "a struggle to treat all deliberate action as a matter of acting on a calculation how to obtain one's ends," and had since doubted that this was right, because "although it is always possible to force practical reason into this mould, constructing descriptions of ends like 'not infringing the regulations about traffic lights,' 'observing the moral law,' 'being polite,' 'playing a game according to its rules,' and so on," she had come to see "a contrast between such constructed descriptions of ends, and the means–end calculations which really do—at least implicitly—take their starting point from some objective one has."[2]

Notice that all of these un-end-like considerations would belong to the befitting region of good. Because of this it seems safe to conclude that unless befitting-style practical characterizations are assimilated to useful-style practical considerations—this is, notice, precisely the dubious move she complains of as leading to "constructed descriptions of ends,"—then if the argument works, it will work against the supposition that we could retain the concept of intention by focusing solely on befitting-style desirability characterizations. That is why I think that my revision of the suppositions is a matter of adapting one her argument rather than subjecting it to a hideous misconstrue.

The two suppositions together allow that we can have intentional action without the calculative order taking us toward any further, future end. They keep the practical force of practical reason by keeping action. What the suppositions exclude is useful-style desirability characterizations. That is why it is an argument about the centrality of useful-style practical considerations to understanding intention. Pleasant-style considerations, recall, can be offered in support of doing this very thing *now*, or having done that very thing *then*. They attach to present action. Befitting-style considerations are more subtle, but if a befitting-style desirability characterization can be given accurately on behalf of what one is here and now doing, then, paradigmatically:

1. what one is doing is the sort of thing that can be done from the relevant patterning principle under these circumstances ("Why are you ignoring your son's birthday and staying late at the office?"—"It befits a man of the world to occupy his hours with business, and in staying late, I am doing that.") and
2. the relevant patterning principle is established in the agent's life in the right sort of way to lend credence to the implicit suggestion that he so patterns his affairs (it is true of our man that he is a man of the world and conducts himself accordingly, or at least that he aspires to be such a man).

What is excluded by Anscombe's suppositions is that our man has any future-directed intention in staying late, any further end in doing what he is doing. It is very hard to stick to the terms of this thought experiment—for example, we have excluded that he is working in order to be better prepared tomorrow, in order to take advantage of market conditions, as a means to securing a promotion, in order to be in a position to take the weekend off, and so on. But, in light of the threefold division, this excludes all and only practical considerations drawn from the useful. So, rather than getting bogged down in trying vividly to imagine the case, we can note that Anscombe is going to argue that the availability of useful-style desirability characterizations is crucial to the concept of intention.

"I just am, that's all" is at best a highly tendentious way of characterizing what can be said on behalf of actions done for the pleasure in doing them or on account of an agent's insight that it is fitting for her to do them. What Anscombe is inviting us to imagine is that there is no such thing as having a further intention in A-ing, no such thing as A-ing with an eye to B-ing, unless in A-ing you are thereby also B-ing. We can redescribe our suppositions accordingly, letting the first supposition remain the same but altering the second:

(a) *intention* only occurs as it does in *intentional action,*
(b) the only answers to the question "Why are you A-ing?" granted that the question is given application are
    (b₁) "I just feel like it" (treat this as ambiguous between "I enjoy A-ing/A-ing is pleasant" and "No reason") and
    (b₂) "I am supposed to A" (where "supposed to" is allowed to range across all of the true befitting-style desirability characterizations that can be given on behalf of the present action, except befitting-style characterizations that involve future ends the attainment of which is secured or made possible by A-ing).

Let's start with the first assumption. The concept of intention occurs centrally in three contexts: in expression of intention (for instance, "I am going to work late tomorrow"), in discussion of intentional action, and in considering the intention with which one does something. Assumption (a) directs our attention to intentional actions, the observable proceedings that were the topic of my crossing-the-road thought experiment, and asks that we isolate these from the larger concept of intention. In my thought experiment, it turned out that the calculative order was important to getting a certain kind of description of intentional action going. Directing our attention to intentional action in Anscombe's argument requires directing it to present proceedings quite apart from any concern with the calculative order. So there is initially a question about what sorts of descriptions of the proceedings we are allowed to help ourselves to for the sake of making sense of supposition (a). Anscombe is allowing in many descriptions that are hard to get going in the right way without the calculative order. All she is leaving out is the A-ing-in-order-to-B variety.

How, then, are we to understand (a), the supposition that *isolates* intentional action from useful-style practical considerations? Anscombe gives two interpretations. The first lets in *any* true description of what is happening when the agent acts, in the absence of the calculative order serving as a filter for which descriptions, A, are (and which are not) in place in asking the reasons-for-acting-seeking question "Why are you A-ing?" The second is more restrictive.

First interpretation of (a): "intentional" has become a kind of style characterization for an action. One As intentionally, and the adverb indicates the manner of A-ing, but any true description of what is happening is allowed in.[3] The problem with this interpretation is that proceedings are describable in more than one way, and are intentional under some descriptions but not others. If all that is indicated by "intentional" is the *manner* in which the agent is engaging in the present proceedings, then there is no room for the question "Why are you A-ing?" to be rejected for any true description of those proceedings. "Why are you sawing the plank?"—"Why are you sawing *my* plank?"—"Why are you making that racket?"—"Why are you scattering sawdust around the room?"—"Why are you increasing your heart-rate / perspiring / scaring the cat / generating chemicals *x,y,z* in your brain / and so on?" Provided that it is true that all these things are happening, there is no room for you to refuse any of the questions "Why?" application. What is happening is just happening on purpose, rather than, say, because of a seizure or during an episode of sleepwalking. And this is so far removed from the concept of intention that it is no longer clear that the question "Why?" has its reasons-for-acting-seeking sense.

On this interpretation, notice, we lop off not only future ends served by A-ing, but also expressions of intention as these are normally understood. "Intentional" is used only to indicate *how* one is doing *what* one is doing. Expressions of intention are future-tensed descriptions of one's own actions that are normally understood to be distinct from predictions: "I am going to take a walk" is usually an expression of intention, whereas "I am going to be sick" is usually a prediction.[4] On this interpretation of (a), however, the agent has no special authority to exercise in saying *which* descriptions of what she is doing are (or will be) integral to her intentions, and so is (in principle, at least) in no better position than anyone else to say what in fact she will be doing in A-ing. She expects she will be A-ing, and she expects that what she will in fact be doing in A-ing she will be doing on purpose, but since she no longer has the authority to reject any true description of what she does as a description of her purpose, she likewise has no special authority in saying what she means to do tomorrow, or this afternoon, or next year. It is in the possibility of *rejecting* the question "Why?" for *some* true descriptions of what one is doing, after all, that the shape of what is intended in the action is made clear. We have here an adverb, "intentionally," attaching to descriptions in an extensional context.[5] This allows in too many descriptions, because intentional actions are intentional under some true descriptions but not others, so we reject the first interpretation of supposition (a).

What has all this got to do with the determinate future? How is part of what hangs us up on this interpretation coming from the fact that we left out useful-style practical considerations? Anscombe's underlying point is, I suspect, that one very important way of determining *which* questions "Why?" are given application and which can be refused application is by thinking about where things are headed, about how the proceedings are *supposed to* come out, and, in light of this, what might count as taking alternate means to achieving the sought-after result. The end, that is, is part of what determines the kind of action that is taking place.

If the end is scaring the cat, then one need not make a mess of the room in order to attain it. If the end was making a bookcase, then the fact that sawing makes noise and dust is incidental to attaining the end—these are foreseeable consequences that are not normally part of the *point* of sawing. If, however, the end is covering the room with sawdust, then it is usually easier to get a bag of sawdust from a woodshop, bring it home, and scatter its contents around.[6] Leaving no room to refuse application of a "Why?" question is in part a consequence of excluding the calculative order as shaping our intuitive sense for which questions do, and which do not, get at the heart of what is intended. The link between what one has in mind in doing what one does and the calculative form of intentional action is tight. For while the future is not *in* the present action, it is in light of how things are *supposed to go in the future,* of, say, the agent's intention in sawing, that we tell the difference between messing up the room in the course of making bookcases and making bookcases in the course of messing up the room. In the latter case, inefficient means have been taken to making the mess. In the former, messing things up happened while one was making bookcases, but was not the point of what one was doing. Whatever the case, in the first way of leaving the useful out, we have let too much in.

This brings us to the second interpretation of (a). Here, "intentional" is not an adverb attaching to observable proceedings under *any* of indefinitely many true descriptions. We allow that a man can reject the question "Why are you *A*-ing?" if *A* does not pick out the kind of thing he means to be doing, if *A*-ing, say, is an incidental effect of what he is up to, which is no part of what he is setting out to do (for example, scaring the cat, or making sawdust), or if he does not know that what he is doing is correctly described as *A*-ing (for example, sawing *my* plank, producing chemicals *x*,*y*,*z* in his brain). This interpretation *does* leave room for a thin sort of expression of intention: *because* you have the inside track on saying what it is that you mean to do, you also have the inside track on announcing what it is that you *will* do. On Anscombe's second interpretation, what you do is intentional under some descriptions but not others. So this interpretation, at least, has a fighting chance of having something to do with intentional action. But here, we have to be careful. Because we are excluding useful-style practical considerations, even if what you are doing or will do is or will be intentional under several descriptions, these descriptions are not linked after the fashion of representation of the calculative order. You shift weight to one foot *and* step off the curb *and* step onto the street *and* walk across the road *and* enter the café at the other side. This is true and, we may suppose, what you intend. What we cannot say is that you *A*, *B*, and *C* in order to cross the road, or that you cross the road in order to get to the other side, or that you intend anything that might be expressed in this idiom. Let this be our interpretation of supposition (a): it gives us a way of looking at intentional action *apart from* calculative reason, and so of focusing our attention on whether noncalculative backing for it is enough to give us a grip on intention.

And now, what of supposition (b)? What happens when the "Why?" question is given application on this interpretation? Very generally, there are two sorts of answers: "I'm *A*-ing because I feel like doing it" and "I'm *A*-ing because I'm supposed to."

The first sort of answer gives a kind of characterization of the spirit in which one is *A*-ing. And this is rather like a nonextensional version of a style characterization. Notice that any criticism of what one does will involve some kind of doctrine about whether one is in decent shape if one *A*s when one is in the mood to *A*. But, by our suppositions, such criticism will be mounted *in the absence* of any account of whether it is in one's interests, serves one's further ends, or is useful to people generally, or some such, to avoid *A*-ing when in the mood to *A*. It will not even be possible to mount an evolutionary argument to the effect that, *because* it would have untoward consequences for the species if people in general were to *A* when they felt like it, any individual member of the species who acts on such urges displays some defect, since we have excluded the whole apparatus of such judgments from consideration. One might criticize the action as being unseemly, or otherwise objectionable; but notice that even if the criticism is accepted, it is not as though we have any reason to suppose that the subject *ought to* or *will* take steps in order to see to it that she does not do that again. Our agent cannot reason in that way (namely, about what to do *in order to* improve anything), and, by the supposition, neither can we.

What of the second sort of answer? Under our supposition, the second sort of answer—"I am supposed to *A*"—the answer that we are allowing to range across the whole of noncalculative befitting-style practical considerations, degenerates into another kind of style characterization. Even if you are wrong in thinking that you are supposed to *A,* we ought not to expect you to do anything in the direction of seeing to it that you do not make this error again. The direction you would look to improve yourself is to the future, and we would have to give you access to a mode of reasoning that has been excluded by hypothesis if we held that you could do anything *in order that* things change. Criticism, discovery of one's own faulty judgment—such things cannot, by assumption, be taken to heart in any way that would lead one to take steps in order to improve. Nor, if one's judgment is sound, could one take steps in order to ensure that one conducts oneself in the same way next time. There is no such thing as doing anything *in order that* anything else might happen. That is precisely what has been excluded.

Is anything left? Do we even have voluntary action left if we have retained noncalculative desirability characterizations but have lost the form of judgment central to the whole business of practical self-correction when one errs, practical self-improvement in order to decrease the chances that one will mess up in the future, and the many little things that a person struggling to act well does by way of working to hold herself constant in doing as she is supposed to do? Here, Anscombe's argument takes the turns I traced in Chapter 6.

A concept of voluntary action does remain, Anscombe assures us, and, in light of the reformulation of supposition (b), it takes exactly the form you might expect. Voluntary actions can be commanded. Accordingly, "I am A-ing because I feel like A-ing" indicates that there is no special authority backing up the action and "I am A-ing because I am supposed to A" indicates some sort of authoritative source for A-ing. And this even leaves room to sort things through a bit: there is doing something because and on account of being ordered to do it, doing something just because you feel like doing it, and doing something that was commanded, but not *on account of* the command.

How important is this distinction? All that remains are two sorts of desirability characterizations. These are, in effect, one that says "The buck stops here, I did it just because it was what I felt like doing" and one that points a finger upward toward some "higher" source and indicates that the A-ing was done in obedience to that. Again, it does not much matter *which* higher source because the distinction is otherwise completely idle. And this, Anscombe concludes, is enough to show that further intention with which one acts is absolutely central to the concept of intention. In the view I have been urging, it is enough to show that useful-style practical considerations have a special place in thought about reason in action. The calculative order in doing things is crucial to work on intention generally, and it is this order that explains how and why it might be to the point to determine such things as the distinction between voluntary and involuntary action.

Anscombe's Objection to Donald Davidson

In this book, I largely sidestep Donald Davidson's work on actions and reasons for acting, in spite of the facts that he has been more influential than Anscombe, that, like Anscombe, he is a great reader of Aquinas, and that some of the terms I have employed in discussing moral psychology ("pro-attitude," for instance) are his. In this appendix, I explain Anscombe's objection to Davidson's work on reasons as causes. I realize that there is tremendous controversy over how to interpret Davidson's work. I do not claim that the objection to Davidson that I discuss gets him right. Rather, I think, it gets at where, on Anscombe's reading, Davidson goes wrong.[1]

Anscombe's most pointed complaint about Davidson comes in dense, cryptic objection to what she took to be the thrust of his work on reasons for acting. She begins this way:

> True, not only must I have a reason, it must also "operate as my reason": that is, what I do must be done *in pursuit* of the end and *on grounds* of the belief. But not just *any* act of mine which is caused by my having a certain desire is done in pursuit of the object of desire; not just *any* act caused by my having a belief is done on grounds of the belief.[2]

As I argue throughout this book, much of Anscombe's work on practical reason, ethics, and intention turns on refusing to take action as a given. In this appendix, I use this refusal to explain her complaint.

Davidson's View

Davidson holds that my beliefs, judgments, con- and pro-attitudes show the point of what I do, they "rationalize" my action.[3] Moreover, rationalization is a species of causal explanation. But sometimes attitude-based causal explanations miss the mark:

> A climber might want to rid himself of the weight and danger of hold-ing another man on a rope, and he might know that by loosening his hold on the rope he could rid himself of the weight and danger. The be-lief and want might so unnerve him as to cause him to loosen his hold, and yet it might be the case that he never *chose* to loosen his hold, nor did he do it intentionally. . . . [S]ince there may be wayward causal chains, we cannot say that if attitudes that would rationalize x cause an agent to do x, then he does x intentionally.[4]

Davidson thinks that introducing practical reasoning into the discus-sion might improve the account of intentional action: "For a desire and a belief to explain an action in the right way, they must cause it in the right way, perhaps through a chain or process of reasoning that meets stan-dards of rationality."[5]

And here we might ask: why not just claim that it is nevertheless *nec-essary* that an agent's A-ing be caused by attitudes that constitute reasons for A-ing if the agent's A-ing is to count as intentional action? Inten-tional action is a pretty broad topic. It is hard to see why we would ex-pect to get a singular, abstract causal framework that will characterize the antecedents of intentional action generally. Practical reasoning seems a likely addition in cases where I work out some practical prob-lem in advance of taking action. It looks much less plausible in cases where my act is grounded in a skill that I acquired before reaching the age of reason, as when I make such-and-such movements in order to rise from my chair and walk. Executing an elaborate stratagem in order to defraud my employers and standing up in order to move about are, alike, intentional actions. The latter is not only rarely the product of ex-plicit practical deliberation, but my ability to do it without thinking about it developed well before I was a fully fledged rational animal.[6]

Davidson agrees, basically. He argues that we should *not* expect to get a single account of the "right" sort of causal link between action and atti-tudes.[7] But now look how odd his response to the climber case is—the action wasn't caused in the right way; it may be impossible to give a gen-eral account of the right causal link; had the climber's act been caused by practical reasoning, *that* would be a right causal link. In short, had the climber case not been a climber case, it would not have involved climber-style wayward causation. When a philosopher responds in this sort of way to a potential counterexample, one suspects that the case has struck too close for comfort.

The project of investigating reasons-based explanation as a species of causal explanation began for Davidson in seeking to understand the *because* in "the agent performed the action *because* he had [such-and-such] reason."[8] Davidson's thought was that this *because* indicates that reasons-based intentional action explanation is causal. Since reasons-based action explanation casts action in the favorable light that it has for agents, Davidson supposed that reasons for acting were given by propositional attitudes toward actions of the kind at issue.

The problem lurking in the climber example may not be merely that the agent met the necessary conditions for intentionally loosening his grip, but failed to meet the sufficient conditions. Potentially, at least, the problem is much more serious. Davidson identifies reasons with suitably connected, action-directed propositional attitudes. We have those in the climber example, and we have the action *because* of *those very* psychological states. But the idea that he could just drop his companion unnerves the climber. From the climber's point of view, notice, these psychological states may not provide *any* reason for action *at all*. The threat is that the "rationalizing" relation *cannot* be cashed out as a relation between the contents of psychological states on the one side and descriptions of behavior on the other. As Anscombe puts it, Davidson "realizes that even identity of description of *act done* with *act specified in the belief,* together with causality by belief and desire, isn't enough to guarantee the act's being done *in pursuit of the end* and *on grounds of the belief.*"[9] That is, tight links between the contents of propositional attitudes and true descriptions of behavior caused by those attitudes may shed no light on the character of intentional action and reasons for acting.

Davidson thinks that it might be possible to avoid the problem posed by the climber example if, instead of just looking for a causally efficacious, content-sensitive link between what a man has on his mind and what he does, we ask whether the man's action was a product of practical reasoning, or backed by considered judgment. Practical reasoning is reasoning toward action. Such reasoning surely should rationalize any action that it explains. Here I focus on two interpretations of Davidson's suggestion.

First, my *judgment* about what I should do might be treated as the conclusion of my practical reasoning, my action then caused by my judgment. This won't solve the problem of freak causal chains, however. Take Davidson's example:

> A man might have good reasons for killing his father, and he might do it, and yet the reasons not be his reasons in doing it. [S]uppose, contrary to the legend, that Oedipus . . . was hurrying along the road intent on killing his father, and, finding a surly old man blocking his way, killed him so he could (as he thought) get on with the main job. Then not only did Oedipus want to kill his father, and actually kill him, but his desire caused him to kill his father.[10]

In the example, Oedipus judges that he has good reason to kill his father, means to kill his father, and kills his father because he has set out to kill his father. But, again, the causal chain is "wrong."

On the second interpretation, A-ing itself might be treated as the *conclusion* of practical reasoning in two senses: it *follows* logically from the practical inference and it is the *outcome* of the deliberative episode. The suggestion has the advantage of making the link between the inferential and causal orders in action very tight: one As in response to the force of the practical argument, as one might come to believe that p in response to a compelling theoretical argument in support of p.

There are several ways that the second interpretation might go. One likely to be favored by some Davidsonians is that the action itself could be understood as intentionally making-the-proposition-that-one-As-true. In the Oedipus example, Oedipus *unintentionally* brings it about that he As. By requiring that he deliberately make it the case that he do what he thinks he has good reason to do, and treating the "good reason" clause as suggesting that his action arises from solid practical deliberation, we unite the causal and inferential orders in action in the right sort of way.

Anscombe's response to this kind of move is subtle. Rather than enter into the fray in attempting to explain what practical reasoning contributes to the causes of action, she draws our attention to the fact that it takes time to determine what to do, that practical reasoning comes in what I called *episodes*. Practical reasoning is itself an event. Hence, something might always intervene before an agent acts on the basis of her considered judgment about what she should do. And because of this, we can neither predict nor prescribe how an episode of deliberation ought to / will come out solely on the basis of discussing the practical considerations entertained in the course of deliberation. In short, for any given episode of practical deliberation, it is possible that the rational order in the reasoning might come apart from the causal order in intentional action. Worse, sometimes one *ought* to leave one's practical conclusions idle.

For instance, if armed assassins burst through the door just as I am about to telephone the travel agent and book my perfectly planned holiday, then, far from being rationally required to place the phone call, I will be foolish to continue on as if nothing had happened. Under such circumstance, even if I had a moment to place the call and begin making the proposition that I vacation in such-and-such spot true, it would be a bad use of my time to do so. Meditating on such difficulties, we could conclude that it isn't the rational order in practical reasoning, but rather facts about what sort of day I am having, that determines how an episode of practical reasoning on my part *will* or *should* come out. And this kind of point casts doubt on any attempt to force an inextricable link between the inferential content of practical deliberation and subsequent intentional action.

What has gone wrong here? If I understand her, Anscombe thinks that the problem comes of failing to attend to the calculative link obtaining between practical reasoning and the act it underwrites. Practical reasoning is usually a stage in a course of action. One engages in practical deliberation in order to decide what to do. In this sense, it is a means to determining one's course of action. Understanding the calculative role of practical reasoning with respect to the act it underwrites is crucial to understanding how practical reasoning can inform action at all. What happens when the would-be murderers arrive, then, is that I leave off doing one thing (vacation-planning as a first stage in vacationing) and take up doing something else entirely (fleeing, fighting, hiding, ducking, or some such) for good reason. We do not assign the evasive or confrontational acts I engage in immediately following the assassins' entrance to the same calculative order that had me planning my perfect holiday, setting out to implement my plan, and so on. Another sort of end is thrust upon me by circumstance, and I need to drop everything for its sake at that moment.

The Importance of Refusing to Treat Action as Given

As I insist throughout this book, *action* functions as a primitive in many contemporary accounts. By "primitive" I mean that we don't bother analyzing the structure of intentional action as such. On Anscombe's reading, Davidson is one of the philosophers who treat action as a primitive. She gives an open question argument against Davidson in order to leave behind worries about the causal antecedents of intentional action, and, hence, worries about wayward causation, with an eye toward discussing the calculative articulation of intentional action:

> [Davidson] can do no more than postulate a "right" causal connexion in the happy security that none such can be found. If a causal connexion were found we could always still ask: "But was the act done for the sake of the end and in view of the thing believed?"[11]

In both the climber example and the Oedipus example, the answer to the open question is: no.

How does Davidson manage to miss that the *persistent* possibility of asking—no matter what caused the action—whether it was done in pursuit of the end and on grounds of the belief suggests that seeking out the causal antecedents of action won't help us to understand practical reason? Anscombe writes:

> I conjecture that the cause of this failure of percipience is the standard approach by which we first distinguish between "action" and what merely happens, and then specify that we are talking about "actions." So what we are considering is already given as—in a special sense—an action, and not just any old thing which we do, such as making an involuntary gesture. Such a gesture might be caused, for example, by realising something (the "onset of a belief") when we are in a certain state of desire. Something I do is not made into an intentional action by being caused by a belief and desire, even if the descriptions fit.[12]

Her most obvious target here is the climber example. In that example we don't have intentional action at all. Davidson knows this, but seems to think that there is an action nevertheless. Anscombe's point is that if you are not going to restrict *action* to *intentional action,* and you are willing to treat the climber's response as an action, you have opened the door to the whole gamut of involuntary gestures.[13] What we have in the climber case is not an action missing the extra "intention" ingredient. What we have is a startle response. Any number of things might have startled him as he was making his way up the face, resenting pulling extra weight. Since there is no action in such cases, there is no wayward cause of action in them. We only thought there was because we noticed the link between what was on the climber's mind and an accurate description of the ensuing involuntary movement. This is exactly the kind of thing Anscombe points to in charging us with assuming that we can take the action as given: supposing that finding a content-sensitive link between psychological cause and behavioral effect is enough to give us an action.[14]

What of the Oedipal drama? There we have intentional killing, we have that the man killed was his killer's father, we have a killer who takes it that there is good reason to kill his father and means to do it, but we do not have intentional patricide. Anscombe argues that an intentional action is one to which the reasons-for-acting-seeking question "Why are you A-ing / did you A?" is given application.[15] If, gesturing toward the old man's corpse, we asked Oedipus why he killed his father, Oedipus would refuse to give the relevant question "Why?" application by responding that he didn't know that he had done so.[16] The action is not intentional under this description.

Davidson tries to capture this by insisting that "the expression that introduces intention . . . must be intensional," that is, we are not licensed to substitute coreferring expressions into a statement of intention.[17] The stipulation captures *one* part of Anscombe's observation that intentional actions are intentional under some descriptions but not others. What it misses entirely is her detailed account of the calculative links *among* those descriptions under which the act is intentional.

Without even posing the question "Why have you killed your father?" we can see that we don't have intentional patricide in Davidson's example because Oedipus will (we assume) *continue* to search for his father, intent on killing him, after the deed is done. This by itself would render the subsequent hunt irrational on the supposition that Oedipus has knowingly killed his father. Where Anscombe sees Davidson getting himself in a muddle, then, is in thinking that we need to look to what is in place *before* Oedipus kills the old man in order to handle the case. Obviously, if we explain an action, *A*, by reference to a cause, *C*, then we are committed to holding that *C* happened or obtained, that *C* happened or obtained before *A* happened, and that *C* brought it about that *A* happened.[18] But, given that Davidson's Oedipus intends to commit patricide, we can as fruitfully direct our attention to what happens *after* he kills the old man.

It belongs to the rational structure in intentional action that once the intended end is *attained,* there is no reason to continue to pursue its attainment. An "end" is, in this sense, a *stopping-place* for intentional action. Davidson's Oedipus kills Laius, and will then keep seeking to kill Laius. His failure to stop his pursuit once the natural, intended stopping-place is reached signals that something has gone wrong. Either he has failed to grasp his own success or else he is exhibiting a serious failure of practical rationality, in roughly the way that I would if, having succeeded in discharging my debt to my creditor, and knowing this, I kept seeking to repay that very same debt to that very same creditor. By failing to notice that reason informs what people do as they go along—rather than just being in people before they do things, and causing them to act—Davidson is unable to take advantage of the rational structure in action to handle his own examples.[19] But once we notice that there is reason in intentional action, we should, Anscombe thinks, drop the assumption that the scene of reason is confined to some states or events that are in place *before* action happens, and this is enough to call off the hunt for the rational cause. It is also enough to show that we cannot treat actions as given.

What we see in intentional action is pursuit of an end on grounds of the thing believed. It should be true of the agent that he seeks to attain his end just as long as he is in pursuit of it, and that what he does in pursuit of his end is done for the sake of attaining it and on account of his insight that doing these things will contribute to attaining that end. Anscombe uses the asking and answering of "Why are you A-ing / did you A?" questions as a device to reveal this fit between what one has in mind and what one does, step-by-step, as one goes along. Imagining the exchange of questions and answers *closes* off the open question by allowing us to display the calculative, rational articulation of the event as it is taking place.

Getting an accurate description of the event in question, of the intentional action *as* an intentional action, is (at least) getting a description of its calculative articulation, of the intended end, and the means or parts done in order to attain, or make it possible to attain, the end. Moreover, getting an accurate description of an event *qua* intentional action takes us a long way toward showing the grounds of the act. This is why Anscombe thinks that we get ourselves in a mess if we treat the action as given. We cannot so much as accurately describe our explanandum, *qua* intentional action, without attending to its intended means–end or part–whole articulation. This, in turn, opens a window on practical reason. The reason in the act shows us part of the agent's grounds for acting, part of what she has in view in doing what she does.

Once we have appreciated the calculative structure in intentional action, Anscombe thinks, we can approach discussion of practical reasoning from a different angle.[20] It is not that we have, on the one side, someone with a lot of things in mind, and on the other an event describable in indefinitely many ways, and now confront the onerous task of connecting mental representation to event. It is rather that some of the salient descriptions of what one has in mind will (if all goes well) line up with the salient descriptions of what one does. Representation of practical inferences, on Anscombe's reading, is partly a device for understanding intentional action, not by giving its cause, but by revealing its grounds, by showing "what good, what use, the action is."[21] It may or may not happen that the agent thinks out what to do explicitly along the lines suggested by the argument. Whether or not she does, the argument gives the grounds, the point, of the action by showing what the agent has in view in doing what she does. The practical argument displays an order in action that could likewise be retrieved by asking the agent why she is A-ing or B-ing, and tracing the order in her responses to the questions that are given application. The questions are given application when our descriptions—A-ing, B-ing, C-ing—are accepted by the agent as descriptions of what she is doing and shown to be relevant to her understanding of her own end and to the grounds she has for thinking that what she is doing contributes to its attainment. Notice that both Oedipus and the climber will refuse to give the relevant questions application.

On Anscombe's view, then, there is no mystery about explaining the connection between the agent's rational powers and the agent's intentional action. Rather, understanding practical reason is understanding how the reason in the agent is likewise in the acts. Because there is no mystery about the connection between intention in agents and the calculative order in their intentional actions (these come to us bound up together), there is no temptation to try to solve the mystery by giving a special kind of causal account of the act. Davidson assumed that he needed some such account, Anscombe suggests, because he wasn't paying attention to the rational structure *in* action, and thereby wasn't noticing that, if the event-to-be-explained involved intentional action, then it had an intended means–end or part–whole articulation relevant to its representation and to understanding its grounds. This is also why, on Anscombe's view, the fact that practical deliberation can be derailed by significant interruptions does not count as a problem for a theory of practical reason. The ends pursued as a result of the interruptions are not the ends pursued in deliberation.

A Note about Kant and Befitting-Style Desirability Characterizations

One curious feature of contemporary work on practical reason is that very few of us accept instrumentalism about practical reason but almost all of us have been willing to treat it as the standard view. One curious feature about contemporary secular work in moral philosophy is that very many of us have accepted one or another aspect of Kant's understanding of morality, but very few of us have been willing to take up the detail of Kant's arguments, even though it looks very much as though in Kant we find a distinctive understanding of morality emerging from the argumentative structure of the theory.

In the way I urge we think about practical reason, Kant's moral theory rests on an series of arguments designed to show that there could not be calculative reasons for acting unless there were moral reasons for acting, that is, that there could not be useful-style desirability characterizations if there were not moral reasons for acting. In the course of making these arguments, Kant produces a singular account of the status of moral reasons, and a picture of the character of calculative reasons that is in keeping with contemporary instrumentalism. I am unconvinced by Kant's arguments, in spite of having worked through a series of initial points of raw confusion surrounding his use of "will" and his claims about universality. My doubts are not doubts about transcendental idealism, exactly (which I have some faith might be reinterpreted to be made more acceptable). Rather, my doubts center on Kant's understanding of what law has to be like, and on the whole project of finding a picture of practical rationality as law-governed in a way that makes no essential reference to the kind of organism or species of being that has some share in it. Kant's arguments seem to me either (on some readings) to rely on a notion of law at once so narrow, so strangely authored and promulgated, and so demanding as to be mysterious, or else (on other, more Aristotelian readings) to rely on a notion of law that has its home in thought about the principles determining kinds of beings as such, which Kant then marries to a picture of the good that is no longer geared to thought about kinds of beings at all, even if we treat rational wills on the order of a species of being and the moral law as the principle governing finite, dependent rational creatures. For all that, Kant's is, as near as I can tell, the most impressive, sustained, and strict attempt to provide an argument that calculative reasons for acting owe their force to noncalculative reasons for acting. Accordingly, I provide some notes here about how one might go about fitting Kant's approach to the threefold division. There might be other ways of doing it, and it might also be that, on the best possible reading of Kant, his project is so unlike traditional moral philosophy as to have no relation to the kind of work found in Aquinas or Aristotle at all. I hope that we will not decide that Kant was *completely* original. Kant insisted that he was making his arguments about morality as it shaped the lives of plain people. And morality in the lives of plain people in Kant's world owed much to the moral tradition that is articulated and theorized in work of the sort we find in Aquinas. If the break between the two is too radical, there will be a real question what Kant was going on about. That is to say, even if Kant succeeds in demonstrating that the finite rational will is free and bound by the moral law, too radical a departure from the substance of older moral thought will make it an open question whether people are, in the relevant sense, finite dependent rational beings, or whether anything a human being might recognize as moral comes under the governance of the moral law.

Kant's argument that the good will operates from the motive of duty and is unconditionally good, and his insistence that thought about the human good, the good for our kind, is *as* unacceptably "conditional" as is thought about private advantage when it comes to understanding morality, have the effect of detaching thought about the good from thought about our kind. This in turn leaves the question of what will count as acting well wide open for anyone impressed by the analysis of morality, but uncertain that Kant's argument gives it substance in action. To see how to connect Kantian practical philosophy with the threefold division, it is helpful to return to Kant's discussions of motive.

Kant's discussions of motive are, I think, best interpreted as discussions of broad, patterning principles that give rise to many actions of various types, as well as to motivated omissions. Kant insisted that there are two sorts of motive: self-love and duty. These are not ends. Rather, both are principles for choosing among ends. Considerations of self-love do not tell me what to eat or how to win friends and influence people. They tell me to side with the action in prospect that seems most likely to further my other pursuits or bring me pleasure. Considerations of duty do not tell me how to make a budget that will permit me to both repay my debts and feed my children. They tell me that, even though I can think of many more enjoyable things to do with my paycheck than go grocery shopping and write checks to my creditors, what I *owe,* rather than what would be most gratifying to me, is what should come off of the top of my pay. What unites the many calculative episodes of a life, the intentional actions, into a single life with a discernible shape for Kant is the motive and, on Kant's scheme, the motive of duty is the primary ordering principle in the lives of finite, dependent rational beings as such. The motive of self-love, on the other hand, lends an essentially calculative shape to a life.

On the old-fashioned way of carving up the good, the sort of good at issue in a life governed by the motive of self-love is good in the sense useful. Considerations of self-love belong to sophisticated calculative reason, involving a mixture of short-term and long-range goals, and devoted to attaining the complex by attaining the various ends that are its parts. Useful-style good in Kant stands in sharp contrast to *bonitas moralis*—moral good—the good at issue in acting from duty.

The distinction between the motive of self-love and the motive of duty cannot be worked out solely in terms of patterning force. Self-love and duty are both patterning principles. The distinction comes to the fore, however, if we concentrate on the difference between the kind of care of self involved in discharging one's duties to oneself and the sort involved in the flat operation of the motive of self-love. Duties to oneself are *duties*. Hence, they fall within the scope of the motive of duty. They are not, however, the stuff of self-love.

The prohibitions on suicide, self-maiming, servility, and masturbation, and the duty to perfect oneself by, say, developing some skills and cultivating one's tastes, enter into Kant's scheme of things under the rubric of "duties to oneself." For example, the duty to refrain from suicide when I see no hope of attaining my ends and every likelihood that the continuance of my life will mean nothing but the increase of my already considerable sorrow is the requirement that I not permit myself to take the only option I see that might halt the catastrophe that my life has become. This is not a matter of scheduling or trade-offs. *Ex hypothesi*, I think it virtually impossible that I should be able to attain any cherished end, save the end of taking my own life, and I am deliberately forgoing *that* pursuit simply because one ought not to commit suicide. Learning Latin when I have no end that would be served by knowing Latin and do not especially take pleasure in language learning, or developing horticultural skills and tastes when I have no gardening ends, merely because it is a good thing to know Latin and to be able to tend a garden, likewise involve changes in my current ends, and may shift them considerably. Again, this is not a matter of scheduling and trade-offs. In the suicide case, it is a matter of not making my own end my end. In the Latin and gardening cases, it is a matter of end acquisition. What makes Kant's treatment of this distinction especially unusual and challenging is how very far removed from calculative reason morality becomes.

Kant's discussion of duty centers on the radically detached, majestically impersonal moral *must*. Because of this, thought about a special, noncalculative *should* (the *should* that would have involved discussion of the human good, rather than mere short-term advantage in Aquinas) has come to seem synonymous with discussion of a Kantian moral *must*, the *must* of duty. In turn, discussion of how it befits a human being to live has come to seem morally second-rate to many of us: merely empirical, or some such, rather than properly normative.

Kant argues that considerations of duty, unlike other sorts of practical considerations, enjoin finite, dependent rational beings to action *directly*, not *via* considerations about what is good for members of their species, what will further their private ends, or what will be pleasant to do. This is part of how Kant argues that morality is universal. When I do my duty from duty, I do what I ought to do simply because I ought to do it. At that moment, none of my other ends—ends that serve to distinguish me, *qua* practically rational creature, from every other such being—comes into play in determining me to my duty. Considerations of Kantian duty do not get their grip on me because doing what I must will further my other pursuits or be pleasant or befit me to do *qua* human, woman, mother, and so on. Private pursuits, characteristically human ends (say, those associated with friendship), pleasures in prospect—all are stripped away when I do my duty from duty: "Here bare conformity to universal law as such (without having its base in any law prescribing particular actions) is what serves the will as its principle, and must so serve if duty is not to be everywhere an empty delusion and a chimerical concept."[1]

If this is what morality is like, then it is impossible to treat the motive of duty as an advanced form of individual calculative practical reason. It is likewise impossible to see morality as grounded in a redirected, but still calculative, form of thought about how morality makes possible and is implicated in the characteristic ends of some kind of being—of people, for example. *Ex hypothesi* there is no private end of mine served by doing as I must because I must. *Ex hypothesi* morality is not even of special interest because there is a characteristic human end made attainable by individuals forgoing private advantage for the sake of right relations with their fellows (a style of argument Geach favors in discussing virtue, which finds some ground for the ethical in what *serves the ends* characteristic of our kind, even if it is a burden for the lone individual to operate on the basis of that kind of calculation). Instead, what can be said on behalf of doing my duty merely because I should in Kant's scheme of things is what could be said on behalf of any finite, dependent rational being doing its duty from duty.

If understand him, Kant holds that if I merely do my duty because it befits a *human being* to do things of certain kinds, I will be seeking a ground for my action in a characteristic of members of my kind that is, from the point of view of pure practical reason, an accidental empirical regularity lacking in the sort of necessity that attends morality. When I do my duty from a properly Kantian motive of duty, on the other hand, I am responding to the *same* sort of practical consideration in the *same* way as would a dutiful blob of nearly indestructible, extraterrestrial, practically rational goo. If there were such things as the angels one meets in Christian theology, then, since the Lucifer story shows that they can stray, I would be responding to the same kind of consideration as determines good angels to their duty from duty when I do mine. Puddles with wills, angels, sound adult human beings, and the like all wind up in the same boat from this perspective.

Notice that it is hard to come up with an account of reasons for acting that will otherwise make it out that there *is* a single boat here to contain all finite rational wills. For example, humans reproduce sexually, for the most part, and undergo a longish period of immaturity when they rely on adults for their care. The goods and duties of family life range themselves around these facts. Angels may, in some sense, have a father, but angel lore does not suggest that there is much in the way of family feeling between God and his angelic creations. One gets the impression that angels come into being fully formed, for example, and have no real infancy. Extraterrestrial blobs, on the other hand, might merely sometimes divide, and sometimes join together again: a legion of blobs might have a *single* rational will. Again, humans are mortal and more fragile than our imaginary blobs (who could, say, divide themselves many times over in order to dodge a blow). For all that, blobs and men might both be capable of suicide in moments of despair. Angels, by contrast, may not be by their own "hands" destructible (they are, for all that, creatures whose lives *begin,* and I suppose that an act of God could extinguish angelic life). And of course, what members of our three kinds of finite dependent rational beings *can* do (hence, concretely can *will* to do), varies accordingly. Whether there are angels or science fictional blobs of this sort, the point is that if there *were,* then they would be bound by the moral law in exactly the same way as we are by Kant's lights: each kind of thing could be the appropriate addressee of imperatives, and hence, of the categorical imperative. And this, in turn, makes the Kantian moral law as magnificently abstract as the Kantian moral *must* is impersonal.

Kant does connect the right operation of the moral law in life to an ultimate end, and does give a kind of account of the patterning principle for a life going in that direction. The ultimate end for finite, dependent rational beings is happiness in proportion to virtue, and the patterning principle for a life going in that direction is the motive of duty. Faring well in the sense attaining one's ultimate end and acting well in the sense having a will governed by the motive of duty to some extent thereby come together again.[2] The motive of duty limits my pursuits. If my will is good, then I will seek to deserve such happiness as I get; in short, I will forgo pursuit of advantage when the ends I might otherwise adopt, or the means available to attaining them, are morally impermissible.

However commonplace it has become to find philosophers discussing morality as if we all understood that the mere fact that I have a purpose, or, even, the mere fact that my purpose is in accordance with the human good, is not all by itself a guarantee that there is *any reason to do anything* in the vicinity, and easy as it is to treat this blitheness somehow vaguely

Kantian, it is hard to understand the operation of the Kantian motive of duty. Kant thought that it took a transcendental deduction to show that it was even *possible* that there could be a being who could act on the basis of something like the motive of duty, and his account of that possibility turned on noumenal freedom and the character of the will as practical reason. Neither will nor noumenal freedom has enjoyed anything like the popularity accorded to some parts of Kant's account of morality (for example, the popularity of one or another formulation of the categorical imperative divorced from its kin), and this should give us more pause than it does, I suspect.[3] The good realized by acting on the basis of the motive of duty, according to Kant, is conditioned neither by irrelevant facts of merely human nature, nor by the idiosyncrasies of one's private plans, projects, or tastes. The highest good, on the contrary, is the unconditional good.

I don't think that Aquinas would have known what to make of the suggestion that there was such a thing as "unconditional good" in the Kantian sense of the term. If there was, then it would be God's lot rather than ours to traffic in it. Our business would rather have been the human good, the good for our kind, about which Aquinas went on at considerable length. I find myself on the side of Saint Thomas here, Kant's point about the good will shining like a jewel while straining against "some special disfavour of destiny or . . . the niggardly endowment of step-motherly nature" notwithstanding.[4] It is, admittedly, a bit of a strain to accommodate the Kantian motive of duty to any of the three regions of the good that are my topic, although clear enough that if it has a home in the threefold division, its region will be the befitting (the other contenders, the useful and the pleasant, are complete nonstarters). The closest we come to a desirability characterization of one of the relevant sorts here is that it befits a finite, dependent, rational being to do its duty. It will come into play under the same sorts of circumstances as the Thomistic or Aristotelian versions: to show what one is doing in a favorable light when what one is doing looks to involve forgoing private advantage.

Moral Actions, Virtuous Actions, Expressive Actions

In the foregoing, I argue that all ordinary intentional actions exhibit a means–end or part–whole calculative form. Some theorists might want to deny this. After all, some classes of actions seem essentially noncalculative. The two that come to mind right off are moral action and expressive action. They are at different ends of a spectrum of purposes—at the one end the perfectly principled act, at the other the spontaneous release of feeling. (Notice that the first involves something on the order of the befitting, and the second something related to pleasure as a source of action.)

While I would hope that the arguments from Chapter 6 on useful-style desirability characterizations would work against raising this objection, my sense is that the approach to thought about instrumental reason that I am urging is sufficiently unfamiliar to make it worth going through some more cases. I mentioned early on that we have become very interested of late in how agents take it into their heads to do various things, in something like a genealogy of rational action. Calculative practical reasoning is one way that agents can take it into their heads to do things. Such reasoning is *not* how one winds up doing something by way of spontaneously expressing feelings, nor is it how one determines what, say, justice requires in the hard case. In short, the cases of ethical action and expressive action come to mind as possible counterexamples to the thought that intentional action as such is calculative because it is hard to imagine that one could arrive at a decision to act ethically or expressively on the basis of calculative practical reasoning. And practical reasoning is the source of reason in action that has been most discussed in recent years. (My adaptation of Anscombe's argument relied on another source—intention—and before making that argument, I gave some reasons not to worry overmuch about still other possible sources of reason in action.)

Although I have not tied my version of the standard picture to a claim that all intentional action is selected for during episodes of calculative practical thinking—"calculation," for short, that is, the business of figuring out how to attain some end you want to attain—calculation is not alien to the version of the standard picture I am trying to defend. Looking to the calculative form of intentional action is looking to something that could have been worked out in advance by an agent who wanted to attain or make possible the attainment of the whole or some part of her primary end. So it will help to work through expressive and moral action in order to show that both have calculative form and also that occasions for calculation might crop up in the course of either sort of action. These are separate points, of course. The crucial bit for my purposes is the calculative form. Whether one has to work things out as one goes along is another matter. But because I am urging a shift in focus for contemporary work on practical reason, it will help to work through examples of ethical and expressive action in order to show what they look like from this alternative point of view, even if my reader was easily won to the point that intentional action as such has a calculative form.

Ethical action is sometimes thought to be thoroughly reasoned in a way that has nothing to do with calculation. For instance, morality (at least since Kant) is generally seen as involving acting from principles that *forbid* trying to get some sorts of results at all (although which ones are prohibited may be a matter of circumstance, if you part ways from Kant and insist, for example, that I could be required to lie under sufficiently strange circumstances), *restrict* one's choice of means, *require* seeking other results by permissible means (again, on some contemporary views, depending on your situation), and *permit* what they do not prohibit in choice of means and ends. Nothing in the standard picture would set such limitations on choice, except insofar as choice of some means might preclude attainment of other ends pursued in a single course of action. In effect, if our picture of reasons for acting involves nothing but the calculative relation, *and* we are committed to the view that morality provides reasons for acting, then we must treat acting from moral principles as a peculiar sort of primary end for moral agents—a very queer objective that is never completely attained over the course of the agent's life, and crops up again and again, perhaps whenever the moral agent does anything at all. (In a way, this is how things go for Aquinas.) The philosopher interested in post-Kantian moral philosophy will counter that this explanation essentially distorts the phenomenon. If he goes so far as to argue that the distortion infects the very character of moral action, then he will be inclined to claim that no moral action is informed by the calculative relation.[1]

To see the problem with supposing that the depth of principle in morality infects the form of any process that might count as a moral action, consider the things one might do in order to contribute to famine relief: make out a check to Oxfam, put it in an envelope with a note, address and stamp the envelope, take it to the post office, mail it. This much can be said for any good deed: it can be completed (as the contribution to Oxfam is completed when the check is in the mail, or when Oxfam cashes it or applies the sum to famine relief, depending on how you like to mark such things), it can be interrupted or stopped (for example, if one has one's purse snatched on the way to the post office), it can succeed or fail to reach its intended end (the attempt to contribute to Oxfam could fail if one absentmindedly left the envelope on the counter at the post office), it is done on purpose, and it may display a bad bit of calculative reasoning or a sound grasp of means and ends (as, for example, putting the check in a bottle, casting it into the Atlantic, and counting on the grace of God to carry it to England and Oxfam displays inferior calculation).[2] There may well be noncalculative moral practical considerations, but there are *at least* calculative reasons for the means and parts of moral actions, and taking these is part of leading an ethically sound life.

I realize that setting out to lead an ethically sound life or always to do one's duty in spite of having a temperament that isn't especially ethically inclined or dutiful is a lifelong struggle. The struggle doesn't have an *end* in the same way that setting out to do such things as post a check to Oxfam, pay the light bill, keep a promise, or deliver truthful testimony in court has an end. Some befitting-style practical considerations are, as I stressed in Chapter 8, interestingly un-end-like—interminable, for short. But the lifelong struggle will be conducted in moments when one is called on *to do* something, and these doings, like the doings of vicious criminals or practical jokers, will have a means–end / part–whole articulation. By their very nature, considerations of duty are in principle inexhaustible in a single course of action. By their very nature, calculative practical considerations attach directly to actions and courses of action of the relevant kinds, and have the same shelf life as the action or course they inform (which may, of course, be identical with the span of one's maturity, if one has, say, a whole life plan or a ground project). But if morality or virtue or some such provides reasons for acting, it will be because of the calculative force such considerations have for the ethically laudable person, or the person who is doing as morality or virtue requires in order to improve herself. That is, it will be because the ethically/morally good pattern in her is a source of ends, or else because she is working to establish such a pattern in her affairs.

The exception might appear to be the person who, say, only undertakes one obligation-generating action in the course of her whole life (for example, makes exactly one promise) and can discharge the whole of that obligation in a single action or course (for example, by keeping the one promise she makes). Here, however, if she has the motive of duty or fidelity in her in the way the ethicist praises, it is an *accident* that she only has one chance to show her virtue. What is *not* an accident for the virtuous or moral person is that she does as she morally ought to do when the time comes. Moral practical considerations are supposed to exert long-term influence on the will. This makes them unlike my interest in making a sandwich now, which will be gone once the sandwich is made. For all that, while morality is not a calculative practical consideration, moral *actions* have calculative form and moral *reasons for acting* are such because of the ends involved in them, ends that have either to do with ethical self-improvement programs or the need to work to realize one's ethical or moral principles in practice. In this sense, it is because they carry something of useful-style practical considerations in them that they have practical significance.

I have just argued that moral actions do not provide counterexamples to the claim that all intentional action has a means–end / part–whole articulation. In the course of doing so, I have repeated the conclusion of the argument I took over from Anscombe in a slightly altered form. The other threat to that claim about the calculative order in intentional action comes from consideration of expressive actions—purposive acts born of mood, sentiment, or temperament which primarily express the agent's state of mind. Moral action threatened to prove the exception to the rule because the reasons for it seemed to go too deep. Expressive action is supposed to pose a problem because the reasons don't go deep enough. Expression is supposed to be *essentially* spontaneous. *Calculated* expression, it is sometimes thought, would be mere affectation, not real, heartfelt outpouring.

Morality and expressivity approach each other in some accounts of virtue born of the thought that virtuous action involves direct perception of what must be done and immediate response to that call, and is by its nature too spontaneous to leave any room for vulgar calculation. According to this view, the virtuous man *always* acts expressively, but his immediate impulses are in accordance with the highest good because he has a perpetual good state of mind, a good character, or a noble grasp of how it befits a human being to live. In general, action that appears a spontaneous expression of temperament, character, or feeling—virtuous or otherwise—seems to elude the calculative form of description because calculation truly is not in the spirit of the thing.

Now, the dividing line between deliberate action and eruption of feeling is not always easily drawn. There are borderline cases. There also are cases that fall squarely on the eruption end of the scale. Blushing, fainting, and sobbing, for instance are usually eruptions.[3] In order to prove an exception to the rule, an event must both have the spontaneity of expression and enough to it to land on the action side of the action–eruption border. Consider a man's cursing the heavens, sinking into a chair, beginning to weep, and reaching for a framed photograph of his friend Jack, upon learning that the train carrying Jack home for the holidays has been derailed and Jack has died in the wreck. The grieving man's response is not a calculated reaction to Jack's death in the way that selling off shares is a calculated reaction to market conditions. However, the response is complicated and involves, among other things, a definite sort of "speech-act"—cursing—that makes sense under the circumstances.

The spontaneity of the bereaved man's action is such that he could not have planned to do it in advance. In order to find the sense in which reacting to a friend's unexpected death could have been selected by calculative practical reasoning, we would have to imagine someone wanting to make a show of grief and choosing this way over, say, smearing ashes on her face and rending her clothes. (Such calculated expression is sometimes seen in stage plays and movies, and nonfictional calculated expression is involved in choosing cards, gifts, or flowers in order to express feelings.) But the clearest indication that expressive action has the calculative form is to be found in the structure of the action itself, and a kind of calculation can crop up in its course.

If the grieving man reaches for Jack's photograph because he wants to hold Jack's image close to him, then he will *stop* reaching when he gets hold of the photograph, and *start* pulling the photograph toward him. If, blinded by tears, he does not get his hands on the picture at first, then he has *failed* in his first attempt to get hold of the image in order to hug it close to his heart. If he gets his hands on the picture right off, then he will have *succeeded*. (If Anscombe asked "Why are you stretching your arm out?" and if he had the presence of mind to reply, then, presumably, he would tell her that he was reaching for the photograph.) Now, if one of us steps between the man and the picture as he reaches out, then she has *interrupted* his progress. If he pulls back his hand and asks that she give him the picture, then he is taking an *alternate means* to his end (this is how a kind of calculation could crop up in the course of the event—he could switch means upon seeing that the first way wasn't going to work after all). Strong emotion can take various primary ends (for instance, to get hold of a photograph or to smash things). The kind of calculation that happens in expressive action with such ends happens when one, say, takes aim in smashing things or uses some means to get hold of a photograph. What matters is that the calculative articulation of events is in place here. If we station our "Why?" questioners at various points along the path of an agent acting expressively, this becomes clear.

In light of this, it should be apparent that the standard picture will cope with spontaneous acts of virtue in the same way it handles other spontaneous, expressive intentional actions. Again, we need here to distinguish between virtue itself (whatever that might be) and virtuous actions in order to make the point stick. Like morality, virtue is not amenable to the calculative form of representation. But virtuous actions ought to display the calculative form. A good man sees a girl fall from her bicycle across the street and feels called on to help her, quite spontaneously. He glances at traffic. Why? In order to see if it's safe to dash across the street. He dashes across the street. Why? In order to get to the other side. He lifts the bicycle off the child. Why? In order to free the child. He bends down, speaks to her briefly, and lifts her up. Why? He is helping her to her feet and checking to see that she is not hurt. As near as I can tell, he wants to help her and does various things to that end. In this case, he doesn't work it all out in advance (but may, of course, work out bits as he goes along—for example, figuring out how to lift the bicycle without risking dropping it on her). Frankly, however, one would hope that a good person's virtue might lead her to do things that required, say, planning. That is, vulgar calculation.

For example, virtue does not only account for how the virtuous person responds to what happens, but sometimes also for how she gets herself into places where what happens calls for a virtuous response. In this sense, lived virtue may be much less like playing a video game (that is, pressing the right button when something that should be attended to flashes across the screen) than some contemporary accounts seem to suggest. A benevolent person does not merely feed those hungry who wander into her part of town and faint on her doorstep, but also sometimes goes to places where (she suspects) people may be going hungry, bearing food. Some benevolent people set up facilities where free food is served, and the hungry come find them. What is involved in setting up a successful facility of this sort is considerable ingenuity, imagination, financial planning, management, and so on. That is, it cannot happen without a lot of calculation, which is at odds with the picture of the virtuous person as bursting out into goodness when the occasion calls for it.

I confess that refusing these descriptions would seem to me to leave us with a picture in which virtue is much less interesting than we might have thought—more like an inner tendency to blush or swoon in various circumstances than a useful and praiseworthy human power exercised in intentional action.[4] Notice that the problem with bursting-out-in-goodness images of virtue is that they have *no* essential link to useful-style practical reason. What is wrong with them is that they focus on responses to passing events, without pointing the agent in the direction of future doings—without, that is, serving as a significant source of further, future ends. Which is just where one would expect the trouble to show itself after marrying Aquinas's threefold division to Anscombe's argument about future-directed practical considerations.

I have argued that neither expressive actions nor moral actions provide counterexamples to the claim that all intentional action lends itself to the calculative form of representation. But my interest in taking us through the calculative order in expressive and ethically praiseworthy action was also to underscore the conclusion of the argument I took from Anscombe, by looking to the calculative order *in* moral and expressive actions. I chose these two classes of actions because they are the two that some philosophers might have thought had no share in calculative practical reason, and I wanted to motivate the claims that all intentional action is informed by the calculative relation and that, because of this, all intentional action has a share of calculative practical reason at its core. This is the ground I see under the feet of the standard picture.

Some Notes about the
Standard Picture and Formal Work

Instrumentalism, Anti-Instrumentalism, and Formal Work on Decision and Choice

Instrumentalism has it that all reasons for acting are based in desires. Desires supply ends. Thought supplies ways of attaining ends. End of story. One virtue that instrumentalist practical philosophers sometimes claim for their view is that elaborating on this story produces elegant, formal models of reason in action. While the formal models generally concentrate on relations *between* ends represented as ordered "preferences," the basic thrust stays the same.[1] Formal work of the sort found in expected utility theory, Bayesian decision theory, and game theory, accordingly, seems to provide a clear target for a lot of anti-instrumentalist criticism. One style of complaint brought against instrumentalism by way of criticizing formal work trades on hard truths about desires.

The kind of criticisms I have in mind here begin by, say, mentioning that tastes can change daily and conclude that you seem to need more than plain desire to get desires to conform to a transitivity axiom. Human fickleness, the sensitivity of desire to context, and, in the trick cases, people's inability to multiply out probabilities and prizes in social science test-taking situations provide a wealth of material to draw on in complaining about independence axioms, suggesting, for example, that if you are indifferent between getting a and getting b, you ought to be indifferent between getting a with a probability of p and some irrelevant x with probability $(1 - p)$ and getting b with a probability of p and x with probability $(1 - p)$. The so-called incommensurability of values is invoked when one suggests that a completeness axiom might be an uncontroversial requirement on preference since one symptom of incommensurability is an inability to weigh various things one wants on a single scale. And so it goes.

In recent years, a minor but burgeoning intellectual industry has sprung up around churning out and chewing on such criticism. Here is how to make your own contribution to the genre: pick a formalization, choose your target axiom and a formal theorist who believes it to express an obvious truth about wanting, think about sets of things people might want that will lead to a violation of that axiom, write these down, find two responses the author might make to your counterexample, come up with an even more subtle, but still plausible counterexample. If you choose your target and examples wisely, you will be empowered to conclude that the formalization you have criticized does not live up to the instrumentalist promise to analyze practical reason plainly and simply as the power to figure out how to satisfy desires. And so, in an especially good essay of the sort I have described titled "The Failure of Expected Utility Theory as a Theory of Reason," Jean Hampton remarks, "It is amusing to me that [von Neumann / Morgenstern's] theory is regarded as 'psychologically abstinent' when they interpret it such that it takes a stand—and a highly implausible one—on human psychology."[2]

While this kind of criticism doesn't argue that it would be impossible for human desires to conform to the relevant axioms, nor even that there would be any defect in a system of axiom-conforming desires, it does suggest that by the time we have theorized reason in action along the lines suggested by formal work, we no longer have a picture of practical reason as the power to figure out how to get what one anyway wants. Instead, we have a picture of the *species of wanting* that fits the models. That kind of wanting is not plain old human wanting at all. Axiom-conforming wanting is much more orderly than the sort responsible for internally generated human misery and scandalous results in economics experiments. The axioms may give us a finish line to head for in trying to rein in and direct desire, but they do not describe human desire as we know it.

Now, there are numerous responses to this style of criticism in the relevant literatures. An important one is to deny that formal work is instrumentalist, a response sometimes made by formal theorists and sometimes made by anti-instrumentalists. But my favorite is Leonard Savage's reaction on discovering that his own preferences violated his own axiom: straightaway, he wanted to change what he wanted.[3] Critics have complained that the response was question-begging, but some of the most interesting responses in the genre center on generating higher-order preferences in order to tidy up the first order. The problem is that it is hard to make the responses seem compelling to people adept at deploying psychological insights about desires.

Some formal theorists are disturbed by the kind of attack I have outlined because they want their formal models to be good predictive tools for social science, and some are concerned because they want models that are close enough to human life to describe reason in human action, whether or not descriptively powerful models will function as sound predictive tools. Surely, however, the more abstract, philosophical concern about the criticism is coming from thought about ethical neutrality. Instrumentalism promises to account for reason in action without importing any tendentious or moralistic claims about what people are supposed to desire. The critics I have described interpret the axioms of formal choice theories as *constraints on desires,* as, for example, assertions that, under some conditions, people are *supposed to* prefer playing Lottery *A* to playing Lottery *B.* Hampton's aside about "psychological abstinence" was *not* meant to suggest that formal work is supposed to employ no psychological vocabulary or apply no matter how we think about mental states and processes. She meant that if the formal work is interpreted as instrumentalist work, then it is supposed to take you from desire to choice no matter what you happened to desire.

In formal work, preferences are treated as expressions of ends. Since instrumentalism is not supposed to be about the rationality of *ends,* arguing that the theories (a) are instrumentalist and (b) place substantial constraints on preferences makes it look as though an illicit move has been made offstage somewhere. It looks this way because instrumentalism is supposed to be neutral with respect to the content of preferences/ends/desires. Concern over the rationality of ends almost invariably leads one toward thought about the good, the noble, the prudent, the beautiful, or some such, and the ambition was to account for reason in action *without* taking a stand on these topics. But you can't plug just any old sets of desires into the models and get decisions or actions as outputs. Thus, it looks as though one of the best features of instrumentalism—neutrality with respect to ends—is lost in formal work. That is, it looks as though, rather than telling you how to get what you anyway desire, the models tell you *what you are supposed to desire.* So, either the formal work is *not* instrumentalist work at all, or it is instrumentalist in a subtle way that is misinterpreted by the critics, or it is correctly interpreted by the critics and unsupportable.

I think that formal work is *not* instrumentalist, that it *is* misinterpreted by the critics, and that it *may be* supportable. I think that the intuitions that drive formal work find their home not in instrumentalism, but in something more like the standard picture. My aim here is to begin to sketch what a standard picture interpretation of the formal work might look like, and to explain why I suspect that it is the better way to go. In the course of doing so, I deploy some points about desire by way of arguing that "preferences" of the sort that are discussed by formal theorists are *not* psychological states akin to desire. As I put it, "preferences" (the subject of the axioms in formal work) are not preferences (psychological states akin to desire). But I mean my contribution to the genre as a way of clearing ground in order to argue that intention and calculative wanting, rather than desire and preference, should be seen as the topic of the axioms. I am not a formal theorist. My concern will be with the conceptual core of formal work, not model-building. By arguing that this core is lodged in the standard picture, not in instrumentalism, I mean in part to give additional support to my initial claim that the standard picture, not instrumentalism, is responsible for the conviction that calculative work on practical reason deserves the status of "default" or "standard" work on reason in action. I argue that formal work is *not* instrumentalist, but that it *is* calculative, and that it *could be read* as a formalization of the standard picture.

Revealing Preferences

There are many ways of approaching formal work on decision and choice, many kinds of mathematical models, many proposals about axioms, and so on. What they share is an intuition that preferences can be inferred from behavior, and can then be modeled by applying to them some points about probability distributions.

For example, suppose that an agent chooses one outcome, o_1, over another, o_2. Infer that she prefers o_1 to o_2.[4] To give a systematic representation of an agent's "preferences" over outcomes, o_1, o_2, and o_3, next offer her a choice between (1) a lottery ticket, $[p_x: o_1, o_2]$, that offers her o_1 with probability p_x and o_2 with probability $(1 - p_x)$, and (2) getting o_3.

Suppose that for some ticket [p_3: o_1, o_2], the agent is indifferent between getting the ticket and getting o_3. Armed with this information it is possible to construct a systematic representation of the agent's "preferences" based, essentially, on the probabilities attaching to the various outcomes (the lottery ticket, notice, is defined by the probabilities of getting two of the three outcomes and the *risk-free* alternative involves an offer in which $p(o_3) = 1$). In so doing, you can calibrate the "preference" scale as finely as you need to by offering additional lottery tickets, provided that the outcomes (the lottery prizes) are such that you can use the probabilities attaching to the prizes in order to get your scale,[5] and the "preferences" meet some conditions that are necessary in order to get them to behave well once linked to probabilities.

The conditions that must be met by "preferences" are standardly given by axioms. Let a and b designate outcomes/prizes and let '$a \geq b$' mean that a is, from the player's point of view, as good as or better than b. The standard axioms include a completeness requirement that for any two prizes a and b, $a \geq b$ or $b \geq a$; and a transitivity requirement that, for any prizes a, b, and c, if $a \geq b$, and $b \geq c$, then $a \geq c$. These first two bring all the items relevant to choice in context under the agent's "preference" relation. Next, there is a continuity requirement that for any prizes, a, b, and c, where a is the most preferred outcome and c is the least preferred outcome, there is some probability p_a, such that the agent is indifferent between b and a lottery ticket [p_a: a, c] giving her a with probability p_a and c with probability $(1 - p_a)$, which establishes the initial linkage between the "preference" relation and the likelihood that "preferences" will be satisfied. In the service of establishing systematic relations between "preferences" and probabilities, we add an independence axiom requiring that if the agent is indifferent between a and b, she will be indifferent between two lotteries whose only difference is that a is substituted for b, an axiom allowing you to make use of the probability calculus to convert "preferences" over compound lotteries (lotteries whose prizes are lotteries) into preferences over simple lotteries with the same expected values (where expected values are computed by multiplying the outcome value by the probability of getting the outcome), and a montonicity axiom that has it that [p_1: a, b] $\geq$ [p_2: a, b] if and only if p_1 is greater than or equal to p_2. Completeness and transitivity establish a "preference" relation. Standardly, axioms covering continuity, independence, the reduction of compound lotteries, and montonicity establish systematic connections between preferences and probabilities (by exploiting the fact that lotteries assign probabilities to outcomes/prizes). The reduction of compound lotteries axiom, incidentally, helps to screen out cases where an agent's attitudes toward gambling might enter in to disrupt model construction. If one loves gambling, one might prefer lotteries over lotteries to lotteries over outcomes. If one hates gambling, things might go the other way round. This kind of thing is irrelevant. The models are abstract, formal devices for representing contexts of choice, not a virtual weekend in Las Vegas.

Axiomatizations of the sort I have described, and variations thereon, make it possible to use the probability calculus to model choice. It is an extraordinarily powerful approach, and however messy some of the axiomatizations get, the approach retains the elegance of the probability calculus. Probabilities, recall, are represented by real numbers on the closed interval [0,1]. The probability symbol, p, stands for a number on this interval, and the operations used to combine probabilities are the familiar arithmetical ones: addition, subtraction, multiplication, division. Because the lottery ticket method attaches probabilities to outcomes, and because we model choice over gambles as displaying "preferences," we are able to get an (essentially) arithmetical system for scaling "preferences" by (hypothetically) offering agents choices over gambles. What looked like a very hard problem, getting some formal method of modeling contexts of choice, becomes vastly simplified.

I mentioned in Chapter 1 that some instrumentalists point to the possibility of giving formal treatments of decision or choice as a point in favor of instrumentalism. This is because, if instrumentalism is true, then all reasons for acting are based in something like desire. Preference is something like desire. "Preferences" are not entirely unrelated to preferences. So we may have found a formal method of investigating instrumental practical reason. In effect, the suggestion is, formal work on decision and choice exploits the mathematically elegant properties of probability distributions for the sake of theorizing reason in action. This will only help instrumentalism, of course, if "preferences" are enough like desires/preferences to read formal work as interestingly concerned with the bit of psychology at the core of instrumentalism. This is what I think *cannot* be shown.[6] Moreover, I think that the problems are clear in the very first, apparently innocuous move: the supposition that what is revealed and systematized with the aid of the probability calculus in formal work on choice are, in the ordinary sense, preferences.

Now, there are notorious difficulties associated with making sense of probabilistic reasoning that center on interpreting the status of the probabilities.[7] Leave these to one side. Pretend that outcomes relative to actions come with probabilities attached of the sort that figure in actuarial tables or games of chance. It is already mysterious why we ought to think we have learned anything about preferences from formal work, because it is unclear why preferences ought to be systematically sensitive to the likelihood that they will be satisfied. "Preferences" display such sensitivity, but why should preferences?

Preference and Probability

Suppose, for example, that I think that there is a probability of 0.23 that D will fall in love with me if I spend time with him, and a probability of 0.77 that J will fall in love with me given ample opportunities to enjoy the pleasure of my company. Suppose that I want to become the object of romantic attention and that J and D are the only two candidates on my romance horizon. The construction of my preference scale begins, therefore, with

A: Someone falls in love with me.
B: No one falls in love with me.

I prefer A to B, so we can arbitrarily assign a "desirability" of 2 to A, 1 to B. Now, by my estimation, A has a probability of 0.23 given that I spend time with D, and a probability of 0.77 given that I spend time with J. So it looks like we should be able to get a measure of my preferences over companions by multiplying the likelihood of romance by the desirability of becoming someone's object of affection. This gives time with D a desirability of 0.46, time with J a desirability of 1.54. Perhaps, then, I can be expected to choose time with J over time with D, and thereby reveal a preference for time with J.

But is there as yet any reason to expect me to prefer spending time with J over spending time with D? If you offer me a choice between a weekend with J and a weekend with D, have I any reason to prefer the former? Not really. D might be a god in my eyes. I might think J a monster. "Better solitude than coping with J's amorous attentions," I think.

But, hang on, let's try something else. My refusal to take up your offer of a weekend with J could be a clue that you have misrepresented the initial preference ranking. Perhaps what I have is a preference ordering more like this:

A: I spend a weekend with D.
B: I spend a weekend alone.
C: I spend a weekend with J.

What is the desirability of solitude? We know that I think it about as likely (given a weekend together) that D will fall in love with me as that I draw a face card when taking a card at random from a standard deck of fifty-two playing cards. We know I think it about as likely (given a weekend together) that J will fall in love with me as I that I will draw a nonface card in a random pick from the same deck of cards. This ought to be more than enough to work with in constructing my preference scale by considering my choices over gambles. For some p, there might well be a lottery ticket [p: *A, C*] offering me D's companionship with probability p, J's companionship with a probability $(1 - p)$ such that I am indifferent between getting that ticket and solitude. We have our end points and enough information to locate solitude precisely. By the continuity assumption, there should be such a ticket. We expect it to be one where p is very high. Getting me to choose among such tickets should be enough to construct a systematic representation of my preferences.

Or should it? Again, not necessarily. I may have been interested spending time with D *because* I suffer in my love life from the same syndrome affecting Groucho Marx in his feelings about club membership: I would not join anyone likely to have me as a partner, and tend rather to seek out people who are likely to reject me. It will be very hard to correlate *that* kind of preference system to choice by means of the likelihoods attaching to outcomes.

On the other hand, I may be an amorous adventuress: without the effort of conquest, the romance is scarcely worth having, hence no opportunity for romance "won" in a lottery will do. And so I make my choices among tickets with two aims in mind:

1. to choose the least desirable partner as the "prize" person,
2. to avoid any set-up that will make a romance bloom as a result of a lottery.

Choice (2) will lead me to go for tickets that offer me a better chance of getting a weekend of solitude than a weekend with company. Choice (1) will lead me to favor time with J over time with D. To be safe, if D is my quarry, then solitude or time with J will be the prizes I shoot for. In this kind of case, it is hard to see why we would expect to see preferences clearly reflected in choices over lottery tickets.

The formal theorist will object that the lottery is merely a device to enable representation of preference, and that this purpose will of course be defeated if we have agents who object to gambling over some outcomes. But while some features of the romance example distort the abstract purposes of the technique, more generally there is a problem about reading preferences from choices. On an ordinary understanding of preference, to say that you prefer *a* to *b* is to say that you think *a* in some respect better than *b*. But the "better" of preferable is not necessarily the better of more choice-worthy. As I mentioned in Chapter 2 in connection with specific good, I prefer good dinner tables to bad ones—deeply prefer the good to the bad in dinner tables, actually—but straightaway will choose a bad dinner table over a good one for a particular sort of stage set. More generally, however, it is hard to see why we would expect preferences to vary systematically with estimates of the likelihood of getting this or that outcome *at all*. And, in a way, the core intuition captured by the formal modeling device is that "preferences" *are* sensitive to the likelihood that they can be satisfied. That is why you can be expected to go for lottery tickets systematically, provided that the arithmetic doesn't confuse you. That is what makes the probability calculus available for use in modeling choice. "Preference" operates that way. Preference does not. Preference is a bit like desire. "Preference" is not. Suppose, for example, that you have very good taste in some area, and very good taste there as elsewhere often draws you toward what is relatively rare and hard to get. Think how strange it would be to suggest that the seasoned art collector's preferences over potential acquisitions ought to be sensitive to his estimates of the likelihood of procuring the various works that strike him as aesthetically meritorious.[8]

On any ordinary understanding of preference, preference is not interestingly sensitive to the possibility that one's preferences will be satisfied. Neither is preference necessarily revealed by choice behavior. I can even choose a thing *in order to* mislead someone about what I prefer, as, for example, when I put aside a plate full of wonderful food and consume three bites of little M's baby food with apparent gusto in order to make it appear that I would gladly trade my meal for M's, thereby getting M to take a lively interest in eating his food (he has been, say, trying to reach my food, and I fear that he will choke if he tries to eat what's on my plate). I can choose a thing that I expect will be very bad indeed when something I expect to be decidedly better is available to me, and this need reflect no failure of reason on my part, no weakness of will, and so on. It need not even arise from a deliberate attempt to mislead anybody: I may be experimenting or I may be out to make a point. Whatever the case, the kind of link that allows one to formulate axioms governing "preference" with an eye toward making use of the mathematical tools familiar from probability theory would not appear to be a link between plain preference and estimates of the future. It is hard to see what these two have to do with one another at all, if *preference* is the name of a psychological state that is in some respects akin to desire or wanting.

Shifting from Preference to Intention

Suppose, then, that what is revealed in choice is *not* preference. Will this mean that formal work is all washed up? No. It will just mean that formal work is not strictly instrumentalist. There is another way to interpret this work, however. Recall that, even though I can want just about anything (for example, to wake to discover that a Fra Angelico fresco has been magically transferred to my living room wall, and Lucas Cranach the Elder's *Adam and Eve* now hangs in my bedroom), I cannot intend to do what I take it that I cannot do. *Desire* may be blithely insensitive to the chances that it will be satisfied, but *intention* is highly sensitive to one's estimate of the likelihood that one can carry out the thing one means to do. So first off, notice that intention (as I have been using the term), at least stands a chance of being what formal work is about, whereas the prospects are dim from the get-go if we think we are on about preference.

Second, notice that, while there is no special reason to restrict one's preferences to future states of affairs (I would prefer that various things about my upbringing had gone differently, for instance), or to things it is in one's power to do or affect (I would also prefer that certain large-scale, ongoing injustices end now), intentions are, paradigmatically, directed at future events that it is in one's power to make happen or make possible. Part of why intention is sensitive to the likelihood that one can succeed in doing what one means to do is that it looks to the future, and it is irrational to intend to do a thing one has no reason to expect one can do.

Third, intention is intention to do something. Its object is intentional action, an end-directed *event*. Probabilities of the sort involved in a lot of formal work also attach to outcome-directed events—rolls of the dice that end up this way or that, drawings, card picks, and the like. Preference is not in this way restricted.

Fourth, notice that some portion of a man's intentions *are* revealed in what he does, even if he is acting in order to disguise some other aspect of what he has in view. On this topic, I quote Anscombe at length:

> [H]ow do we tell someone's intentions? or: what kind of true statements about people's intentions can we certainly make, and how do we know that they are true? That is to say, is it possible to find types of statements of the form "A intends X" which we can say have a great deal of certainty? Well, if you want to say at least some true things about a man's intentions, you will have a strong chance of success if you mention what he actually did or is doing. For whatever else he has in mind, or whatever may be his intentions in doing what he does, the greater number of the things which you would say straight off a man did or was doing, will be things he intends.
>
> I am referring to the sort of things you would say in a law court [if] you were a witness and were asked what a man was doing when you saw him. That is to say, in a very large number of cases, your selection from the immense variety of true statements about him which you might make would coincide with what he could say he was doing, perhaps even without reflection, certainly without adverting to observation. I am sitting in a chair writing, and anyone grown to the age of reason in the same world would know this as soon as he saw me, and in general it would be his first account of what I was doing; if this was arrived at with difficulty, and what he knew straight off were how precisely I was affecting the acoustical properties of the room (to me a very recondite piece of information), then communication between us would be rather severely impaired.[9]

Not only is intention interestingly sensitive to estimates of the future, restricted to things it is in one's power to make happen or make possible, and directed at events, some part of it *is* revealed in intentional action. This is a fourth reason to suppose that formal work has much more to do with the standard picture than it has to do with contemporary instrumentalism.

But if this is right, what are formal models models *of*? How are we to motivate the axioms that effect the transition from probability theory to intention and intentional action? I suggest the following: the axioms should be considered (and assessed) as proposals about the constraints that must be met by *systems of potential ends* that the agent wants to attain in a *single* course of action; they place constraints on what sorts of things an agent can reasonably seek to attain in a single pursuit within a clearly defined context of choice. I do not run through the many proposed axiomatizations here. Nor do I give a very detailed assessment of the axioms I focus on as constraints that must be met if ends are to be jointly considered in a single context of choice. I simply give a sample sketch of how such an interpretation of the point of the axioms will go.

A Sample Reinterpretation

What are constraints expressed by the axioms constraints *on*, from the view of intention? Means and ends, parts and wholes, basically. First, for simplicity's sake, restrict the outcomes/prizes at issue such that each is something I want to do or make possible. That is, let the outcomes/prizes be treated as potential ends that are framing a single context of choice. Second, let lottery tickets serve as (rather severely impoverished) representations of means that might be taken to those ends. Third, treat lotteries over several and various outcomes as complex means that might make possible the attainment of any of several ends I seek to attain. Winning becomes attaining an end by the chosen means. And "preference" becomes interestingly related to the kind of wanting relevant to the standard picture.

We get:

> *Completeness:* the requirement is that for any two separable ends I
> want to attain within a single course of action, I must be able to direct my efforts such that I am devoting more to one, or to the
> other, or that I am working equally in order to attain both. A violation of this axiom could involve such things as starting six projects
> and finishing none because I cannot manage to set priorities.
> *Transitivity:* if I am at least as concerned with attaining *a* as with attaining *b*, and at least as concerned with attaining *b* as attaining *c*,
> then I must be at least as concerned with attaining *a* as with attaining *c*.

These two axioms establish the rough basis on which it becomes possible for me to handle pursuit management by means of scheduling and trade-offs. How does probability come in? First, we will have to do away with the relevant version of the "attitudes toward gambling" problem by restricting our attention to *acceptable* means. What makes means acceptable to an agent may involve a noncalculative filter, of course, if noncalculative befitting-style principles are helping to shape decision for her. Still, it is a bit of a stretch to get probabilities into the interpretation in the right way:

> *Continuity:* I want to attain a, b, or c (in that order). My wanting obeys the completeness and transitivity axioms (that is, it enables scheduling and trade-offs). For some probability, p, I must be indifferent between taking acceptable, adequate means to b and taking acceptable means that will result in a with probability p, c with probability $(1 - p)$. (We might call this a "good faith" requirement of sorts; it renders more precise the willingness to make trade-offs.)
>
> *Reduction of compound lotteries:* I want to attain a, b, or c. I should be indifferent between various acceptable means that give me the same chance of attaining my ends.
>
> *Independence:* I want to attain a, b, or c. If I am indifferent between attaining a and attaining b, I should be indifferent between taking acceptable means that will result in a with probability p, c with probability $(1 - p)$ and acceptable means which will result in b with probability p, c with probability $(1 - p)$.
>
> *Monotonicity:* I want to attain a, b, or c. If I am most concerned with attaining a, and least concerned with attaining c, then given a choice of acceptable means that will result in a with probability p_1, c with probability $(1 - p_1)$, and acceptable means which will result in a with probability p_2, c with probability $(1 - p_2)$, I should be at least as willing to take the former as the latter if and only if p_1 is greater than or equal to p_2.

My sense is that the sort of calculative thought involved in this reading underlies and drives some of the intuitions in formal work. My sense is also that the axioms look much less implausible if we think of them in this way. They do so because calculative wanting and intention are much better candidates for governance by such axioms than desire and preference. I will not go into it here, but the tremendous emphasis on strategies (that is, means–end calculative plans) in game theoretic work makes it even clearer that we are on about the structure of intention in formal work, not about desire.

It is vital for my reinterpretation of the axioms that we consider singular courses of action/contexts of choice. Of course, a singular course can be a very complex and long-term affair, the result of long-term financial planning, or career planning, or an agricultural scheme involving planting orchards that won't yield an appreciable harvest for decades. But it is important that we make the restriction because, on the interpretation I have sketched, what the axioms concern is ends *internal* to something on the order of a single course of action or context of choice. Violations of the axioms *outside* these bounds will not, on this proposal, count as problems.[10] The standard picture concerns the structure *internal* to a means–end process. There is no requirement that I pursue the same things with the same seriousness from one day to the next or one year to the next. I might, and if I do, it will be possible to extend a formalized picture accordingly. But that will be up to me.

Notes

Introduction

1. Rosalind Hursthouse, *On Virtue Ethics,* pp. 15–16.
2. Philippa Foot, *Natural Goodness,* p. 21.
3. Elizabeth Anscombe, "Von Wright on Practical Inference," p. 378. The quote concludes a dense, cryptic objection to Donald Davidson's work on reasons for action. I discuss the objection briefly in Appendix B.
4. See his "Are Moral Requirements Hypothetical Imperatives?" pp. 18–19.
5. See, for example, Christine Korsgaard's discussion of the place of reflective practical endorsement in life in *The Sources of Normativity,* pp. 90–130, and Elijah Millgram's discussion of selfhood and noninstrumental reasoning in *Practical Induction,* pp. 43–85. Both would argue that they are not giving end-based justification for noninstrumental exercises of practical reason. The forms of argument at issue in each are "transcendental" arguments, arguments that aim to display something like the conditions that make possible what we already know happens. But the phenomenon in question in each case is "unified" individual human agency, and the account of the place of practical induction or reflective endorsement in making possible duly unified agency is rather more causal than conceptual. What we are given is stories about how this phenomenon comes about, what things would be like if it didn't come about, and what sort of psychological exercise contributes to the production and maintenance of appropriate selves. That is why I am taking these two as examples here.
6. See, for example, Michael Slote, *Morals from Motives,* pp. 169–196. Slote ties the crude picture of human motivation at issue in instrumentalism to consequentialism in ethics. Robert Nozick sees a similar link. I set it to one side in note 1 of Chapter 1.
7. "The Book of the Death of Arthur," in *The Collected Books of Jack Spicer,* p. 211.
8. There are, of course, contemporary moral theories that accept instrumentalism about practical reason and argue that there is a strong calculative in-

centive to be moral no matter what the content of one's ends might be. But since we can imagine that someone's most cherished end might be to die before he is twenty-five and take out as many other people as possible on the way (he might even have a view of contemporary life to offer in support of this end), it is very hard to get the result independently of setting substantive constraints on the content of the ends that find their best hope of attainment under, say, circumstances of justice. It may even be that a kind of trust between people that flows from justice is what our would-be mass murderer is banking on in setting out to die-while-murdering, but that only shows the we have provided the background conditions he requires in order to attain that end. Notice, some species of fraud are impossible outside the whole institution of contract, but *that* does not show that the person intent on fraud has miscalculated how to get what she wants, given that contractual institutions are in place. It just shows that her mode of acting ill is parasitic on a conventional mode of acting well.

1. Instrumentalism about Practical Reason

1. Nozick, *The Nature of Rationality,* p. 133. Nozick makes two assumptions that I reject. First, he assumes that the standard theory is broadly desire-based (133–136). I argue that the strongest version of this view is not desire-based. Second, he assumes that the standard theory concerns "causally expected utility" (134–139). Throughout this book, I will treat a part–whole relation among acts of given types as one instance of the relation central to the standard theory. In order to treat a part–whole relation as a species of causal relation, one needs to resort to antiquated causal vocabulary, claiming, for instance, that the parts "materially cause" the whole and the whole "formally causes" the parts. That *cannot* be what causal decision theorists had in mind.

2. I take it that the Groucho Marx preference is not a convoluted expression of the desire to avoid club membership; rather, it represents a desire *to* join any clubs that *won't* have him as a member. The preference is both in principle unsatisfiable (others are, for the subject, desirable companions just as long as they reject him) and familiar enough to make the joke work. In principle unsatisfiable preferences could also include wanting to find integral roots for $[n^2 + 2n + 2 = 0]$, or wanting the planet's geological past to have gone differently so that the piece of land one just bought would have the ten-to-twenty-foot layer of loess that the neighboring county enjoys.

3. As an aside, some traditions have it that a positive *desire* to attain enlightenment is enough to hinder one's progress in Buddhism (i.e., whatever kind of

reason for acting that apprehension of the Four Noble Truths is supposed to provide, it is not a desire-based reason for acting).

4. I cast this remark in terms of act types rather than, say, states of affairs or objects. The quick explanation for my formulation is that we are concerned here with the justification of *action*. The claim is that secondary ends (A-ings) are shown to be justified in terms of how they contribute to attaining primary ends (B-ings). The relation in question is most naturally expressed this way: I am/will/was A-ing in order to B. For example, I am breaking eggs in order to make an omelet. Obviously, this kind of account can be extended to other actions—I am tapping the eggs on the side of the bowl in order to break them; I am making an omelet in order to feed myself a nice breakfast. Because it is possible to extend the account in these ways, it is easy to see that ends that are secondary with respect to one end (breaking eggs is a means to or part of making an omelet) are primary with respect to another end (tapping the eggs against the side of the bowl is a means to or part of breaking them). Casting the whole account in terms of act types is the easiest way to capture this point about the justification of action. There is a deeper reason to employ the act-type formulation. I take up the deeper reason in the following chapters.

5. A firm could not have intentions, of course, unless some of its officers had psychological states directed at realizing them. However, it is entirely possible that complex corporate intentions, established, say, through the votes of board members on policy matters, will not be identical with *any* individual member's intentions. Such corporate intentions only coincide with what officers have in mind to the extent that officers are determined to carry out the will of the board. For a representation of the voting difficulty, see Elizabeth Anscombe, "On Frustration of the Majority by Fulfilment of the Majority's Will."

6. Some intuitionists, some virtue theorists, and some early moral sentiment theorists have such a view.

7. See, for example, David Gauthier, *Morals by Agreement*, pp. 21–59. Gauthier accepts (1), (2), and (3). His emphasis on maximization implies a rejection of (4).

8. For example, Henry Richardson argues against instrumentalism by arguing against (3), taking it that a sound argument against (3) will undercut (2) and cast some doubt on (1). See Richardson, *Practical Reasoning about Final Ends*. Again, Richardson takes it that (1), (2), and (3) are crucial to instrumentalism. His own system sets very stringent requirements on the form of action guidance given by practical reasoning. It is not enough that some act be *a* way of attaining some end in order for the agent to have a justification

for action. The grounds must instead in some way *necessitate* the action that they support. This much, he takes it, he shares with the instrumentalists. In this sense, he does not see (4) as central to instrumentalism.

9. Elijah Millgram, for instance, takes Robert Audi's views on practical reason as a paradigmatic instance of instrumentalism because Audi holds that practical reasoning is solely concerned with matching means to ends (see Millgram, *Practical Induction,* p. 4). Here, it seems that (3) is at the heart of instrumentalism. But in the work to which Millgram refers, Audi thrice denies instrumentalism on the grounds that some ends are rationally desirable in themselves (see Audi, *Practical Reasoning,* pp. 179, 183, 191). Audi takes some variant of (4) to be crucial to instrumentalism. Jean Hampton focuses upon the metaphysics of value in arguing against instrumentalism (see Hampton, *The Authority of Reason,* pp. 6–7, 125–216). She takes (1) to be the central instrumentalist thesis. Christine Korsgaard initially takes (2) (bifurcationism about motivation) and (3) jointly to describe instrumentalism in practical philosophy (see Korsgaard, "Skepticism about Practical Reason"). She later shifts her attention to (1) (the metaphysics of value view) and to (4) (the claim about rational justification) (see Korsgaard, "The Normativity of Instrumental Reason," pp. 215–254). Warren Quinn takes it that (2), (3), and (4) form a single thesis rightly identified with instrumentalism, which he calls *neo-Humeanism.* His argument against this view proceeds on the basis of a denial of some versions of (1). See Quinn, "Rationality and the Human Good."

10. By "otherwise unrelated" I mean, for example, that some philosophers take some passages of David Hume as the *locus classicus* of instrumentalism, others take the views of Thomas Hobbes as definitive, others take work in neoclassical economic expected utility theory as the best statement of instrumentalism, others focus on Bayesian decision theory, and still others head for Aristotle. The most common trend is to blend the diverse moral psychological doctrines of early modern British philosophers and then mix the result with formal work on decision and choice, in order to produce an instrumentalist theory of practical reason. Hume argued against Hobbes's account of motivation. Both Hume and Hobbes offered substantive accounts of human psychology, which neoclassical economics refuses to do—indeed, getting distance from empiricist psychology is generally regarded as an instance of significant conceptual progress in economics. In some variants of Bayesian decision theory, preferences—the "volitional" element in rational decision—are a *function* of subjective probability distributions (the "cognitive" element), and there is absolutely no room left for any version of substantive motivational bifurcationism. Think how odd it would be to call reason a "slave" to the products of formal derivation!

11. See, for example, Jean Hampton, "The Failure of Expected Utility Theory as a Theory of Reason."

12. See, for example, Jean Hampton, *The Authority of Reason,* pp. 167–206; Christine Korsgaard, "The Normativity of Instrumental Reason," pp. 215–254; and James Dreier, "Humean Doubts about the Practical Justification of Morality," pp. 81–99.

13. If I understand him, some such query may have inspired Thomas Nagel to distinguish motivated desire from unmotivated desire. See *The Possibility of Altruism,* pp. 27–30.

14. What follows is a bit of creative reconstruction. Instrumentalists have not in general addressed the question about volitional transfer.

15. This particular field of controversy is especially vexed. It seems to me that to the extent that formal work on decision and choice has severed all ties to substantive doctrines about the nature of psychological states and processes, formal theorists could rightly reject both instrumentalist appropriations of their views and anti-instrumentalist criticisms of their views. Nevertheless, it is the prevalence of formal modeling techniques in some regions of social science that is most often taken to provide a guarantee of instrumentalism's intellectual credentials.

16. I discuss Dewey's instrumentalism, and contemporary instrumentalism in moral philosophy and in philosophy of science, in *John Stuart Mill's Deliberative Landscape,* ch. 2.

17. I do not discuss individuation of act types at any length. For my purposes, the following crude account of what is at stake in calling *A* and *B* "different kinds" of acts will suffice. *A* and *B* are acts of different kinds just in case completing an act of type *A* need not coincide with completing an act of type *B.*

18. I have used terms like "principally" and "primarily" to foreshadow a caveat. My claims about the centrality of the standard picture are drawn from a point about (the representation of) intentional action: namely, that intentional action paradigmatically has a means–end/part–whole calculative form. There may be "atomic" acts, human acts that lack this form. I argue that these could not be the central or typical cases of intentional action.

19. "MacGuffin" is a term for the seemingly irrelevant item on which the whole plot turns. It helps explain the success of Alfred Hitchcock's work as filmmaker. Part of Hitchcock's skill was in noticing that the audience's stakes in a narrative film need not coincide with the characters' stakes. What is, from the audience's point of view, irrelevant, is often at the center of the action on screen. That there are solids concealed in bottles of wine, that $40,000 has gone missing, that a psychiatrist suffers a phobia—these facts move a plot along. They are not the facts that hold the audience's attention. Such a plot

device is the MacGuffin. I take it that what makes instrumentalism a recurring topic for us is the bit we that have been least inclined to analyze. In this sense, we have played audience to our own story's MacGuffin.

2. In Some Sense Good

1. Thomas Aquinas, *Summa Theologiae* [hereafter *"ST"*], I–II, q. 94, a. 2.
2. *Nicomachean Ethics* [hereafter *"NE"*], 1094a, 1–3.
3. *Ethics and the Limits of Philosophy*, p. 58. More recently, David Velleman complains that by seeing all action as aimed at the good, moral philosophy makes us all out to be "squares" (see "The Guise of the Good"). I share Velleman's impatience with moralism, but think the problem is not with the association between goodness and action, but rather with the pinched, moralized account of the good. Elizabeth Anscombe, whom Velleman takes as one of his targets, likewise had little patience with moralism in action theory. Lauren Tillinghast pointed out in conversation that one peculiar feature of Velleman's complaint is that it makes no sense unless we hold that it's bad to be a square. In this sense, he is complaining that moral philosophy makes us all out to be *bad* in the sense of "un-hip," *by* making us out to be *good* in the sense of "moral." That he doesn't notice this is, I think, a symptom of how deep moralism about the good has gone.
4. *Intention*, §4.
5. Some contemporary theorists are unconcerned about this. One such view has it that in learning and practicing seeing circumstances in different ways, one stores up things that might later be of use (or not, as the case may be), and that the whole business of building one's practical repertoire should be treated as practical reasoning. I think it better to avoid this outcome if possible, and would rather confine "practical reasoning" to using what one has in figuring out what to do.
6. Alain Robert, a French climber, scaled the Golden Gate Bridge several years ago in this way, and chose the bridge because it was very challenging and beautiful.
7. Aquinas takes up the division from Ambrose's *De Officiis* I, 9, PL 16, 31 (see *ST*, I, q. 5, a. 6) and first connects it to Aristotle in the *Commentary on Aristotle's Nicomachean Ethics* [hereafter *"CNE"*], 1095b, 16–17, bk. I, lect. 5, pp. 20–21.

   The first place Aquinas interprets Aristotle using the threefold division is with reference to Aristotle's discussion of the three kinds of lives. I find it very hard to follow the link Aquinas makes between the sensual, the public, and the virtuous lives and the threefold division. The virtuous is pretty close to the Thomistic befitting, so that correspondence seems clear enough. The sensual will, of course, line up with the sensual portion of pleasure, but the pleasant as a region of the good is not solely concerned with carnal enjoyment, so the fit is less clear. This leaves public life aimed at honor as life lived in light of what is useful. The chief problem with a public life is that it places one's happiness in others' hands. I suppose that there is a sense in which this makes all of what one does in one's public capacity a mere *means* to attaining a good reputation, but, again, it's a stretch. Basically, the kinds of lives seem substantively distinct: the three kinds of men have different aims. The threefold division is at its best, I think, in its more formal aspect. Things are clearer when Aquinas sees the threefold division underlying Aristotle's discussion of the three forms of friendship. There is always the danger, of course, that if one has misunderstood the first link, one will have misunderstood the second as well.

8. See *NE* 1555b–1556a. For Aquinas's use of this material in a general account of reasons for acting see *CNE*, bk. VIII, lects. 2 and 3, pp. 480, 483–484.

9. *ST,* I, q. 5, a. 6.

10. The kind of source at issue in each region of the division for Aquinas is the sort one used to call a *final* cause. What was at issue was how the movement of rational appetite *stops*. In a sense foreign to us, Aquinas was a calculative theorist of practical reason. This is one of the reasons it is worthwhile for friends and foes of instrumentalism about practical reason to devote some attention to his work.

    Contrast this with Gavin Lawrence's stress on the good as a *formal* cause of action, (see "The Rationality of Morality," pp. 130–134). Lawrence is working with Platonic and Aristotelian treatments of reason in action in his essay. What the two have in common, among other things, is that their source material predates the serious philosophical exploration of varieties of wickedness that animates work on action done by the Catholic schoolmen. Aquinas argues that the point of an act is what gives us a grip on the good of it, and *that* emerges from consideration of its end-directedness.

11. Michael Thompson, "Relations of Right."

12. Ibid. Thompson argues that an agent is a *locus* of concept-involving end-orientation. It is an excellent definition, applicable to people, to firms, and so on.

13. Nation-states, corporations, and other such bodies can also act. Moreover, corporate agents can do acts of types that plain collections of individuals cannot do: e.g., even if 90 percent of U.S. citizens decided to contribute a dollar each to relief funds annually, this would not count as levying a tax. This is one reason to avoid treating a corporate agent like a nation-state as identical with a sum of particular individuals. In what follows, unless otherwise specified, I focus on individual human action and individual adult human agents.

14. *Natural Goodness,* pp. 53–56.

15. I would insist that the same point *must* be made about what is seen as good, given the thrust of Aquinas's account of practical reason.

16. I discuss the special place of pursuit of pleasure among the sources of *akrasia* in Chapter 4. The kind of end that pleasure provides, on a neo-Thomistic account, is one especially likely to lead one to choose the lesser good. What is important, on this view, is that dignifying a moment of incontinence with the term *"akrasia"* will require taking it that there *was* a lesser good that "won out" over a greater good. That is how such a "defect" in behavior can be assigned to rational will (hence, intentional action) rather than, say, to illness or other loss of control over bodily functions.

17. *Natural Goodness*, p. 56.

18. Anscombe devotes several sections of *Intention* to this point (suggesting that it is crucial to her argument—*Intention* is a work of frightful economy). She is at once arguing that, paradigmatically, the ends of intentional action are pursued *sub specie boni* and that the good in question must be, as such, intelligible. Since the account focuses on one's descriptions of the point of what one is doing, she can, I take it, treat these as a single claim. I cannot be said to have succeeded in *describing* something (e.g., the point of what I am doing) unless someone else can understand what I have described. For her various discussions of the connection between wanting (in the sense relevant to action) and good, see *Intention*, §§35–40.

19. It may be worth noting here that the account is in no sense consequentialist. An *as-such end* is no mere "result" of action, distinguished from other "results," say, by being both foreseen and welcomed. How consequences figure in action-assessment on this view is complex, and involves such thoughts as that you get *no* credit for the inadvertent, generally beneficial consequences of an act you mean to be harmful, but may be blamed for even more of the act's harmful consequences than you meant to bring about in so acting.

20. There is considerably more to Aquinas's answer than this. Part of his answer turns on a discussion of the sense in which human evil is parasitic on human good. Evil is not a freestanding object of pursuit. Kant takes this matter up in arguing that there could be no such thing as a devilish human will (see *Religion within the Limits of Reason Alone*, bk. I, ch. 3, pp. 27–33). Anscombe takes it up in giving a reading of a line from Milton (see *Intention*, §39).

21. There are serious questions about how to interpret Aquinas's account of practical reason (that is, *goal-directed*, calculative reason rather than speculative or theoretical reason). My claim about action-assessment is *not* that it involves no more than straightforward application of principles to particular cases. Nor is it that practical conclusions about particular actions or the scope of secondary precepts can be simply *derived* from more general principles. My claim is rather that consideration of the last end provides a kind of overarching frame for assessment of kinds of act in kinds of circumstance.

22. For remarks about the usefulness of virtues (i.e., the point of cultivating them), see, for example, *Summa contra Gentiles* (hereafter *"SCG"*), bk. IV, ch. 54; *ST*, I–II, q. 57, a. 5. Peter Geach argues that we do not need to identify the content of a last end in order to offer an account of the usefulness of the cardinal moral virtues, although the point of the theological virtues is only clear in light of the relevant dogmas (see *The Virtues*).

23. "Roughly" because divinely infused virtues are among those at work in the account, and one cannot calculate how to coerce God's granting of faith, hope, and charity, even though revealed doctrine has it that we have been subject to this providence.

24. I do not mean to pretend that there are no arguments out there that aim at bringing together discussions of different kinds of reasons for acting. There are in fact myriad modern and contemporary secular arguments that aim to unify calculative practical considerations and ethical ones (considerations of pleasure have no single definite sort of place for us). However, there is *no* agreement among contemporary philosophers that any one, or one kind of them, works. I see no reason why we would expect any of them to work. If the threefold division is as powerful as I expect that it will turn out to be, then the way to think about different kinds of practical considerations is in terms of how they relate, temporally, to what one is here and now doing. I see no reason to suppose, e.g., that what justifies the present act—and looks to neither past nor future in doing so (the pleasant)—will have any essential tie to what looks to the future (the useful) or to the larger practical direction of one's life (the befitting). Shorn of something like an account of the ends of man, why would we think unity was to be found in practical good? Even given such an account, it is a bit of a stretch to get the good of trimming my nails to be of a piece with the good of sending checks to Oxfam, and to show these as somehow unified with the good of rolling in fresh grass clippings on a fine summer day. Aquinas, at least, thought it took a lot of arguments to try to counter the many obvious objections to a claim that there was unity among the departments of practical good.

25. So too are Kantian critics who argue that any account of the form of acting well that belongs to morality that ties morality to inclination, to a practical orientation the having of which is a matter of one's education or circumstances, or to long-term interest thereby fails to be about morality at all.

26. It could be objected that nothing removes risk of natural disaster from human life for bad people either, and that the difference is that Nature's second, culture or society, makes it no accident when good people fare well. I agree that we have found a problem in a social order if it turns out that its institutions (e.g., its juridical institutions) do not work to prevent manmade blocks to flourishing in the lives of decent people. But Kant's question concerns individual practical reason, i.e., what the individual has good reason

to hope will be the case, and (1) the lone individual is not generally in a position to engineer social institutions so that they will reward his good conduct, and (2) there is good evidence that social institutions can and have operated in ways that reward institutional and private viciousness, and also actively prevent decent people from faring well. There are too many examples of work on this topic to list, as any casual enquiry into, say, the operation of race as a category of social organization will attest. For one interesting recent turn on this topic by a philosopher best known for his work on theoretical (rather than practical) reason, see Michael Dummett, *On Immigration and Refugees*.

27. For an excellent reading of Kant's argument about God, see Carol Voeller, *The Metaphysics of the Moral Law*, ch. 1.

28. I mean what follows as a kind of response to neo-Aristotelian virtue theorists' accounts of practical reason and the human good. Traditionally, Anglo–North American moral theory treats morally reprehensible action as having one of three sources: ignorance of the greater good (emphasized by neo-Aristotelians), weakness of will (sometimes also emphasized by neo-Aristotelians, and discussed at some length by neo-Kantians), or imprudence (a favorite among neo-Hobbeseans, and also sometimes discussed by neo-Kantians). All three suggest that immorality betrays a failure of practical reason. Shorn of the theology, acting from capital viciousness has none of these kinds of sources and hence, I argue, need betray no defect of practical reason.

29. Aquinas discusses sin and vice in various works. I have special fondness for *On Evil* (hereafter "*OE*"), qq. 7–15, because the systematicity of the account is very clear there.

30. *OE*, q. 8, a. 1, p. 312.

31. I use "acedia" rather than "sloth" on purpose. Most of us have come to associate sloth with plain laziness. Acedia is more interesting. In acedia apprehension of some spiritual good becomes painful to the agent. Sometimes this is because he does not want to leave off doing things he otherwise wants to do for the sake of helping to realize the spiritual good, and, while this version involves laziness in spiritual matters, our "lazy" man can be exceedingly busy with his own affairs. Sometimes it is that he is unwilling to allow himself to hope and work for a spiritually better circumstance in his life or the life of his community. And here, it is much more akin to an important form of depression, and carries some of the underlying anger that one associates with depression, tinged with an anxiety that he is on the verge of despair. Here, he may be practically paralyzed, but not because he is in any ordinary sense lazy.

32. *OE* q. 8, a. 1, p. 313.

33. Bradley, *Aquinas on the Twofold Human Good,* p. xiii. A *caveat:* although I have found reading Aquinas and the work of scholars of Aquinas illuminating, I do not regard myself as a proper scholar of Thomas or Thomism. Genuine Thomistic scholarship has a kind of magnificence rare in the history of ideas, in part because many of the most able scholars have more than an intellectual relation to Saint Thomas. There are enormous controversies surrounding the reading of Aquinas. I have only begun to be equipped to think through some of them. For all that, it is an occupational hazard to form opinions at points of controversy, and mine on Aquinas have been most strongly influenced by Bradley. In various respects, I take it that Aquinas's moral science constitutes a significant advance over Aristotle's ethics. But, as Bradley put it, "the thrust of Aquinas's authentic doctrine . . . leads to an *aporia:* any moral philosophy inspired by Aquinas cannot legitimately return to a quasi-Aristotelian form of eudaimonism; but neither can it, as [secular] philosophy, go forward to a theological affirmation of man's ultimate supernatural end" (ibid.).

I also offer here a note of apology. I take it seriously that I am relying upon the work of a Catholic saint. This is a delicate business for one who is variously agnostic. I recently learned that one of my Catholic students has been asking Aquinas to help me. The student's act brought home to me how different a relation one can have to Aquinas if one can just ask him things. My hope is that I do no inadvertent violence to Aquinas's work on practical reason by putting it to secular use. It is bad enough to take it out of its theological context, but *this* badness is one I understand.

34. *Intention,* §13.

35. Backward-looking motive is much more interesting if one is thinking exclusively about divine law ethics. The whole structure of God's past gifts to humanity enters into thought about reason in human action in theological moral philosophy. But, to the extent that I understand my sources here, the overall picture of practical reason that informs them is calculative. Backward-looking motive has a clear calculative form, which is why I place it among useful-style practical considerations. I do not think that the other two regions need be, strictly, calculative, from a secular point of view.

36. I am grateful to Elijah Millgram for discussion of this point, and for the suggestion that I use "local," "nonlocal," "terminable," and "interminable" in discussing the distinctions at issue.

37. This is, I take it, the result established in *Intention*.

38. Donald Davidson has also made a study of Aquinas. Davidson has not, however, made the structure of intentional action his topic. I will take up Davidson very briefly in Appendix B, largely in order to explain Anscombe's objection to his account.

39. A caveat: it is standardly assumed that you can perform some kinds of action (generally very bad kinds) without quite understanding that you are doing a thing rightly described as an act of that kind. If asked "Why did you rape her?" when I have, in fact, raped her, I might respond in all sincerity "I didn't," thereby refusing the question application. In such cases, however, there will be many other descriptions of what I was doing that I *will* accept (if I am truthful). These descriptions are what a police officer will use in arresting and charging me, and what a prosecuting attorney will turn to in arguing that I raped someone. If I really am ignorant of the illicit and wrongful character of the act, and if I believe that police officers serve the ends of justice, and if I am not advised not to, I may well supply the relevant descriptions myself.

40. *Intention,* §40.

41. I take up this connection when I discuss specific good in the next chapter.

42. *Intention,* §§20–21, 26, 41.

43. Ibid., §§38, 39.

44. Ibid., §§39, 40.

45. Ibid., §17. Anscombe goes on to consider some restrictions on when this is a sensible answer to give. It is sensible when the action at issue is one that can ordinarily be done as an idle action. Aquinas's examples of kinds of actions that might be done idly include picking up a straw from the ground and walking in the fields (*ST* I–II, q. 18, a. 8). Anscombe mentions doodling.

46. *Ethics and the Limits of Philosophy,* p. 59.

3. Medieval and Modern

1. *Ethics and the Limits of Philosophy,* p. 58, emphases added.

2. In Aquinas, in the context of the theology, this move has a point, of course. Goods are good insofar as they have places in the larger scheme of things, and their places link them to the pursuits of various kinds of creatures. Pursuits are good insofar as they tend to the good of the kind of being that the pursuer is. The things pursued are good insofar as they belong to the practical orientation of the pursuer, and on their own account as created things. Etc.

3. *ST,* I, q. 5, a. 6. For one thing, he thought that the threefold division concerned appetitive movement generally. All species of appetitive movers move in ways governed by the threefold division. But what they move toward, their substantive good, varies in accordance with their species. In the passage of the *Summa* that I have cited, he contrasts ontological good, good that belongs to being as such, with the threefold division, making the point

with reference to Aristotle's ten predicaments: substance, quantity, quality, relation, place, time, position, state, action, and undergoing. The whole of the threefold division falls under the single predicament: *action.* The question of where specific *differentia,* the nonaccidental properties of members of kinds of things connected to specific good, find their proper home in the ten categories is notoriously vexed (for a succinct summary of some of the troubles, see D. P. Henry, "Predicables and Categories").

For the sake of simplicity, I claim that what makes a kind of being the kind of thing it is for Aquinas will fall under *substance.* Here, then, the distinction between different specific goods and the threefold good of the division is a distinction between what belongs to substance on the one side, action on the other. For Aquinas this involves, I think, a distinction in part between good as a formal cause (substance) and good as a final cause (action). In Aquinas, as in his sources, the two are not unrelated, and it is hard to get the details of the distinction right. Roughly, however, granting the distinction without attempting to sort matters out cleanly, Aquinas's argument covers the place of the threefold division in the Aristotelian categories generally, hence how it is unlike those features of the good involved in thought about substance in particular. The threefold division centers on action, and hence the character of purposes. What makes a good horse good is relative to its species. A good horse might be sought/pursued/wanted because one takes *pleasure* in riding good horses, or because one hopes to win the race by fair means and having a good horse and a good rider are *useful* for this, or because one is, say, a horse breeder whose aim in breeding horses is to aid in the generation of good horses (i.e., it belongs to one, *befits* one, *qua* horse rancher, to have and breed exemplars of equine excellence). Aquinas takes it that the primary sense of "good" connects goodness with action. For contemporary work on specific goods more generally, see Lauren Tillinghast's *The Thought of Art,* ch. 3. She there focuses on Peter Geach's essay on good and evil, defending him from a host of objections.

4. Neo-Aristotelians nowadays also stress the unity of a view about virtue, a view about action, reason, and motivation, and a view about the good for our kind. The neo-Aristotelian view of human specific good is beholden neither to the theological commitments that frame Aquinas's view nor to Aristotle's deplorable hierarchy of types of humans and the lives suited to different types. But contemporary neo-Aristotelians are not noted for the depths of their theoretical engagement with viciousness (the one recent and notable exception is Philippa Foot). Aquinas, on the other hand, theorizes viciousness as the complex, cultivated result of determining one's will to the pursuit of genuine human goods. This in turn suggests that a secular account of the goods of human life may not lead as quickly to an argument in

favor of virtue as some contemporary theorists suggest, unless we are very careful about the goods we choose as the primary, specifically human goods. I discuss this point, and Foot's engagement, at some length in Chapter 8.

5. See Pat Califia, "Shiny Sharp Things."
6. See Foot, *Virtues and Vices.*
7. One interesting feature of this suggestion is that it will produce an interpretation under which, say, engaging in the proceedings constitutive of successful, consensual erotic knife play from and for the sake of pleasure counts as good intentional action.
8. See, e.g., "'Under a Description.'"
9. *ST* I–II, q. 51, a. 1.
10. I have slightly adapted the example to include excessive moralism as a failure to exercise due amusement. The example is Aristotle's and is treated at length by Aquinas. See *CNE*, bk. IV, lect. 14, pp. 270–271.
11. I mean: one important root of the incommensurability literature may involve philosophical resistance to treating modern pressure toward commodification as a force siding with wisdom in value theory.
12. He argues for this point in his essay "How to Make Something of Yourself."
13. The relation between what I do and how I understand that it befits me to live may be subtler still, having to do with, say, the *a priori* structures of practical reason, which may never be clear to anyone outside speculative accounts of Reason, but are nevertheless presupposed in the giving of any sort of reason for acting. Following Carol Voeller, I take it that this is Kant's position. See Voeller, *The Metaphysics of the Moral Law.* If Kant is right, then there is a sense in which the moral law always informs intentional action. It need not inform intentional action as such, however, since I can know perfectly well that I morally ought to do a thing that I don't do, and since I anyway may not understand the link between moral conduct and practical reason. My topic is intentional action as such.
14. See, for example, Denis J. M. Bradley, *Aquinas on the Twofold Human Good,* pp. 323–360; Daniel Westberg, *Right Practical Reason,* pp. 199–197. Ralph McInerny argues that because, for Aquinas, acts of will are immaterial acts, and because Aquinas follows Aristotle in holding that our powers or capacities can only be known through their acts, the analysis of the sources of voluntary actions in volition and intellection must be inferred from an analysis of the structure of intentional action. See McInerny, *Ethica Thomistica,* p. 76.
15. I have been taking it for granted that an account of the essential linkage between practical reason and ethics will need to propose a substantive view of human good in order to ground ethics. If I understand her, Philippa Foot has recently argued that a formal account of the good of our kind will be

enough to get the reason–morality link going in both directions—not just by finding reason in the ethically sound acts of decent people, but by finding irrationality in the characteristic acts of vicious people. See her *Natural Goodness*. I will take up Foot's account briefly in the final chapter.

16. For David Gauthier's view, see *Morals by Agreement*.
17. *OE*, q. 13, a. 3, pp. 399–400.
18. Ibid., q. 8, a. 1, pp. 307–316.
19. *Intention*, §38.
20. Ibid., §39.
21. Ibid., §5.

4. Pleasure

1. For work by a contemporary philosopher sensitive to the apparent trouble who devotes himself to arguing that there is no such systematic link between failures of ethical self-governance and sense pleasure, see Michael Slote, *Morals from Motives*, pp. 141–168.
2. C. C. W. Taylor and J. C. B. Gosling set the philosophical scene for Plato's discussions of pleasure this way: "There were those who made the pleasures of the Life of Pleasure their goal in life, and those who thought some overall balance of pleasure over distress in life should be pursued. There were those who insisted on a contrast between a life of virtue and one of pleasure, and those who thought that a life of virtue was pleasanter than a life without it" (*The Greeks on Pleasure*, p. 2).

    Plato insisted that one must believe one is doing well in order to enjoy oneself, and seems to have held that nonhuman animals might seek pleasure in roughly the way that humans do. Aristotle took up the suggestion about thinking one is doing well and developed it in terms of actualizing potentials (one must at least think one is acting well with respect to an activity in order to enjoy it). He rejected the claim that human pleasures are the same as nonhuman pleasures (because a being takes pleasure in what perfects beings of its kind, and our kind is distinctive).
3. Modern philosophical treatments of pleasure, for example, tend to emphasize aesthetic pleasure, which I do not discuss, largely because nearly all modern philosophers hold that aesthetic pleasure has more to do with a private experience of inner harmony or expansion than with anything one happens to be doing at the time.

    The sense in which modern aesthetic pleasure explains action is highly attenuated because such pleasure is not especially practical. Its source is in *disengaged* stillness (rather than the active, cultivated stillness of Aquinas's "rest in the thing desired"). As such, aesthetic pleasure is better equipped to explaining stopping and smelling the flowers, or reading, or listening, or watching, or burying one's hands in the softness of fur, than it is to explaining more vigorous sorts of pursuit. Moreover, modern views of aesthetic pleasure have a slightly narcissistic taint that I resist: modern aesthetic pleasure is grounded in a glad apprehension of one's cultivated discernment, one's social standing, one's harmonious personality, the conformity between one's object and the wondrous faculties of one's mind or organs of one's sense, and so on.

There may still be ethical danger in modern aesthetic pleasure. For example, many modern theories of aesthetic pleasure can be read as theories of what might be worthwhile in the leisurely occupations of a comfortable and privileged life. Because the lives at issue in the development of modern aesthetics were often lives made economically possible by ethically egregious material relations, aesthetic pleasure could also be seen as potentially at odds with the ethical: the circumstances conducive to experiencing high-end aesthetic pleasure are not circumstances of social justice. Again, there have been many arguments designed to demonstrate that aesthetic pleasure is not necessarily contrary to morality. Mill's treatment of the higher pleasures, for example, and Kant's discussion of aesthetic judgment, make aesthetic pleasure a force for moral good (on two very different accounts of moral goodness).

Outside of philosophy, many critics have discussed these topics at some length. One excellent example explicitly concerned with intersections between philosophical aesthetics and colonial ideology can be found in David Lloyd's "Writing in the Shit: Beckett, nationalism and the colonial subject," in *Anomalous States*, pp. 41–58. See also David Lloyd and Paul Thomas, *Culture and the State.*

For excellent discussion of Aquinas on aesthetic pleasure, see Umberto Eco's *The Aesthetics of Thomas Aquinas.*

4. It might be thought that pleasure has a home in reason-based action explanation because happiness has a home in reason-based explanation of human action, and some portion of happiness involves pleasure. But, on the picture of practical considerations that I am urging be adopted, questions about the relation between pleasure and happiness, and the place of pleasure in a human life, belong to concern about how it befits one to live. These are, if you like, questions about the order of things in human affairs. Accordingly, I leave these questions to one side.

5. *The Concept of Mind,* pp. 107–108.

6. One could aim at sustaining an activity for the sake of the sensations (as with some athletic activities undertaken because it feels great to do them, and sustained on that account). Here, the desire to keep at it as long as one can, and to regulate one's movements to this end, brings the examples into

the purview of pleasant-style desirability. But the kinds of cases I explain in terms of pleasure are rarely of this sort—cases like singing in the shower or while driving, chatting with friends, rereading a favorite novel or poem, or watching a favorite movie for the nth time just because one likes it (i.e., when the viewing and reading are in no sense undertaken as means to attaining some other end: teaching the text, say, or writing a review, or preparing to dazzle others with your knowledge).

7. Enjoyment is not alien to moods, since some days one can enjoy activities that the very next day are a source of anxiety, crabbiness, or frustration. But the point of introducing good moods into the discussion, on my view, has more to do with getting some grip on the phenomenology of being absorbed in what one is doing.

8. Aquinas seems to think that one can find this view of pleasure in Aristotle. See Aquinas, *Commentary on Aristotle's Nicomachean Ethics* [hereafter *"CNE"*], bk. VII, lects. 2–4, pp. 412–429, and bk. X, pp. 589–650.

For an excellent summary of many controversies surrounding commentary on Aristotle's view of pleasure, see J. C. B. Gosling and C. C. W. Taylor, *The Greeks on Pleasure,* chs. 11–16. I am grateful to Martha Nussbaum for discussion of pleasure in Aristotle.

The other reason that Aquinas is untroubled by the apparent tension between Books VII and X of Aristotle's *Nicomachean Ethics* seems to be that Aquinas takes it as obvious that the Book VII account (the account that appears in some ways to treat pleasure as identical with pleasant activity) aims partly at explaining how sensual pleasure can lead you to do what you ought not to do. Because pleasure draws people along in action, it can lead them into immoderate action, and so is crucial to understanding weakness of will. When discussing the place of pleasure in a life well-lived—when discussing, for instance, *where* a virtuous man puts himself in putting himself in the way of enjoyment, which is, Aquinas thinks, the main topic of Book X (the account that seems to argue that pleasure cannot be identical with pleasant activity)—the kind of moral weakness shown in getting carried far away by sensual delights is not an issue.

I leave to scholars the question whether Aristotle is best read in this light.

9. See Aquinas *CNE,* bk. VII, lect. 7, p. 463.

10. The passage is from a letter Flaubert sent to his mother from Cairo, dated 5 January 1850. The translation is taken from *Flaubert in Egypt,* pp. 74–75. That Flaubert vegetated in Egypt is, one suspects, multiply determined by the business of European tourism in colonized places. Several of the ways in which such pleasure is, for such a person, *befitting* or connatural are ethically and politically significant and repellent. For discussion of such matters generally, and of Flaubert's trip in particular, see Edward Said, *Orientalism.*

11. In various places, Aquinas discusses playing or resting in order to make

work go better later on, and contrasts these with play or rest taken for their own sakes. See, e.g., *SCG,* bk. III, pt. I, ch. 2, §9.

12. In the case of aesthetic pleasure, she must have refined enough intellectual or sense powers to savor the relevant perceptual or cognitive delights.

13. Part of the response is in the *sententia* on Aristotle, but is taken from sections where Aquinas gives no indication that he disagrees with his source material.

14. *CNE,* bk. VII, lect. 12, p. 462.

15. See Aquinas, *ST,* I–II, q. 50, a. 4.

16. See ibid.

17. I am grateful to Irad Kimhi for discussion of ecstasy.

18. See Mihaly Csikszentmihalyi, *Flow.*

19. Notice that this is often how one explains things that don't involve happy, good feelings, but that an agent somehow knows to do in the face of conflict: e.g., having just suffered some grievous loss, one might suddenly start a big house-cleaning project, or stop eating altogether, or hold objects associated with the lost object close to one's face for several hours, or start smashing things. There are many different psychological diagnostic accounts of apparently pointless actions undertaken as some part of psychological conflict resolution. For at least some people, intentional action of this sort is neither a means to the end of feeling better nor part of taking one's mind off the loss or expressing one's grief (that is, at least some people don't do such things in order to attain some further end). For the folks who have no further end in view, if we ask, "Why are you rubbing his jacket against your cheek?" the answer will be some version of "I feel like it." Similarly, the answer to, "Why don't you eat something?" will be some version of "I don't feel like it." The close fit between what the agent is doing and who and how the agent is make these cases formally like Thomistic acts done from and for pleasure. The difference is, in part that these sorts of acts are not done from and for the sake of pleasure intentionally, hence, the good of doing them will not be given as a pleasure-related desirability characterization.

20. I discuss these matters at length in *John Stuart Mill's Deliberative Landscape.*

21. I am indebted to Dan Brudney for discussion of the opposite of Thomistic pleasure.

22. "Obsessive Action and Religious Practices," p. 430.

23. One such place might be in childhood. There have been many arguments that pleasure is absolutely essential if the young are to develop anything like a practical repertoire to begin with. Learning to do things is painful. Lacking the powers to do what one wants to do is frustrating. It can be argued, then, that delight in the increase of one's powers is absolutely essential to the kind

of youthful habituation that goes with learning how to do the things one must be able to do as an adult. In childhood, then, pleasure may have an essential place in human life. Of course, it would not follow that *adults* needed to make room for pleasure in their lives. Since our topic is exercise of practical reason, and since the objection concerns the "highest" region of practical good, I leave the place of pleasure in childhood to one side.

5. Fit

1. *Groundwork of the Metaphysics of Morals,* p. 75 [Ak. 407].
2. By focusing on desirability characterizations, I may well have planted myself in a tiny portion of what Kant reviled as a "disgusting hotch-potch" whose home is in "the chit-chat of daily life" (*Groundwork of the Metaphysics of Morals,* p. 77 [Ak. 409]). My aim in part is to show that the kind of "chit-chat" Anscombe drew our attention to, when wedded to some bits of Aquinas, is no mere "hotch-potch," of course. I take up specific discussion of how Kant's account of duty might be viewed as involving a noncalculative befitting-style practical consideration in Appendix C.
3. For such an argument, see Anscombe, "On Promising and Its Justice, and Whether It Need Be Respected *in Foro Interno.*"
4. *Disputed Questions on Virtue* (hereafter, *"DQV"*), Art. 1, pp. 105–113.
5. *The Virtues,* p. 16.
6. Ibid., p. 17.
7. Aristotle likewise would have denied that virtue could be used to bad ends, but Aristotle offers precious little by way of a substantive theory of the rational structure of culpable badness—*so* little that it is hard to turn to him for illumination on this topic. The point I am making is that the very same qualities of character might enable both collective good acts and collective bad acts.
8. "Von Wright on Virtue," p. 278.
9. Shakespeare, *Macbeth,* act 1, scene 5, lines 38–45.
10. Spicer's view of poetry is very similar to views of literary production one finds in Friedrich Hölderlin, Stephane Mallarmé, William Butler Yeats, Rainer Maria Rilke, André Gide, Paul Valéry, and other prominent nineteenth- and twentieth-century authors. Maurice Blanchot's meditations on literary production, creativity, and literary experience offer a sustained development of various aspects of this kind of view. See, especially, Blanchot, *L'Espace littéraire.* I have chosen Spicer as my example for the frank, pragmatic quality of his account.
11. *After Lorca,* in *The Collected Books of Jack Spicer,* p. 34.
12. Ibid., p. 51.

13. *The House That Jack Built,* p. 116.
14. *Admonitions,* in *The Collected Books of Jack Spicer,* p. 61.
15. *The House That Jack Built,* p. 6.
16. Ibid., p. 7.
17. Ibid.
18. Ibid., p. 18.
19. Ibid., p. 8.
20. Ibid., p. 14.
21. Ibid., p. 11.
22. Ibid., p. 10.
23. Ibid., p. 33.
24. Ibid., p. 32.
25. Ibid., p. 86.
26. Ibid., p. 230.
27. On the complexities that attend trying to get a straight read on Spicer's poetics see Peter Gizzi, "Jack Spicer and the Practice of Reading," pp. 173–225.

6. Use

1. *The Holy Grail,* in *The Collected Books of Jack Spicer,* p. 192.
2. "Part–whole" is not the happiest term for this relation, because it usually calls to mind things rather than processes. I have borrowed the term from Aristotle, together with the thought that in the part–whole relation, the whole governs the parts in a way that would lead one to say that the parts materially cause the whole, and the whole formally causes the parts. Robert Audi introduces the term "constitutive means" to cover what I call *parts* in the course of explaining Aristotle's view of action and its structure (*Practical Reasoning,* pp. 29–32). It is a very good term, but we are so accustomed to thinking "efficient cause" when we hear "means" that I have stuck with a less apt term.
3. For an extremely funny list of different ways of expressing one's reason for lying down, see Anselm Müller, "How Theoretical Is Practical Reason?" pp. 100–101.
4. This sort of thought has been central to much of Anscombe's work. See, for example, *Intention,* §§6, 19, 23, 26, 36, 46–48; "The Intentionality of Sensation," "'Under a Description,'" "Intention," "The Two Kinds of Error in Action," "On Brute Facts," and "Modern Moral Philosophy."
5. As some of her readers concluded. Her readers concluded a great many things that were no part of her view, actually. For a list pertinent to this topic see "'Under a Description,'" pp. 208–216. My remarks in this paragraph summarize some of the points she makes in that essay.

6. As I mentioned at the outset, considerations involving plans stand at the border of calculative practical considerations and befitting-style desirability characterizations. For the purposes of the thought experiment, emphasize their befitting-style aspect.

7. In Anscombe's parlance, you have no desirability characterization to provide for what you are doing under that description *B*-ing.

8. I am grateful to Elijah Millgram for pointing out the need for a reminder about the significance of the "Why?" question being given application. The need for such a reminder arose in his conversation with Michael Bratman, to whom I am also grateful.

9. In order to capture the sense in which calculative considerations look to the future, it is crucial to distinguish proper parts of an action from the whole of it. This is the reason that I have not borrowed Jennifer Hornsby's "by" locution in discussing parts of an action. Hornsby concentrates on cases where I *B* by *A*-ing. While it is true that I walk *by* taking one step, then another, then another, the steps–walking relation has the element of temporal distance required to treat it as a species of calculative relation. For Hornsby's basic discussion of individuating actions and her complaint against part–whole accounts of action, see her *Actions*, pp. 1–32.

   Michael Thompson adopts a related approach in "Naïve Action Theory." If I understand him, his approach is closer than Hornsby's to the one I am taking. The insistence on distinguishing proper parts from wholes is thrust on me by the future-directedness of the useful region of practical good, together with the sense that part–whole relations must be included here to make sense of both Aquinas and Anscombe.

10. I am grateful to Elijah Millgram for asking about atomic actions. He called them *primitive* actions, because we were talking about the primitive operations ordered in computer programming. I have renamed them because their chief feature is that they have no intentional parts.

11. I take these matters up briefly in Appendix B.

12. Kant, *Groundwork of the Metaphysics of Morals,* p. 62 [*Ak.* 394].

13. Kant is, of course, the source for this kind of use of the term "will." There are ways of reading Kant such that he is not suggesting that the characteristic activity of practical reason is narcissistic fantasy. What is shocking to me is that commentators have not been more worried to produce such readings generally, since, on the face of it, the use of "will" in the context makes no sense. I do not mean to impugn Kant on the grounds that he turns "will" into a nonsense syllable. I don't think that he does, although I have little confidence that my preferred way of saving him from the charge would meet with general acceptance among Kant scholars.

14. A version of this adaptation of Anscombe's argument that follows her text fairly closely is to be found in Appendix A. I operate at some distance from

the text here, on the advice of readers who pointed out that Anscombe is largely opaque to most of us, and that the relevant bit of Anscombe took me a very long time to understand.

15. The way things happened in secular philosophy was rather the other way around: modernity pulled the plug and God drained out of things, taking the order of design in nature (hence, a kind of calculative order discussed extensively in medieval Christian philosophy) with him.

7. The Standard Picture of Practical Reason

1. Some theorists might seek to deny that this is true of moral actions, virtuous actions, or expressive actions. I take these up in Appendix D. If there are such things as "atomic" actions, actions with no parts, then these will be the exceptions. My arguments in Chapter 6 are meant in part to establish that these could not be ordinary intentional actions.

2. It is not necessary that the course *was* so selected. It is necessary only that it might have been, given what she meant to accomplish and did in order to accomplish that.

3. *Groundwork of the Metaphysics of Morals,* pp. 84–85 [*Ak.* 417]. Some philosophers make similar claims about necessary means without directly quoting Kant. See, for example, R. Jay Wallace, "How to Argue about Practical Reason," pp. 365–366.

4. See *Lectures on Ethics,* p. 15.

5. I am grateful to Stephen Darwall for raising this objection.

6. For apparent disinterest in the modal, see, for example, Christine Korsgaard, "The Normativity of Instrumental Reason," pp. 235–239. Korsgaard quotes Kant, and then slides quickly into discussion of "the" means, masking the trouble spot by use of the definite article. Kant, as near as I can tell, may have been doing one of two things in employing the modal. He may have been indirectly alluding to his view about the conditions that must be met if a statement is to express a *law* of any kind. As I mentioned, his conception of law is peculiar, and his requirements on what might count as a law are exceedingly stringent: a law is at the very least an exceptionless universal generalization. The hypothetical imperative is a law. Therefore, the hypothetical imperative may be formulated to suggest that there will be a *uniquely* good solution to any practical problem that is governed by the hypothetical imperative. On the other hand, Kant might have in mind *standard* techniques for attaining ends, rather than calculative reasons for acting generally. For example, there is a prescribed series of keystrokes, execution of which is how one is supposed to go about saving text in the word processing program I am using. Any moderately clever computer user, however,

can get the same result using other means. Here, it is true that executing the prescribed keystroke sequence *is* how you save text, and that you *can* save text other ways. This latter interpretation doesn't quite solve the puzzle about Kant, however, since even in Kant's day there were many different standard techniques available for attaining some ends. Kant's own example of what he has in mind is a particular geometric construction employed in order to bisect a line segment (*Groundwork of the Metaphysics of Morals*, p. 85 [*Ak.* 417])—a very restrictive sort of example, actually, and not one that would seem pertinent to most kinds of calculative practical considerations.

7. I do not mean to impugn Kant, but rather to suggest that one ought to explain the modal if one is going to quote the claim, because the modal does not on the face of it make any sense if it is supposed to apply to all calculative practical considerations. The claim is meant to be (a) analytic and (b) accounted for by the arguments in Chapter 3 of *The Groundwork of the Metaphysics of Morals*. Kant's topic is not ordinary calculative practical considerations versus other kinds of reasons for acting, but rather the conditions of the possibility for reason having practical employment. He takes it (for complicated reasons) that the conditions on reason having a practical employment are the same as the conditions under which it is possible that a rational will could be the addressee of imperatives. I expect that close attention to these matters will show that Kant was not making the claim indirectly ascribed to him by the usual use of the passage in contemporary literature on practical rationality, that he was not, for instance, urging that wanting to B was a sufficient condition for having calculative reason to A. I am grateful to Carol Voeller for discussion of these matters.

8. The example is taken from the movie *Die Hard 3: Die Hard with a Vengeance*, Fox, 1995.

9. In conversation, Carol Voeller suggested that ordinary calculative practical considerations are not happily expressed as *imperatives* in Kant's rather precise sense of that term.

10. I am concentrating on the means–end relation here, but parallel remarks could be made about some part–whole action descriptions too. While one cannot walk without moving one's legs, indefinitely many routes and rhythms are available to the Sunday stroller. While one cannot play fetch without tossing something for the dog to retrieve, many objects can be so tossed. While one cannot swim out of water, one can use many strokes and combinations in swimming, etc. Again, the problems I am on about here seem to me to be problems for philosophers who try to apply this bit of Kant directly to questions about calculative reasons for acting, not problems with Kant's own employment of the claim.

11. Anscombe, *Intention*, §33. She draws the example from some remarks by R. M. Hare.

12. Some theorists interested in noncalculative matters have hesitated to concede even this much. *Without* conceding this much, however, without providing the future-directedness of an end-to-be-attained, we are in the world of Anscombe's two-supposition argument, and I hope to have shown that this is precisely where ethicists ought not wind up. Stephen Darwall refuses to concede a related matter (that intention based solely in desire gives one reason to perform the actions one intends to perform) in *Impartial Reason*, pp. 46–49.

13. What makes means unacceptable can be noticing that taking some means will preclude attainment of other ends (calculative restriction on means), or the dictates of some patterning principle that restricts my choice in means (e.g., I will not take murderous means to any end—befitting-style restriction on means), or noticing that taking some means will impede my attempt to put myself in the way of pleasure (e.g., artlessly combining kinds of practical engagements that cannot be undertaken at the same time in my search for a pleasant thing to do—pleasant-style restriction on means).

14. Anselm Müller takes this up implicitly in "How Theoretical Is Practical Reason?" Michael Thompson argues for the point in some detail in "Naïve Action Theory."

15. Anscombe, *Intention*, §36. Because she was working with a calculative picture of practical reason in *Intention*, Anscombe treats this kind of wanting as wanting in the sense relevant to action. Georg Henrik Von Wright later convinced her that some wanting that bears on action does not take as its objects ends in the sense of stopping places or ends in the sense of whole activities undertaken with no further end in view. See the "Introduction" to *The Collected Papers of G. E. M. Anscombe*, vol. 3: *Ethics, Religion and Politics*, p. viii.

16. Velleman, "The Guise of the Good," p. 17.

17. An end, after all, is an end *relative* to some means or parts: stepping off the curb is a *means* relative to the end of getting to the other side of the road; relative to weight-shifting, foot-lifting, etc., however, stepping off the curb is an *end*; and, in turn, getting to the other side of the road may be *part* of walking to school. Insofar as deciding what to do gives one something different to do, it gives one new ends, even if these ends are means or parts relative to other ends. *Any* form of practical deliberation generates new ends in the sense that after the deliberation is successfully concluded, one is determined to do things that one had not initially intended to do.

18. I take it that part of the reason Kant thought that considerations of happiness were the business of calculative practical reason is that he thought that

there were quasi techniques for attaining happiness. His lectures on anthropology are, I take it, meant to aid in such calculation.

19. "Deliberation and Practical Reason," p. 228.

20. Elijah Millgram argues that many such preferences are formed on the basis of limited thought and experience, and that the pervasiveness of novelty in human life requires that we adjust ends often in light of how little goes into the initial end-setting. See *Practical Induction*, chs. 4–5.

21. See Anselm Müller, "How Theoretical Is Practical Reason?"

22. Aquinas, *SCG*, bk. 3, pt. I, ch. 2, §7, p. 37.

23. Ibid., §8, p. 37.

24. I assume that this is in part a mark of the material privilege of those of us who devote ourselves to the study of practical reason. Relative to most people (roughly 75 percent of people live in what one would have called the Third World when there was a Second World), we are very nearly a leisure class, and so rarely find ourselves faced with having to work out how to get enough to eat, clothe our children, obtain some kind of medical attention for ourselves or those in our charge, and so forth. Although the late medieval schoolmen were very like us in having lives in an academic institutional setting, these lives were not marked by the extraordinary material advantages that we enjoy.

25. Müller, "How Theoretical Is Practical Reason?" p. 97. Müller holds that any exercise of practical reason is irreducibly goal-directed, whether the exercise involves ordinary intentional action or thought. The irreducibly goal-directed character of exercises of practical reason enters in at the ground level of understanding any event as involving intentionally making something the case. This "element" of practical reason is not a thing that is added by thought. If the thought is practical, its goal-directedness is already in place.

26. See, e.g., David Gauthier, *Morals by Agreement*, p. 8.

27. I am grateful to Elijah Millgram for raising a version of this objection.

28. I am grateful to Paul Benacerraf for pointing out that the lofty and the earthy are in the same boat with respect to the "rather than" problem.

29. One reader suggested that the fact that this problem is aptly characterized as a neurotic tic suggests that it is not a form of irrationality. I would suggest, however, that neuroses as such involve action, thought, or feeling that is neurotic to the extent that it is maladjusted to one's circumstances from the point of view of reason: a phobia is an irrational fear, a compulsion is a drive to do things for which there is no reason, anxiety disorders of various kinds involve free-floating fear that does not take a clear and reasonable object, and so on. Interestingly enough, the traditional explanations of neurosis involve the suggestion that the psychological condition is a means to attaining an end the neurotic agent herself is not consciously, intentionally seeking to

attain (for example, repression of trauma, symbolic appetite satisfaction). This is, I take it, what is going on when clinical psychologists discuss "symptom choice."

30. Anscombe, *Intention,* §§22–24.

31. Anscombe, *Intention,* §23.

32. As Gideon Rosen pointed out to me, children routinely make mistakes of this sort but we don't think them irrational for it. I take it that there is no defect in the young child who thinks she can do card magic by mixing up cards at random. The would-be magician at the party was a grown-up, which is why she blushed when she admitted what she was(n't) doing.

8. Ethics

1. "Marginalia" (June 1849), p. 1457. Not that Poe thought it preferable to remake social institutions in the service of virtue instead: "The fact is, that in efforts to soar above our nature, we invariably fall below it. Your reformist demigods are merely devils turned inside out" (ibid., p. 1456).

2. Only "partly" a matter of this, because no one who is isolated, impoverished, unwell, in danger, and, for all practical purposes, friendless, and who has wound up in these circumstances through injustice or grave misfortune, is required to take it that his own good character removes all sting from the misery he faces.

3. *Without Stopping,* p. 367.

4.1 "Replies," p. 188.

5. "Might There Be External Reasons?" p. 78.

6. "On Promising and Its Justice, and Whether It Need Be Respected *in Foro Interno,*" p. 18.

7. Ibid., p. 19.

8. Bernard Williams, "Internal and External Reasons," p. 111.

9. Although I think it mere prejudice to assume that conversion is by its nature nonrational, particularly in light of work on faith as a virtue (see, e.g., Geach, *The Virtues,* pp. 20–44). Even Kant, after all, thought that we found ourselves committed to belief in the existence of a just God simply in virtue of our reasonable hope that regularly acting from the motive of duty might not bring ruin to the man of good will and those around him, and ought not to destroy the prospects of a happy life. It is *not* the physical or chemical order of the world that grounds such assumptions.

10. In *On Immigration and Refugees,* for example, Michael Dummett argues that racism and racist immigration policy are inherently destabilizing under current international social conditions.

11. See her "Modern Moral Philosophy."

12. See his "Putting Rationality in Its Place."

13. For example, the unity that obtains between his character and his acts is *not* the unity that obtains between being a strange, impulsive person and acting on strange impulses.

14. A point illustrated with devastating clarity in Nathaniel West's novella *A Cool Million,* a dark turn on the Horatio Alger story in which a deeply good young man, Lemuel Pitkin, falls prey through his goodness to the viciousness of life in New York.

15. It may be a smallish part of their social context, of course. For example, they might have found a handful of friends and make a kind of haven in a miserable world with these few people.

16. "Moral Incapacity," p. 54.

17. I am grateful to Lauren Tillinghast for this suggestion.

18. I know of no theologian who takes this line, but it was the Christianity of a Sunday school teacher I had when I was very young.

19. "Internal and External Reasons," p. 110.

20. *Ethics and the Limits of Philosophy,* pp. 22–23.

21. Williams raises the question why an amoralist would care about our arguments in ibid., p. 22.

Appendix A

1. What follows is a summary of the argument in §20 of *Intention.*

2. *The Collected Papers of G. E. M. Anscombe,* vol. 3: *Ethics, Religion and Politics,* p. viii.

3. There is something deep in the suggestion, I think. Although I do not pursue the point at all in what follows, I would tend to favor offering something on the order of an adverbial analysis of how pleasant-style practical considerations hook up with intentional actions of specific sorts.

4. *Intention,* §2. Anscombe maintains that the intuitive distinction between predictions and expressions of intention is a kind of baseline that must be explained by a sound account of intention. A contrary view is argued by David Velleman in *Practical Reflection.* As near as I can tell, Velleman's hypothetical story about what rational agency might be like at root obliterates the distinction that gets Anscombe's *Intention* going: the distinction among future-tensed descriptions of my own doings between predictions and expressions of intention. Rather than argue against Anscombe on this point directly, he ranges very far afield. His position is to this extent in keeping with the spirit of her project (which he treats seriously): her point in noticing the distinction between predictions and expressions of intention and showing how many dead ends we encounter in trying to explain it inter-

nally is that we do better to start with intentional action than with expressions of intention if our quarry is the concept of intention. Velleman has taken to heart the many dead ends we run across if we try to make out this distinction internally. In a way, his conclusion is that there is no very hard and fast distinction to be made out.

5. The suggestion here, which I do not pursue, is that the calculative order is responsible for the distinction between intensional and extensional descriptions of ordinary actions.

6. My use of "usually" here is in reference to another end. When one wants sawdust for paths and the like, in my experience it is easiest to visit a woodshop and take some away. Woodshops generate a lot of sawdust that has no role to play in shop operations, so friendly woodshop owners are often glad enough to let you cart some off.

Appendix B

1. I discuss this matter in greater detail in "Anscombe on Practical Inference."
2. "Von Wright on Practical Inference," p. 378.
3. See, e.g., Davidson, *Essays on Actions and Events*, Essays 1, 2, 4, 5, and 12.
4. Ibid., Essay 4, p. 79. Ernest LePore and Brian McLaughlin take it that in cases like the climber case there is a primary reason (belief-pro-attitude couple) that causes the act without rationalizing it. See LePore and McLaughlin, "Actions, Reasons, Causes, and Intentions," p. 5.
5. *Essays on Actions and Events,* Essay 12, p. 232.
6. Two *caveats* about the stand-and-walk example are in order. First, a general point. On some contemporary views, skill-based action is grounded in practical reasoning insofar as it is grounded in learning. See, for example, Elijah Millgram's account of learning as practical reasoning in *Practical Induction.* Now, if a man has learned how to be a lead climber, he likewise has learned that keeping a grip on the rope matters because loosening his hold will pose grave risks to his companions. By parity of reasoning, he has learned how to let a companion fall. Davidson suggests that finding practical reasoning among the causal antecedents of the event could make the difference between treating the case as involving intentional action and seeing it as a climbing accident. The suggestion makes no sense unless we are so strict about the application of practical reasoning that the climber's know-how won't automatically make loosening his hold into a product of practical reasoning.

Second *caveat:* I have in mind being restless and standing in order to stretch one's legs. I take it that some such cases involve nothing even remotely like the elaborate stratagem of the political example, that one does what one does because one feels like doing it, and has no more than this to offer on behalf of having done so. Here, the Davidsonian should be content with an explanation in terms of beliefs and pro-attitudes—I want to stretch my legs a bit, know that I need to get out of my chair and move around to do so, etc. Davidson leaves ample room for such examples.

7. Davidson, *Essays on Actions and Events,* Essay 4, pp. 78–80.
8. Ibid., Essay 1, p. 9.
9. "Von Wright on Practical Inference," p. 378.
10. *Essays on Actions and Events,* Essay 12, p. 232. The exact wording of Davidson's example obscures a point that Anscombe sees, but his allusion to "good reasons" makes it possible to think that his Oedipus sets out to kill Laius on the basis of considered judgment.
11. "Von Wright on Practical Inference," p. 378.
12. Ibid.
13. See *Intention,* §19. There, she argues that treating "intention" as the name of an added ingredient to action dissolves the distinction between voluntary and involuntary movement, and makes it well-nigh impossible to give a principled account of intentional action.
14. Ibid., §§9–11 treat these matters.
15. See ibid., §§5–9.
16. On this way of refusing to give the question application, see ibid., §6.
17. *Essays on Actions and Events,* Essay 6, p. 122.
18. For Davidson's discussion of these matters, see ibid., Essay 7.
19. Consider: in the climber example, thinking we have an action would generally involve thinking that the climber intends to injure his companion or else to effect an alteration in their arrangement. Suppose that the companion manages to catch hold of a rocky outcrop and hang there. If the lead climber intended injury, we would expect to see him make his way down and, say, stomp on her fingers. If the lead climber just wanted a change, and loosened his grip *to that end,* he might continue on, having attained his end. The point is that if he loosened his grip in pursuit of an end and on some grounds, then the calculative structure of events should inform his subsequent acts.
20. For example, she reads Aristotle's practical syllogisms as displaying the rational structure in intentional action, as showing both what the agent has in mind and the point of what he does.
21. "Von Wright on Practical Inference," p. 380.

Appendix C

1. Kant, *Groundwork of the Metaphysics of Morals,* p. 70 [*Ak.* 402].
2. The story is more complex than this sentence suggests, of course, and goes by way of certain practically necessary postulates, if I understand it.

3. Barbara Herman argued as much in "Neo-Kantianism in Ethics—or—'Back to Kant.'"

4. *Groundwork of the Metaphysics of Morals*, p. 62 [Ak. 394].

Appendix D

1. Stephen Engstrom made such a proposal in a series of lectures on Kant's moral philosophy a few years back. I do not know whether he still would side with the claim.

2. Kant discusses what's wrong with treating God's grace as a means to attaining an end in *Religion within the Limits of Reason Alone*, pp. 40–49.

3. There are techniques for getting people to blush, faint, or sob, of course, and some people even can use these techniques on themselves when doing so serves some purpose. However, deliberate deployment of techniques designed to make someone redden, swoon, or weep is clearly calculated, and so cannot quite rescue the claim about intentional action.

4. It is unclear that the virtue theorists in question—principally British moral realists indebted to the work of John McDowell—would reject this way of describing acts of virtue. What McDowell is at pains to deny is that the virtuous man engages in self-interested calculation, not that virtuous action has an end in view (see, for example, "Are Moral Requirements Hypothetical Imperatives?" p. 26). Jonathan Dancy comes closer to a position that apparently would rule out planning as an exercise of virtue when he argues that the role of imagination in ethical action is severely circumscribed—I take it that planning involves various exercises of imagination—but would not seem to give any grounds for refusing my description of concrete acts of virtue ("The Role of Imaginary Cases in Ethics").

Appendix E

1. The models treat ordered groups of ends as single, complex primary ends, and investigate such matters as strategies by which an agent can expect to attain them, the basis for bargaining or negotiation they provide, the trade-offs commensurate with the ranking of component secondary ends, and how that ranking is sensitive to the probability of attaining the complex primary end or its constituent secondary ends.

2. "The Failure of Expected Utility Theory as a Theory of Reason," p. 220. In this essay, Hampton gives an excellent review of a wide range of criticisms directed at formal work and belonging to the genre to which I am alluding.

3. *The Foundations of Statistics*, pp. 101–103.

4. From here on out, let scare-quoted "preference," "prefer," etc. pick out what

is rendered systematic by formal work; "preference" and cognates refer to any of many and various desiderative psychological states of the sort instrumentalism treats as the basis of reasons for acting.

5. The provision itself is tricky, actually, and some of the more controversial axioms introduced by rational choice theorists in economics seem to be attempts to meet it. Wesley Salmon's exceptionally lucid adaptation of Hans Reichenbach's axiomatization of the probability calculus makes use of classes of events, *A, B, C,* and class operations. The axioms turn on such points as whether one class is a subclass of another, and whether classes are mutually exclusive (i.e., can have no members in common). When the classes involve objects of choice, drawing conclusions about preferences based on the probabilities attaching to prizes for lottery tickets requires specifying the objects in such a way that they can be cleanly sorted, one from another, that adding a prize won't alter the preferences over the past gambles dramatically, etc. For instance, if you have already determined that the agent will choose the first outcome over the second, and you are using outcome three to help you build your preference scale, you operate on the assumption that there isn't anything about outcome three that will alter the agent's preferences over outcomes one and two. You are also assuming that outcomes one and two are distinct enough for the agent that she is in a position to determine whether to go for one over the other. For Wesley Salmon's axiomatization, see *The Foundations of Scientific Inference,* p. 59. For Reichenbach's, see Hans Reichenbach, *The Theory of Probability,* §§12–14.

6. For a very interesting survey of some of the many ways in which it is not possible to get measures of desire satisfaction from economic models of choice, see Jean Hampton, *The Authority of Reason,* pp. 217–281. For a relatively early cautionary note on this matter, see Daniel Ellsberg, "Classic and Current Notions of 'Measurable Utility.'" Ellsberg explains very clearly why one cannot draw conclusions about welfare based on conclusions about Von Neumann / Morgenstern utility.

7. For summary and discussion see Roy Weatherford, *Philosophical Foundations of Probability Theory.* Weatherford provides a survey of various interpretations of probability, a discussion of their virtues, and criticisms of each approach.

8. There are, I take it, various problems with the suggestion, among them that most serious collectors do some dealing in order to help finance collecting, and you can't turn a good profit dealing in the commonplace.

9. *Intention,* §4.

10. In this sense, I think it may be possible to motivate what Amartya Sen calls *internal consistency* requirements on choice as central to the standard picture, provided that we reinterpret the internalism as being relevant *to a*

single decision rather than to the sets of alternatives at play in decisions. Strictly, the conditions Sen complains of involve, for example, the thought that if you choose one thing when another is available, you must do so again and again, or if you choose an alternative from a set S, and it turns out that S is a subset of T, you must choose the same alternative from T. While these kinds of constraints are "internal" to certain choice functions, they are not internal to particular contexts of choice. In effect, I am urging that choice functions be relativized to choice contexts. This would suggest that, for example, if you choose an alternative in the first stage of a single, multistage lottery, you must be prepared to work from a strategy for the whole lottery consistent with your initial choice. Otherwise, you can't reasonably hope to win. Such requirements are not, in Sen's way of putting it, "purely internal" or "endogenous." The "exogenous" rationale for such requirements is calculative: end attainment is being represented as winning; choice is being interpreted as intending; strategies are being interpreted as means; alternatives are being interpreted as potential ends one takes it that one can seek to attain in the relevant choice context. For Sen's criticism of internal requirements, see "Is the Idea of Purely Internal Consistency of Choice Bizarre?" pp. 19–31.

Bibliography

Anscombe, G. E. M. *Intention.* Cambridge, Mass.: Harvard University Press, 2000.

—— "Intention," reprinted in *The Collected Papers of G. E. M. Anscombe,* vol. 2: *Metaphysics and the Philosophy of Mind,* 75–82. Minneapolis: University of Minnesota Press, 1981.

—— "The Intentionality of Sensation," reprinted in *The Collected Papers of G. E. M. Anscombe,* vol. 2 (q.v.), 3–20.

—— "'Under a Description'," reprinted in *The Collected Papers of G. E. M. Anscombe,* vol. 2 (q.v.), 208–219.

—— "Introduction," *The Collected Papers of G. E. M. Anscombe,* vol. 3: *Ethics, Religion and Politics,* vii–ix. Minneapolis: University of Minnesota Press, 1981.

—— "Modern Moral Philosophy," reprinted in *The Collected Papers of G. E. M. Anscombe,* vol. 3 (q.v.), 326–342.

—— "On Brute Facts," reprinted in *The Collected Papers of G. E. M. Anscombe,* vol. 3 (q.v.), 22–25.

—— "On Frustration of the Majority by Fulfilment of the Majority's Will," reprinted in *The Collected Papers of G. E. M. Anscombe,* vol. 3 (q.v.), 123–129.

—— "On Promising and Its Justice, and Whether It Need Be Respected *in Foro Interno*," reprinted in *The Collected Papers of G. E. M. Anscombe,* vol. 3 (q.v.), 10–21.

—— "The Two Kinds of Error in Action," reprinted in *The Collected Papers of G. E. M. Anscombe,* vol. 3 (q.v.), 3–9.

—— "Von Wright on Practical Inference." In *The Philosophy of Georg Henrik Von Wright,* ed. Paul Arthur Schlipp and Lewis Edwin Hahn, 377–404. La Salle, Ill.: Open Court, 1989.

Aquinas, T. ST. *Summa Theologiae.* Trans. Members of the Dominican Order. 60 vols. New York: McGraw-Hill and Blackfriars, 1963.

—— SCG. *Summa Contra Gentiles.* Trans. Vernon Bourke. Notre Dame: University of Notre Dame Press, 1975.

—— CNE. *Commentary on Aristotle's Nicomachean Ethics*. Trans. C. I. Litzinger. Notre Dame: Dumb Ox Books, 1993.

—— OE. *On Evil*. Trans. Jean Oesterle. Notre Dame: University of Notre Dame Press, 1995.

—— DQV. *Disputed Questions on Virtue*. Trans. Ralph McInerny. South Bend: St. Augustine's Press, 1999.

Aristotle. NE. *Nicomachean Ethics*. Trans. W. D. Ross, rev. J. O. Urmson. In *The Complete Works of Aristotle*, vol. 2, 1729–1867. Princeton: Princeton University Press, 1984.

Audi, R. *Practical Reasoning*. Routledge: London, 1989.

Blanchot, M. *L'Espace littéraire*. Paris: Éditions Gallimard, 1955. Translated by Ann Smock as *The Space of Literature*. Lincoln: University of Nebraska, 1982.

Bowles, P. *Without Stopping*. New York: Echo Press, 1985.

Bradley, D. J. M. *Aquinas on the Twofold Human Good*. Washington, D.C.: Catholic University of America Press, 1997.

Califia, P. "Shiny Sharp Things." In *Ritual Sex*, ed. Tristan Taormino and David Aaron Clark, 13–38. New York: Rhinoceros Press, 1996.

Csikszentmihalyi, M. *Flow: The Psychology of Optimal Experience*. New York: Harper, 1990.

Dancy, J. "The Role of Imaginary Cases in Ethics." *Pacific Philosophical Quarterly* 66 (1985): 141–153.

Darwall, S. *Impartial Reason*. Ithaca: Cornell University Press, 1983.

Davidson, D. *Essays on Actions and Events*. Oxford: Oxford University Press, 1980.

Dreier, J. "Humean Doubts about the Practical Justification of Morality." In *Ethics and Practical Reason*, ed. Garrett Cullity and Berys Gaut, 81–100. Oxford: Clarendon Press, 1997.

Dummett, M. *On Immigration and Refugees*. Oxford: Oxford University Press, 2001.

Eco, U. *The Aesthetics of Thomas Aquinas*. Trans. Hugh Bredin. Cambridge, Mass.: Harvard University Press, 1988.

Ellsberg, D. "Classic and Current Notions of 'Measurable Utility.'" *Economic Journal* 64 (1954): 528–556.

Flaubert, G. *Flaubert in Egypt*. Ed. and trans. Francis Steegmuller. Chicago: Academy Chicago Publishers, 1979.

Foot, P. *Virtues and Vices*. Berkeley: University of California Press, 1978.

—— "Von Wright on Virtue." In *The Philosophy of Georg Henrik Von Wright*, ed. Paul Arthur Schlipp and Lewis Edwin Hahn, 271–280. La Salle, Ill.: Open Court, 1989.

—— *Natural Goodness*. Oxford: Oxford University Press, 2001.

Freud, S. "Obsessive Action and Religious Practices." In *The Freud Reader*, ed. Peter Gay, 429–435. New York: Norton, 1989.

Gauthier, D. *Morals by Agreement*. Oxford: Clarendon Press, 1986.

Geach, P. T. "Good and Evil." *Analysis* 17 (1956): 33–42.

———— *The Virtues*. Cambridge: Cambridge University Press, 1977.

Gizzi, P. "Jack Spicer and the Practice of Reading." In *The House That Jack Built: The Collected Lectures of Jack Spicer*, ed. Peter Gizzi, 173–225. Hanover, Conn.: Wesleyan University Press, 1998.

Gosling, J. C. B., and Taylor, C. C. W. *The Greeks on Pleasure*. Oxford: Clarendon Press, 1982.

Hampton, J. "The Failure of Expected Utility Theory as a Theory of Reason." 10 *Economics and Philosophy* (1994): 195–242.

———— *The Authority of Reason*. Cambridge: Cambridge University Press, 1998.

Henry, D. P. "Predicables and Categories." In *The Cambridge History of Later Medieval Philosophy*, ed. Norman Kretzmann, Anthony Kenny, and Jan Pinborg, 128–142. Cambridge: Cambridge University Press, 1988.

Herman, B. "Neo-Kantianism in Ethics—or—'Back to Kant.'" Paper presented at the American Philosophical Association Central Division meeting, New Orleans, May 1999.

Hornsby, J. *Actions*. London: Routledge and Kegan Paul, 1980.

Hursthouse, R. *On Virtue Ethics*. Oxford: Oxford University Press, 1999.

Kant, I. *Groundwork of the Metaphysics of Morals*. Trans. H. J. Paton. New York: Harper, 1964.

———— *Lectures on Ethics*. Trans. Louis Infield. Indianapolis: Hackett Publishing, 1989.

———— *Religion within the Limits of Reason Alone*. Trans. Theodore M. Greene and Hoyt H. Hudson. New York: Harper Torchbooks, 1960.

Korsgaard, C. "Skepticism about Practical Reason." *Journal of Philosophy* 83 (January 1986): 5–25.

———— *The Sources of Normativity*. Cambridge: Cambridge University Press, 1996.

———— "The Normativity of Instrumental Reason." In *Ethics and Practical Reason*, ed. Garrett Cullity and Berys Gaut, 215–254. Oxford: Clarendon Press, 1997.

Lawrence, G. "The Rationality of Morality." In *Virtues and Reasons*, ed. Rosalind Hursthouse, Gavin Lawrence, and Warren Quinn, 89–148. Oxford: Oxford University Press, 1995.

Lepore, E., and McLaughlin, B. "Actions, Reasons, Causes, and Intentions." In *Actions and Events: Perspectives on the Philosophy of Donald Davidson*, ed. Ernest LePore and Brian McLaughlin, 3–13. London: Basil Blackwell, 1985.

Lloyd, D. *Anomalous States*. Durham: Duke University Press, 1993.

Lloyd, D., and Thomas, P. *Culture and the State*. New York: Routledge, 1998.

McDowell, J. "Are Moral Requirements Hypothetical Imperatives?" *Proceedings of the Aristotelian Society* (supp. vol. 1978): 13–29.

——— "Might There Be External Reasons?" In *World, Mind, and Ethics*, eds. J. E. J. Altham and Ross Harrison, 68–85. Cambridge: Cambridge University Press, 1995.

McInerny, R. *Ethica Thomistica*, rev. ed. Washington, D.C.: Catholic University of America Press, 1997.

Millgram, E. *Practical Induction*. Cambridge, Mass.: Harvard University Press, 1997.

——— "How to Make Something of Yourself." In *Robert Nozick*, ed. David Schmidtz, 175–198. Cambridge: Cambridge University Press, 2002.

Müller, A. "How Theoretical Is Practical Reason?" In *Intention and Intentionality*, ed. Cora Diamond and Jenny Teichman, 91–108. Ithaca: Cornell University Press, 1979.

Nagel, T. *The Possibility of Altruism*. Princeton: Princeton University Press, 1978.

Nozick, R. *The Nature of Rationality*. Princeton: Princeton University Press, 1993.

Poe, E. A. "Marginalia," reprinted in *Edgar Allan Poe: Essays and Reviews*, 1455–1462. New York: Library of America, 1984.

Quinn, W. "Rationality and the Human Good." *Social Philosophy and Policy* 9 (Summer 1992): 81–95.

——— "Putting Rationality in Its Place," reprinted in *Morality and Moral Action*, 228–255. Cambridge: Cambridge University Press, 1993.

Reichenbach, H. *The Theory of Probability*. Berkeley: University of California Press, 1949.

Richardson, H. *Practical Reasoning about Final Ends*. Cambridge: Cambridge University Press, 1994.

Ryle, G. *The Concept of Mind*. London: Hutchinson, 1949.

Said, E. *Orientalism*. New York: Vintage Books, 1979.

Salmon, W. *The Foundations of Scientific Inference*. Pittsburgh: University of Pittsburgh Press, 1967.

Savage, L. *The Foundations of Statistics*. New York: Dover, 1972.

Sen, A. "Is the Idea of Purely Internal Consistency of Choice Bizarre?" In *World, Mind, and Ethics*, ed. J. E. J. Altham and Ross Harrison, 19–31. Cambridge: Cambridge University Press, 1995.

Slote, M. *Morals from Motives*. Oxford: Oxford University Press, 2001.

Spicer, J. *The House That Jack Built: The Collected Lectures of Jack Spicer*, ed. Peter Gizzi. Hanover, Conn.: Wesleyan University Press, 1998.

—— *The Collected Books of Jack Spicer,* ed. Robin Blaser. Santa Rosa, Calif.: Black Sparrow Press, 1999.

Taylor, C. W., and Gosling, J. C. B. *The Greeks on Pleasure.* Oxford: Clarendon Press, 1982.

Thompson, M. "Naïve Action Theory," unpublished manuscript.

—— "Relations of Right," unpublished manuscript.

Tillinghast, L. *The Thought of Art.* Ph.D. diss., University of Chicago, 2000.

Velleman, D. *Practical Reflection.* Princeton: Princeton University Press, 1989.

—— "The Guise of the Good." *Nôus* 26, no. 1 (1992): 3–26.

Voeller, C. *The Metaphysics of the Moral Law: Kant's Deduction of Freedom.* New York: Garland Press, 2001.

Vogler, C. *John Stuart Mill's Deliberative Landscape: An Essay in Moral Psychology.* New York: Garland Press, 2001.

—— "Anscombe on Practical Inference." In *Varieties of Practical Reasoning,* ed. Elijah Millgram, 437–464. Cambridge, Mass.: MIT Press, 2001.

Wallace, R. J. "How to Argue about Practical Reason." *Mind* 99 (1990): 355–385.

Weatherford, R. *Philosophical Foundations of Probability Theory.* London: Routledge and Kegan Paul, 1982.

West, N. *A Cool Million.* New York: Vintage Press, 1961.

Westberg, D. *Right Practical Reason.* Oxford: Clarendon Press, 1994.

Wiggins, D. "Deliberation and Practical Reason." In *Essays on Aristotle's Ethics,* ed. Amélie Oksenberg Rorty, 221–240. Berkeley: University of California Press, 1980.

Williams, B. "Internal and External Reasons." In *Moral Luck,* 101–113. Cambridge: Cambridge University Press, 1981.

—— *Ethics and the Limits of Philosophy.* Cambridge, Mass.: Harvard University Press, 1985.

—— "Replies." In *World, Mind, and Ethics,* ed. J. E. J. Altham and Ross Harrison, 185–224. Cambridge: Cambridge University Press, 1995.

—— "Moral Incapacity." In *Making Sense of Humanity,* 46–55. Cambridge: Cambridge University Press, 1995.

Index

Acedia, 39, 262n31

Acting well or faring well, 35–36, 180–182, 198, 228

Act types, 58–61, 66–67, 132–134, 201, 230, 233, 255n4, 257n17, 273n9. *See also* Part-whole considerations

Aesthetic considerations, 76, 83, 113–114, 116–125, 157, 177–178, 197, 199, 246, 267n3. *See also* Spicer, J.

Agent-relative and agent-neutral considerations, 152

Anger, 39

Anscombe, G. E. M., 1, 2, 3, 27, 45–47, 128–131, 133, 137, 144, 147, 154–155, 166, 173, 174, 183, 187–188, 195, 196, 205–212, 213–222, 230, 233, 235, 236, 248, 255n5

Aquinas, St. Thomas, 4–5, 8, 26, 27, 29, 30–36, 37–40, 48, 50, 62, 66, 68, 75, 81–82, 110, 122, 126, 167–168, 181, 194, 198, 224, 229; and Aristotle, 26, 30–31, 81–82; on practical good, 26, 40, 50–51, 110; on the threefold division, 27, 30–32, 34, 37, 40, 50; on vice, 34, 37, 38–39, 40, 68, 198; on avarice, 68–69; on pleasure, 73, 81–87; on practical reasoning, 167–168

Aristotle, 4, 26, 30–31, 62, 81, 128, 224, 229, 265nn3,4, 271n7, 272n2, 281n20

As-such desirables, 37, 68, 193, 196

Atomic actions, 134

Audi, R., 255n8

Augustine, 75

Avarice, 39, 68–70

Backward-looking motive, 43, 263n35

Befitting. *See* Fittingness; Desirability characterization; Interminability; Threefold division of good

Belief-desire psychology, 1–2, 18–21, 135–136, 213–215. *See also* Bifurcationist psychology; Desires; Instrumentalist moral psychology

Bifurcationist psychology, 7, 12, 13, 14, 18–21, 48, 198, 255n10. *See also* Belief-desire psychology; Desires; Instrumentalist moral psychology

Big head schematic of rational action, 45, 139–140, 144

Bowles, P., 183–184

Bradley, D. J. M., 41, 266n14

Calculative form/structure, 3, 4, 6, 128–129, 133–134, 141, 147, 151–152, 156, 158, 165–166, 173–176, 206, 208–210, 230, 231, 232, 249–251

Calculative justification, 3, 12–13, 14

Calculative reasons, 7, 9, 47–50, 127–128, 139, 147, 158, 173–175, 194–195, 223

Calculative relation, 127–128, 139, 169, 172, 173–175, 249–251

Calculative wanting, 22–23, 156, 171, 249

Capital vice, 38–40, 68–70, 196. *See also* Acedia; Anger; Avarice; Envy; Gluttony; Habit, vicious; Immorality, theory of; Lust; Pride

Cavafy, 74, 75

Choiceworthiness, 29–30, 33, 37, 50, 246

Concept-involving end-orientation, 31, 134

Consequentialism, 260n19

Courage, 6, 30, 108, 109, 194

Dancy, J., 282n4

Darwall, S., 276n12

Davidson, D., 213–222, 263n38

Deliberation of ends, 12, 13, 14, 157, 159.